To Africa and Back
Memoirs

J.D.Fage

This book is a publication of
Centre of West African Studies,
University of Birmingham
Edgbaston
Birmingham B15 2TT
2002

ISBN 0704423308

Birmingham University African Studies Series No. 6

CONTENTS

Acknowledgments

I am deeply grateful for the help and advice given me at various stages in the writing of this work by David Church, Jean Fage, Michael Meyer, Roland Oliver, Michael Orrom, Christine Richards, Joan Tate, and Jean Wilks.
J.D.F.

Editor's Note

We are delighted that John gave us the opportunity to bring out this volume of memoirs in the *Birmingham University African Studies Series*. It seems appropriate – and is also, of course, a great honour for us – that the Centre of West African Studies, which he founded, should have been entrusted with the task of publication.

Karin Barber

FOREWORD

A round of dinners marked John Fage's retirement from Birmingham University. At these John said that he owed his distinguished career to luck and timing. This is both true and untrue. It is true in that John's working life coincided with the purposeful and innovatory post-war expansion of Britain's universities, and ended just as that time of optimism faded away. It is untrue in that John seized upon the opportunities that lay before him and made something significant and enduring out of them. This was a purely personal achievement. Thus, he can lay fair claim (although he would not do so himself) to having been one of that small group who more or less invented African Studies in Britain, institutionalised it in British universities and worked to establish its claims and credentials in the wider world.

John Fage's record speaks for itself. Following military service (an exhilarating time, fondly recalled in conversation and now set down here in a transparent love of flying and aeroplanes) and Cambridge, John taught history at the University College of the Gold Coast (now the University of Ghana at Legon). There, during the eventful years that led up to the coming of independence to Nkrumah's Ghana in 1957, John played an important role in laying the foundations of modern historical study in Britain's first independent African colony. Ghana and its people left an indelible mark on John and in a real sense turned him into an Africanist. Back in Britain he taught at the School of Oriental and African Studies in London, there forging a working relationship with Roland Oliver that still stands as the single most productive academic partnership in African Studies. Among many other things the pair created the *Journal of African History* and over forty years on it remains the leading journal in the field. Clearly, this was an exciting and productive time in John's life but it was still prologue.

In the memoir that follows John describes how – in the world made possible by the Hayter and Robbins Committees on higher education – he came to found and direct the Centre of West African Studies at the University of Birmingham in 1963. In his recollection of this time John man-

i

ages to recapture a lost academic world of almost insouciant possibility. The air of "let's have an African Studies centre", "shall it be in Birmingham or Glasgow?" (I have a memory, perhaps faulty, that he once told me at length about his private debate over the supposed merits and demerits of each place), "where shall we put it?", "what about staffing?", and all the rest are set down below to stir the nostalgia of older academics and excite the incredulity of younger ones. But there was real work to do. John (assisted by his eventual successor Douglas Rimmer) gave shape and direction to what is now the premier African Studies department in Britain and an internationally renowned centre of research and teaching.

John spent two decades (1963-83) as Director of the Centre of West African Studies. Establishing, running and teaching in the department took up much time but this was also the period in which he made massive contributions to the academic and public understanding of Africa's past. Two achievements stand out. One was the general editorship (again with Roland Oliver) of the multi-volume *Cambridge History of Africa*, a monument of scholarly coordination and cooperation. This was a work of tremendous significance within British academia, for the dedication of a series of volumes to Africa (on the model of the *Cambridge Modern History*) was the clearest possible signal to the uninformed or unbelieving that there was an African history and that this could be recovered. The other achievement was more personal. This was the publication in 1978 of John's *A History of Africa*, a controlled, compelling and deeply informed narrative account of the continent from the neolithic to the present. This is a book on the grand scale and academics, students and anyone else interested can read it with profit. They obviously do so, for in 2002 a fourth edition of *A History of Africa* appeared in print – a notable achievement in its own right and one unparalleled by any other scholarly book on Africa in recent times.

The final parts of John's memoir track his administrative career at Birmingham. Two things stand out here. One is John's recognition of the deepening (and still continuing) sense of uncertainty in British higher education. The other is his determination to leave the Centre of West African Studies as well defended as circumstances allowed against the winds of retrenchment blowing through British universities. I know of his efforts in this regard for I was a principal beneficiary of them. John retired in 1984 and he and Jean went to live in Wales. But there was a major scholarly coda. In his retirement John produced the invaluable *A Guide to Original*

Sources for Precolonial Western Africa published in European Languages, a comprehensive survey of books published on Africa to the close of the nineteenth century. This was entirely fitting, for throughout his long and varied career John's central interest was the precolonial history of western Africa.

*

I want to conclude on a more personal, informal note. John Fage is a private man, an exemplary instance, perhaps, of that reticence commonly ascribed to Englishmen. Yet in this memoir we are afforded hints of and insights into some of the paths that his life might have taken. I knew for example about his interest in the cinema and literature, but had no real sense of just how important both of these have been to John. I knew too, from years of interacting with him, that John preferred to persuade rather than to dictate and the search for reasoned consensus in all things is a thread running through *To Africa and Back*. This leaves the question, often asked of me, of what he was like to work for and with. In searching for an answer I often think of (but seldom say) "the single sheet of paper", a symbol for me of the man behind the academic. Allow me to explain.

I met John in Cambridge in 1974. The occasion was my Ph.D. viva and he and Jack Goody were the examiners. Proceedings were short. It was hot and the glass walls of James Stirling's prize-winning History Faculty Building acted to ensure that our talk about Asante was conducted in an appropriately tropical temperature. I was passed, ushered out wringing wet and sent on my way. I felt a sense of anti-climax. It was all over so quickly. That feeling lasted until I read "the single sheet of paper" that John put into my hands as I left. It was a page of A4 crowded with meticulously ordered handwriting in black ink. It was brief, prescient and kind. John had read my work with enormous care.

After I joined the Centre of West African Studies in 1975 different incarnations of "the single sheet of paper" came before my eyes again and again. In those days we had weekly seminars (nearly two dozen in a year) and a feature of them was the sight of John taking notes as he distilled the presentation and discussion down to "the single sheet of paper". He told me that this was his way of "keeping up" with research on a continent-wide scale. "The single sheet of paper" was also emblematic of the way in which John ran his department. It came into play when one of us needed reminding of some administrative dereliction. It descended upon us when John wished to commend or encourage. In all of its incarnations "the single sheet of paper" signalled care and concern, but at a remove that was congenial to John's character.

If all of this sounds odd to contemporary ears then it hardly ever seemed so to us at the time. The Centre of West African Studies was lodged in its own spacious building. We had ample support staff. We had minimal administrative obligations. We were all left to get on with our own research and teaching. John Fage presided over all of this with an even-handed lightness of touch. He was a pleasure to work for and with. Now that I head the Centre of West African Studies – in very different times – I look back with respect and affection to his tenure and example. To echo my opening remarks, I have had the luck and timing to know him.

Tom McCaskie

CHAPTER 1

YOUTH

I was born in June 1921 at Teddington, in the now vanished county of Middlesex. I was born in the first floor front bedroom at the house called Milford in Park Road, and here my sister Christine followed me three and a half years later. In those days it was unusual to arrange for births to take place in hospitals. The house, which subsequently became 171 Park Road, was one of a row of large, three-storey semi-detached Edwardian houses which looked south across Bushy Park towards Hampton Court. It had been bought by my father, Arthur Fage, at the time of his marriage in the previous year. It was the only house which he ever owned. He had chosen it not simply because of its pleasant situation (there were, for example, better situated houses in parts of nearby Hampton), but also because it was within easy walking distance of his place of work, the National Physical Laboratory in Queens Road about half a mile away to the west.

The whole of my father's working life was spent at the National Physical Laboratory. In 1912 he arrived in what was then called the Aeronautics Section of its Engineering Department as the holder of a research scholarship from Imperial College, from which he had just graduated, and when he retired in 1953 he had become a Fellow of the Royal Society and for the last seven years had held the post of Superintendent of what had long before become an independent Aerodynamics Division of the N.P.L. It was important to him to be close to his place of work because, virtually alone among the scientific staff of the N.P.L., he never owned or drove a motorcar. He had once possessed a motor bicycle but, so far as I know, he gave this up to please the young lady who became my mother. She was Winifred Donnelly who, after studying at the University of London's Bedford College and securing a degree in botany, was recruited to the staff of the Physics Department of the N.P.L. in 1916 and remained there until her marriage in 1920.

My father and my mother were alike in that they were the first members of their families to go to university, and it was undoubtedly of major importance to them that their children should receive a good education. In their eyes so far as I was concerned, this meant that I should go to a public school. So, after two years at a kindergarten at the northern end of Teddington just off the road to Twickenham, to which I would go on my "Fairy" cycle escorted by my mother on her very stately "grown-up" bicycle, in 1929 the "Fairy" cycle was passed on to my sister, and I was equipped with a "proper" bicycle, i.e. one which had a crossbar as well as full-size wheels, so that every weekday I might cycle across Bushy Park to Hampton and there attend a preparatory school called Pembroke House. This was a great adventure. I can well remember the first time I rode the "proper" bicycle: my father went with me into Bushy Park to see whether I could safely control so large a machine.

Quite how I passed this test, I do not know, because I collided with one of the two Crimean War cannons which stood outside the park gates of Bushy House (where the Director of the N.P.L. then lived in some state), and while the bicycle could just scrape under the cannon's barrel, there was no space for its rider, who fell winded to the ground. However there was no significant damage to either boy or machine so, after an exploratory trip supervised by my mother, I was passed fit to cycle every morning by myself the one and a half miles to my new school and back again in the late afternoon - even if it were dark or foggy, circumstances which made the journey more enjoyable because they were rather exciting.

Pembroke House was in origin a very substantial dwelling in Uxbridge Road in Hampton to which had been added a wooden extension with a corrugated iron roof so that about fifty boys aged eight to thirteen could be taught in five classes. Opposite on the other side of the road was a rough field which was used for breaks and *ad hoc* games. There were much better playing fields, which may well have been rented, a short distance away in a walled paddock off the road which led to Hampton Court, and near this there was a public open-air swimming pool to which we were taken in a crocodile once a week in the summer term. The school was, I think, the property of its headmaster, a Mr Lee-Jones, a very small, lively man who had served in the Tank Corps in the First World War. His much more substantial wife acted as mother to about a dozen boarders. The rest of us were dayboys, arriving by 9 a.m., lunching with the boarders and, except on Saturday, which was a half-day, leaving for home about 4 or 4.30 p.m. It was a much smaller and less grand prep school than some of those with which we competed at football or cricket, such as The Hall in Hampstead, or Colet Court, the preparatory school for St Paul's. During the Depression of the early 1930s it was able to attract onto its staff attractive young, and often pipe-smoking, Oxbridge graduates; one whom I particularly remember had previously sailed as Spanish interpreter on a Fyffe banana boat. But, like the hero of Evelyn Waugh's *Decline and Fall*, none of them stayed very long. The mainstays of the teaching staff were a very competent woman, a Miss Nesbitt who, though probably no more than middle-aged, seemed awfully old to me, and Lee-Jones himself, though I suspect he was something of an amateur. I think it was he who taught mathematics, and probably also Latin. But the only lesson of his that left any mark on my mind was one in which he taught us, with the aid of rubber bands, matchsticks and pieces of candle, to convert cotton reels into little tanks that would climb lurchingly over small obstacles. I do not think that Pembroke House was any great shakes academically: its boys were able to pass the Common Entrance examination needed to enter into a public school, but I do not remember them winning scholarships. So far as my experience went, I could be inspired in fields like English, French and history, and I became a voracious reader of books from the school library (especially those by G.A. Henty and Percy F. Westerman), but I was never drilled well enough to achieve scholarship level in such vital Common Entrance subjects as Latin and mathematics. In the latter case, my father did the best he could to coach me, but so many things which were so clear to him were so obscure to me that I suspect that he may well have done more harm than good.

Somewhere along the line, a decision was taken that I should go to a public school as a boarder. I am not sure how much my mother approved of this; there were certainly some good day schools within reach of our home, for example Merchant Taylors' and King's College, Wimbledon (to both of which cousins of mine went), not to mention Kingston Grammar School and Hampton Grammar School. But more than once I remember my father saying to me that if I did not do better at my Common Entrance work, I would end up at a *grammar school*. At the time this seemed to me to be an awful threat; it was not until I had got to Cambridge that I began to appreciate that grammar schools could provide just as good an education as public schools - and indeed in some cases a considerably better education than some public schools.

By the time that I was at Pembroke House, my father had consulted among his N.P.L. colleagues and, on the advice of Sir Thomas Stanton, then Superintendent of the N.P.L.'s Engineering Department, I was entered to follow his son (also called Tom), who was four years older than me, to Tonbridge School and its Hill Side boarding house. In retrospect I see no reason to criticise this choice. Obviously my parents were happy with it, and my father felt able to give the same advice to a slightly junior colleague, C.N.H. Lock, whose two sons in due course also appeared at Hill Side, the elder, Robin, in my last year there. Whether this apostolic succession continued any further, I do not know. Something I do know is that Tom Stanton, Robin Lock, his younger brother Michael and I all ended their school careers as Hill Side's head boy (the younger Lock also became head boy of the School); if this has any significance at all, it suggests an unusual genetic inheritance from senior scientists at the N.P.L.

I arrived at Tonbridge in September 1934. Although I had done well enough in the examinations I had taken at Pembroke House to avoid being placed in the Lower School at Tonbridge, where I started in Form Four (and so, if I behaved myself, had the chance of three years in its Sixth Form), I had not won a scholarship, so that my father had to pay full fees for me. While I know that this was a disappointment for my parents, I do not know how much of a financial burden it may have been for them; neither of them ever spoke to me about money matters. In due course my sister was sent for her secondary education, not to a boarding school, but to the nearest school of the Girls' Public Day School Trust. But this decision may well have had nothing to do with any financial stringency; it may have been taken because it was then thought best for schoolgirls to live at home - even though, in Christine's case, this meant daily return journeys by train between Teddington and Wimbledon. But the reputation of Wimbledon High School (as of other G.P.D.S.T. schools) was a good one, and it was also entrusted with the education of other daughters of the scientific staff of the N.P.L. (In passing, I think I should say that I do not think that my parents' reticence in money matters was at that time unusual for people of their class and background. For example, when my mother's sister's husband had a severe stroke and was condemned to spend many years in bed tended by a full-time nurse, I remember my aunt saying that she had no idea whether there was money enough to pay for such care. In fact when, after several years, my uncle was eventually released by death, it was found that he had left quite a small fortune.)

I cannot now recall very much of my earliest time at Tonbridge: the abiding memories are tinted by the autumnal colours and sensations of the season of my arrival. I seem to have been always rushed uncomprehendingly through and across a stage, of house and school and the streets between them, that was dark and cold and sometimes wet, and crowded by strange actors, boys and men and men-boys, who were large and remote and potentially dangerous. I sensed little positive hostility, the dangers of fagging and beatings were much less menacing in reality than they had seemed in prep school folklore, but the other actors on the stage, even my kindly housemaster, seemed unaware that I was I. I was just one of seven *novi* – the Tonbridge term for new boys – who were crowded together in Hill Side's semi-basement, as yet not even allowed to join in pairs to live in their own studies. It was only at night, when I retired to bed in my little cubicle on one of the upstairs floors, that I had time to be an individual and to wonder what the future – tomorrow, let alone next week, next term, next year – might hold for me.

Gradually one climbed out of this darkness. Before the first term had ended, my fellow *novi* and I had successfully persuaded our elders that we had learnt the names of all our fellow Hill Siders and of the School Praeposters, and knew the cap colours and the whereabouts of each of the boarding houses, and much other information of more or less practical value if we really were to move about on the stage of our school and house without endlessly colliding with somebody or some convention. But I think that more than a year was to pass before I began to think that I really belonged to this world of house and school, and that also the school belonged to me, so that I could make something out of it and gain from it. By this time I had survived the Fourth Form, without – I think – learning much except how to survive it, and a decision had been taken that when I reached the Fifth Form, and thus entered a world divided into separate branches of learning labelled "Classics", "Modern Studies", and "Science", I was not to proceed on the science side. This was a decision that was not exactly pleasing to my parents nor, for that matter, to my housemaster, who was a teacher of chemistry. It came about, I am inclined to believe, largely because of an inadequacy of the master who tried to teach me science in the Fourth Form. Like my mother, he had a degree in botany, and I believe in fact that he did very well indeed as a teacher of botany to sixth form scientists; but there were two things he could not do. One was to teach, and to raise any enthusiasm for, the kind of physics, chemistry and biology which in 1934-35 were subsumed under the label "General Science", and the other was to keep order in a class of something like two dozen thirteen and fourteen year old boys. I can still remember the very early lesson on mensuration: when it came to the part of the lesson which dealt with "volume", we very quickly managed to submerge the classroom under a substantial volume of water.

At this stage, it was still open whether I should aim to be a classicist or a modernist, and for some reason of which I am now not entirely sure, I entered the Fifth Form on the classics side. I like to think that I had cleverly perceived that there were far fewer boys concentrating on classics than there were on modern studies, so that I would meet with less competition when it came to promotion to an appropriate Sixth Form and, possibly, that I might receive more individual attention from my teachers. If this were the plan, it miscarried. I made no progress with Greek (which had not been available at Pembroke House), and when in 1936 I took the School Certificate examination, although I secured the credits necessary for university matriculation in English, History, French, Elementary Mathematics, and General Science (!), I did not secure the equally necessary credit in Latin. This had to be added in a resit the following year, when I had already secured a place in the Modern Lower Sixth, and was also able to add German to my list of School Certificate credits.

I think that it was in 1936-37 that I really began to enjoy being at Tonbridge, and then in the following two years I knew that I was thoroughly at home in what I think to have been an extraordinarily good school. This was not the universal opinion at the time. The headmaster from 1922 to 1939 was H.N.P. Sloman, and in both the histories of Tonbridge School which treat of his tenure of the post, it is reported that in his last years a general opinion was that the school's academic standards were slipping and that it had a reputation for slackness. But both writers come to the same conclusion, that Sloman was a good headmaster, but one who, in the succinct words of Barry Orchard, "did not care or bother about public relations. He refused to flatter prep school headmasters, and he did not much like parents, especially stockbrokers". I was one of the editors of *The Tonbridgian* when Sloman retired, and our opinion was expressed in an editorial quoted in part by the other authority, the historian D.C. Somervell: "[Sloman's] reign was distinguished by a wide and tolerant humanity, by a charity of outlook which seldom and reluctantly condemned, which chose to guide and lead rather than to order and drive, which abhorred the idea of a headmaster as 'a beast but a just beast', supplanting it by an unaffected and friendly intercourse with all whom he met, boys and masters alike". Sloman was a gentleman and a scholar: though a classicist by training and in his teaching, he made something of a literary reputation for himself after his retirement (at the early age of 59) by his translations from Maupassant. I spent a term under his successor, E.E.A. Whitworth, the new broom brought by the school governors from Bradfield to sweep slackness out of the door.

Since by that time I was a School Praeposter I saw Whitworth at closer hand than I ever saw Sloman, and I thought the change of headmaster seemed a sad let down. After I had left Tonbridge for Cambridge, Sidney Keyes, the fellow Hill Sider who had followed me as senior editor of *The Tonbridgian*, wrote to me of Whitworth (who taught Second Isaiah throughout the school) that he was "a narrow-minded, uncultured Hebraist, who walks doubtless by the best light he has, but will never be convinced that it is Darkness"!

However for almost all non-curricular activities at Tonbridge, it was the housemaster, not the headmaster, who was the important figure. E.J.H. Eames was always called "Ferdie", even by his wife; the nickname arose from a supposed likeness to the Archduke whose assassination at Sarajevo had precipitated the First World War. He was – as I have already mentioned – a teacher of chemistry. At the time of my arrival at Hill Side, he had only recently become a housemaster, and for that reason I think he was possibly still rather shy of dealing with boys' private lives. He was a tall man who strode quickly about both house and school with a slightly rolling gait, and spoke in a strange manner which was at once upper class and deeply West Country. This combination of factors initially made him something of an enigma to me, and it was not until I became one of his house Praeposters I really began to appreciate what a nice man he was: a thorough gentleman, not in the least hidebound in his opinions, and capable of remarkable enthusiasm for a variety of extra-curricular activities, even those of an aesthetic nature. This last trait, I suspect, had rubbed off onto him from his wife Gladys who, despite (perhaps because of?) having five of her own children, aged something like four to fourteen when I first knew the family, still had room in her heart for the interests of the fifty boys in her husband's care.

In the classroom, I was fortunate to come across two very gifted language teachers. Gottfried Friedrich was a Bavarian who had not found Hitler's Germany congenial, and who after some years at Tonbridge moved further afield to the United States, where he assumed the surname Peters. He was virtually unique among our masters in that he had a Ph.D. and in never being seen without a briefcase; somehow he carried with him an air of being more of a scholar than our other teachers. It was impossible to resist his enthusiasm for German literature. Little time was spent in instructing us in the grammar of his native language; almost immediately, it seemed, he had us reading Schnitzler and Thomas Mann. I would now find this something of a labour, but his most infectious enthusiasm was for the German Romantic poets, so that I can still quote odd bits of Schiller, Heine and Hölderlin, and still enjoy reading some of them. French was taught by Alfred Foster, at first sight a much more ordinary schoolmaster. I first met him in my first year when he was my form master. I suspect that this was a job which he did not enjoy; certainly he was not at his best when trying to control a class of impertinent thirteen and fourteen year olds. At this stage, all I can remember of his teaching was that he insisted on our learning the International Phonetic Alphabet so that we might be better equipped to voice the appropriate unEnglish sounds needed to speak French like the French did; this did not endear him to us but, so far as my experience goes, could produce reasonable results. But when we reached the sixth form, and could read with him works like Alain-Fournier's *Le Grand Meaulnes*, I could appreciate that beneath his rather formal and conventional exterior there was an intellectual who could impart enthusiasms comparable to those which radiated from Gottfried Friedrich.

I have left to the last the teacher who had the greatest influence on me, Tom Staveley, the form master of my two years in the Modern Upper Sixth. Staveley had an ungainly frame, which he propelled with something of a limp (which had induced younger boys to nickname him "Staggers"). Atop this frame was a large head of Roman imperial character, with eyes apparently focused on the remote distance until something was said to him which he thought worthy of attention, whereupon they could look at one alarmingly directly. He was in many respects an unlikely school-master, an Old Tonbridgian with an indifferent Oxford degree, who had entered the profession relatively late, after writing poetry which was said to have impressed W.B. Yeats, and – like many others in his age group, including Eames –

army service in the 1914-18 war. Unusually this service was not on the western front, but in the expeditionary force sent to Greece (it was rumoured that his limp was the result of slipping on the dockside at Salonika). He was apt to go off on exchanges with schools in the U.S.A., and had acquired an American wife. In the school at large he was probably best known as the teacher of geography and as the master who always sang the Pooh Bah type parts in the concert performances of the Gilbert and Sullivan operettas which were given at the school each summer in the 1920s and 1930s. But with his own form Staveley taught history and English literature. His enthusiasm for the latter, the Romantic poets in particular, rivalled that of Friedrich for the poetry and prose of his language. As a historian, Staveley was professionally outranked by Somervell, who had been a scholar at Oxford, had taught at Repton for nine years, and had published brief but pithy historical works somewhat in a Lytton Strachey style. But at Tonbridge, Somervell was condemned to teach history only to the lower forms, and a very dull job he made of it. Staveley's understanding of the subject was instinctive rather than learned, and his style of teaching so inspirational that at times it verged on the manic. If it appealed to you, it was as though you had been enlisted in an evangelical church.

By the time I left Tonbridge, I was one of a small coterie of Tom Staveley's converts, and had entered into friendships which were different from any that I had experienced before, which might for the most part be described as somewhat perfunctory. I began, of course, with "friends" who had in effect been chosen for me in that they were the children of friends of my parents. Then, by the end of my time at Pembroke House, I had become acquainted with about half a dozen boys with similar interests to my own, in particular perhaps in model making. But as it happened, only one of these lived at all close to me in Teddington; the homes of the others tended to be in places like Feltham and Richmond which were towards the edge of a comfortable cycling radius, and my pocket money of sixpence (2½p) a week was inadequate to allow me to travel so far by bus or train other than very occasionally. Then, though they all went on to public schools, none of their parents had had the wit to send them to Tonbridge, so that by 1939 I was beginning to lose touch with them, a process which was completed following the outbreak of war. At Tonbridge, prior to the sixth form and the luxury of "study periods" in which there was no formal teaching, it

17

was virtually impossible to make friends with anyone outside one's own house, and in the houses friendships with anyone outside one's own year were virtually unheard of.

At Hill Side, there were nine boys in my year besides myself. For three years or more, I shared a study with one of them, and I suppose I might say that I was on terms of some intimacy with two or three others (so that, if the distance were not too great, we might visit or even stay in each other's homes during the school holidays). But one of the nine lived in Peru and left after only four years, as did two others, respectively to enter the Royal Navy and to train as a solicitor. Of the remainder, one had no apparent interests other than qualifying to train as a doctor; another was devoted to winning his school colours at rugby and cricket. Out of the nine, there was only one who shared what were becoming my main extra-curricular interests, and academically I was outrunning him.

Outside the classroom, all boys were required to spend part of each weekday afternoon in some sporting or athletic activity. Everyone was conscripted to play in organised games of rugby football in the autumn term, of hockey in the spring, and of cricket in the summer (though in this season, if they were hearty enough they might choose rowing instead, or they might choose tennis if they were good enough at that game to be a candidate for the school team). On days when no game had been arranged for him, a boy had to elect an alternative athletic activity, and if he had not booked one of the relatively few squash or fives courts, this usually meant running through the streets according to one of a number of recognised plans. I was unusually tall and spindly for my age, and this shape did not fit well on the rugby field. Hockey was more congenial and certainly more enjoyable, but my main love was cricket. As a spectator, it still is, but in my school days I fancied myself as a performer. I did well at the game at Pembroke House, but at Tonbridge cricket proved a sad disappointment. Once, after making a high score in one of the compulsory games for second year boys, I was given a trial for the school's Junior Colts team, but this was a miserable failure; while I could demolish bad bowling, better bowling defeated me. It was not until years later that I realised what had been wrong: with my feet so far away from my head, I did not find it easy to put them into the proper positions for anything other than pulling to leg, and there was no coach to point this out to me. Still I did have one cricketing achievement to my credit at Tonbridge that may well have escaped even the most illustrious of its players – even perhaps its most famous Test cricketer, Colin Cowdrey. The only occasion that I ever played on the Head, the First XI cricket ground, was in a house match. In those days these were played in the periods of two hours or so that were available each afternoon between classes and supper, periods so short that a match might continue for quite a few afternoons. Batting about No.9 for Hill Side, my innings extended over three days! (The explanation for this feat is that I went in to bat towards the end of the first afternoon and that rain prevented much play on the second day, so that I was still not out at the beginning of the third day.)

If I were to make any mark at Tonbridge, it had to be outside the sporting world. I held office in the Debating Society; I increased my book stock at no financial cost to myself by winning prizes in the essay, poetry and literary competitions which had been generously endowed for all levels of the school, and – as has already been mentioned in passing – I was appointed an editor of *The Tonbridgian*. So far as I can now recall, my tenure of this office extended over two years, and it was something that I greatly enjoyed. I thought it enormous fun to correct proofs and to take them down town to the Whitefriars Press, one of England's premier printing houses, and there to discuss any technical points arising from them. Most of what was printed was routine news and notes about the school and its old boys, but these had to be collected and often edited as well. However there was usually room for some literary contributions, and by the autumn of 1938 the master who oversaw our activities, C.H. Knott, best known for his cricketing achievements, had agreed that *The Tonbridgian* might have a Literary Supplement. Two issues of this were produced, much to the joy and advantage of the Modern Upper Sixth coterie, before Knott began to worry about the cost, and the supplement's ultimate burial by the outbreak of war.

However my main personal interests as they developed at Tonbridge were music and the cinema. In retrospect, I have little idea of how either of these interests was acquired. There was not much music at home. The family did not own a gramophone and I do not remember much listening to music on what was then called "the wireless". A mid nineteenth century Broadwood grand took up a fair amount of space in our drawing room, but arthritis in her hands made it increasingly difficult for my mother to perform on it, and by the time I had reached the age of about eight I had rebelled against being taught to play it. My sister was learning to play but was reluctant to perform in public. My father had sung in his youth in his church choir, but in my youth his musical contribution did not extend further than occasionally taking us to the opera at Sadler's Wells. However I do remember being much moved by hearing Chopin's "Funeral March" being broadcast on the wireless at the funeral of King Albert of the Belgians in 1934. It may be that it was this that led me to ask for a wind-up portable gramophone for Christmas, and to use pocket money to buy what little Woolworths had to sell in the way of sixpenny records of classical music – Franz von Suppé was about as far as this went. By modern standards, Tonbridge, like other public schools of the 1930s, was not a very musical school. Tom Staveley, in the *avant garde* fashion of the day, was devoted to the music of Sibelius, records of which he used to play to the four or five young Hill Siders who in their early years at the school went to his home for weekly tutorial evenings derived from what Tonbridge supposed to be the practice at Eton (from which Sloman's predecessor had come). Even the most musical of us found a diet of substantial and apparently interminable Sibelius tone poems somewhat indigestible. I think that I was much more influenced by occasional recitals by invited artistes or on gramophone records. While I can remember enjoying a recital by Roy Henderson, with Gerald Moore as his accompanist, I think it may have been a gramophone evening of *Lieder* sung by such artistes as Elisabeth Schumann which first made me appreciate the divinity of music, so that when on leave during the war I would go to concerts in the Orangery at Hampton Court given by the Boyd Neel Orchestra, and later venture as far as the Albert Hall to listen to promenade concerts.

It is just as difficult to be sure about the origins of my interest in the cinema, which for ten years or more from about 1938 onwards proved more compelling than my interest in music. I experienced very little cinema-going in my younger days; it was not thought altogether proper (in some measure, perhaps, because before about 1936 or so the local cinema in Teddington was rather a flea-pit). Such interest as my parents had in the cinema was largely kindled by me. Before then, I can remember a time when if I wanted to see a film, I had to persuade my grandmother (who was then living with us) to take me. So there was little structured film viewing before I went to Tonbridge. But there my study mate would enthuse about the films of Hitchcock or the Astaire and Rogers musicals.

Perhaps more significantly, he introduced me to the film reviews by Caroline Lejeune each Sunday in *The Observer* (the other goddess of this craft, Dilys Powell, started as film critic of *The Sunday Times* only in 1939). But actually going to the cinema in term time at Tonbridge was almost a capital offence until 1938, when a respectable cinema in nearby Sevenoaks occasionally took to showing French films. Our little group in the Modern Upper Sixth suggested to Alfred Foster that it would do our French good if he were to organise trips to see some of these. Rather to our surprise he readily agreed to this (and our opinion of him rose dramatically), and off we went one afternoon on the bus to Sevenoaks and saw Duvivier's *Un Carnet de Bal*. That time was one of the greatest in the history of the French cinema, and from then on we were hooked on the idea of the cinema as a noble popular art. A legacy of this was that, by the time I had become involved in the Cambridge Film Society, friendly cultured masters at Tonbridge like Foster and Eames had managed to persuade the school's governors to provide the money to enable a film society to be started at the school.

Members of what I have called Tom Staveley's coterie in the Modern Upper Sixth shared in all these non-athletic interests. The greatest of them, and the one I was closest to, was Sidney Keyes who, following his death in action in North Africa in 1943, was to be posthumously awarded the Hawthornden Prize for his poetry. Sidney had come to Hill Side a year after me, and I was first aware of him as a boy who was much concerned with natural history (he was quite likely to take a snake out of his pocket), and who entertained his fellow *novi* by telling them stories of his own invention. He had had an irregular upbringing. His mother had died soon after his birth, his father – who, before an early retirement, was an army officer – was not very fit, and though in due course Sidney was provided with a stepmother and a sister, he was largely brought up by his grandfather, a self-made master miller who lived at Dartford in Kent (and was the inventor of the Daren flour that once rivalled Hovis). Two consequences of this upbringing were that Sidney did not go to school until he was nine years old, and that when he arrived at Tonbridge he knew no Latin, and so had to start in Form One. But he then rose through the school literally by leaps and bounds, securing promotion to a higher form, not annually like ordinary mortals, but virtually every term, so that he arrived in the Modern Upper Sixth close on my heels. In those days I too was writing poetry, and we used to criticise each other's work. This continued in the school holidays either by post or by Sidney coming to stay with me at Teddington or I going to his home in Hastings. Poetry was by no means our only mutual interest: his surviving letters to me deal also with the novels he had been reading, the concerts he had heard, the plays he had been to, and – at some length, because I had already begun to think about writing a book on the cinema – the films he had seen. This pattern of interaction continued when I went to Cambridge and he, a year later, to Oxford, and ended only when I went into the Royal Air Force and it sent me off to Africa.

I can say of Sidney Keyes that, despite his occasional moments of introspective depression, it was sheer delight to be in his company, and that he was quite the most stimulating person I have known. I do not know when I came to appreciate that he would achieve a wide reputation as a poet whereas I was no more than passing through an adolescent phase of poetising. I suppose I sensed this when I first read his "Elegy" on the death of his grandfather, but this was essentially subconscious. This poem, written in 1938 and, I think, first published in *The Tonbridgian*'s first literary supplement, later became the first item in the *Collected Poems* edited by Michael Meyer (Routledge, 1945). But Sidney was strangely diffident about his poetic gift. As late as August 1940 he could write to me "Why not make a practice of setting each other subjects [for poems]? It would keep us in training. We both write a poem on the set subject and exchange works"! And in March 1941, after he had had poems accepted by at least *The Spectator*, *The Listener* and *The Fortnightly*, and was in correspondence with people like Stephen Spender, Herbert Read and John Lehmann, he gave me the typescript of the collection which was to see publication as *Eight Oxford Poets* which he and Meyer were then assembling, and asked me for my comments. (Comparing a letter which Sidney wrote at this time with the collection as it was published by Routledge in 1941, it even looks as though my comments may have had a hand in persuading him and Meyer to drop one of the poets they had originally selected.)

However Sidney and I and our friends in the Modern Upper Sixth were not sent to Tonbridge to write poems or to discuss the cinema and other arts. We were there to qualify to enter Oxford or Cambridge and, in my case at least – as my father once put it – "The main thing to do is to get a scholarship". Tom Staveley's idea for me was that I should seek a history scholarship at his old college, Trinity, at Oxford. But he thought that if I were to achieve this aim, I must first have some live practice. He was quite right for, as I can now see, I was still rather a child; in relation to my current or potential future academic achievement, I was not very mature. But this was not something that I understood at the time; I can remember being quite upset when Eames chose as the head boy of Hill Side for 1938-39 a boy who had entered the house a term later than I had. (Born in June 1921, I was not far into my fourteenth year when I arrived at Tonbridge; I can now see from the Tonbridge School Register that half those who entered the school with me were born in 1920 and so, by the standards of the young, were quite a bit older than I was.)

The first target that Staveley chose for me was Magdalene College at Cambridge. Magdalene was a small college which was not then very distinguished academically, but Tom knew that in Frank Salter it had just the right kind of history don to get the best results out of someone like me. So in December 1938, I spent the best part of a week staying at Magdalene, feeling very small and insignificant in its dark enclosures, and going most mornings and afternoons to the great, light hall of Trinity College to write my examination papers. I did not win a scholarship, but Salter had invited me round to tea, and afterwards wrote me a very kind letter saying that he was sorry that I had not got a scholarship, but adding: "if you had put yourself down for an exhibition [a lesser award worth £40 or £60 a year compared with a scholarship's £100], you might quite possibly have got one as your work, although immature, had a good deal of promise in it. I very much hope that you will come up again for Magdalene in 1939..." My second sortie, in March 1939, was to the Queen's College at Oxford, much more splendid than Cambridge's Magdalene but, in my eyes at least, more formal and less friendly. This too was unsuccessful.

The next stage in my competition for academic and financial awards was the examination for the Higher School Certificate, on the results of which State Scholarships were awarded by the Department of Education in London. The normal practice at the time was to offer for examination two principal subjects and two subsidiaries, but there was an alternative pattern by which one might offer instead three principal subjects. This is what I did, the three subjects being History, French and English; I believe I was not eligible for a distinction in the last of these, since it stood in the place of subsidiary subjects. I passed in all three, but achieved distinction only in French. Doubtless for this reason, I did not win a state scholarship;

however there was some consolation in that Tonbridge thought I had done well enough to be awarded one of its leaving exhibitions. I find it interesting that Sidney Keyes, who was having a first, trial run at the Higher School Certificate, also failed to get a distinction in history. He did some research into this, and reported to me that he could not see that any distinctions in history were awarded by the H.S.C. examiners in 1939. Whatever the truth of this, it can be said that Sidney was to do better than I in his competition for awards. Not only did he win a major scholarship in his first essay at one, in the spring of 1940 at the Queen's College at Oxford, but he also got his history distinction and a state scholarship from the H.S.C. examination later in that year. Sidney believed that this distinction may have been not unconnected with the fact that in 1940 one of the Higher School Certificate history examiners was Frank Salter. By this time I was already working under Salter, for I had been successful in my second attempt at a Magdalene scholarship, and I had already had two terms at Cambridge. One consequence of this was that I was able to introduce Sidney to Frank, with the result that afterwards Sidney wrote me a letter in which he said: "I thought Salter the nicest don I have ever met! You're very lucky".

CHAPTER 2
PRELUDE TO WAR

My first contribution towards victory in the war with Germany which began on 3 September 1939 was to evacuate my sister. The received opinion of the day was that massive bombing would follow immediately upon the outbreak of war, and therefore that children should be removed from the cities which would offer the largest targets for enemy bombers. The wife of one of our neighbours at Teddington had a brother, Arthur Chant, an architect in Shrewsbury who had a daughter of about Christine's age, who was a pupil at a school which was a member of the same G.P.D.S. Trust which embraced Christine's school at Wimbledon. So it had been arranged that in the event of war Christine would be sent to live with the Chants and attend Shrewsbury High School. When on the morning of 1 September it was clear that war was imminent, neither my father nor my mother (who was an Air Raid Warden) was in a position to take Christine to Shrewsbury, so the job was entrusted to me. I can vividly remember how strange it all was, travelling by train with Christine to a town neither of us had ever been to before, finding our way to the Chants' house (which luckily was within walking distance of Shrewsbury station), lunching with perfect strangers, and then leaving my sister behind in this foreign environment and making my way alone back to Teddington.

There was of course no serious bombing of London before September 1940, and relatively few bombs fell on Teddington (though 171 Park Road was superficially damaged by the blast from one which fell nearby). Nevertheless Christine spent term-times with the Chants until in 1943 she won an exhibition at Newnham College at Cambridge. This was the beginning of a continuing family connection with Shrewsbury. Christine lived in or near the town for many years after her marriage, and in our retirement in Wales it has become a major shopping centre for my wife and myself. However when the Blitz did begin, I was required to conduct a second evacuation, that of my grandmother to stay with her other daughter who lived in her old home at Kimberley just outside Nottingham. But this was a journey into familiar territory; the abiding memory of this second excursion is of the great twisting network of fire-hoses littering the streets near Marylebone as evidence of the previous night's bombing.

My second contribution to the war effort involved taking a day off from school early in October to visit Armoury House in Finsbury (the headquarters of the Honorable Artillery Company) to attest for service in the army for the duration of the conflict. This requires some explanation. Britain had begun to call up twenty year old men for military service some months before the war began, and with the outbreak of hostilities, all males between the ages of eighteen and forty became liable for service. But time was needed to equip, house and train all these potential conscripts; thus by September 1939, by no means all of the twenty year olds had actually been embodied in the armed services. It was therefore decided that those in full time education might be allowed to continue in it for the time being. However at the same time young men who had already received some military training – as I had in the Officer's Training Corps, membership in which was virtually compulsory for boys at Tonbridge – were encouraged to attest their willingness to serve in the armed forces. Thereupon such persons were officially enlisted in one of the armed forces, and so were not liable to be called up under the 1939 National Service Act. I cannot see in the papers of mine that have survived from this time any mention of how long any deferment of my service might last, but I believe that "subject to the exigencies of the service", it might continue for up to two years.

So on 12 October 1939 I officially became a soldier whose army service had been deferred, and as a consequence, when in December I won entry to Magdalene with my scholarship, it made sense not to wait until the following October and the beginning of a new academic year before going up to Cambridge, but to go up as soon as possible, for the second term of the 1939-40 academic year. With any luck I would then be able to spend the best part of two years at Cambridge before I went off to war. So I said goodbye to Tonbridge at the Hill Side House Supper just before Christmas 1939, and in January 1940 I was matriculated as an undergraduate of the University of Cambridge.

Although leaving home for Tonbridge had been a major break in my life, arriving at Magdalene was in many respects a more significant change.

For one thing, while I seem always to have taken for granted the architectural setting at Tonbridge, I could not escape that of Cambridge in general and of Magdalene in particular. Magdalene was one of the smallest and least wealthy of the Cambridge colleges. It displays none of the grandeur of its immediate neighbour, St. John's College, let alone of King's or Trinity; it is charmingly domestic. Even its finest architecture, in the Pepys Building, is domestic behind its facade. Magdalene was also rather peripheral to the university as a whole. It lies at the northern end of the main street which, under a succession of names, runs south to north through Cambridge until it crosses the River Cam at Magdalene Bridge and assumes the name of Magdalene Street. It is unusual in that it has buildings on either side of this road. On the eastern side there are two little courts, the second of which is made beautiful by the front of the Pepys Building. To its west, fronting the street, lies the First Court, built in stages from the fifteenth century onwards. Today it can be seen in the glow of its original brickwork. In 1940 it looked very different, since eighteenth and nineteenth century tastes had combined to plaster it with stucco, to crown its walls with false battlements, and to clothe it in ivy; these excrescences were not removed until the 1950s. In the first third of the twentieth century, a growth in undergraduate admissions from no more than about twenty a year to a steady sixty-five or so, led the college to expand to the west of Magdalene Street. Behind the row of picturesque cottages and small shops that faced the old college buildings, there arose the grand but not very practical Benson Court designed by Sir Edwin Lutyens, and the much more homely (and usefully less costly) Mallory Court put together by combining modest new building with the conversion of older, originally non-collegiate buildings. Upon my arrival in Magdalene, I was allocated rooms in Mallory Court, and I consider myself fortunate to have been able to continue to have rooms there throughout my time at Magdalene. It followed that when I was *in statu pupillari* I would have to cross the road whenever I needed to see my tutor or supervisor, to go to chapel, to visit the college library, or to lunch or dine in hall. Thus at least three or four times a day, after dodging the buses and cars thronging the narrows of Magdalene Street, I would arrive on its eastern shore and see as if for the first time the enfolding First Court and – if it were evening time – its candle-lit Hall. If these occasions were somewhat less frequent after I became a Bye-Fellow, their friendly magic was no weaker.

While big, powerful and rich colleges like Trinity and St. Johns were so devoted to the advancement of scholarship and science that relations between their dons and their undergraduates might sometimes go little further than what was thought necessary to achieve the best possible examination results, the atmosphere at Magdalene was more that of a family of elders and offspring. This could be restrictive, as with the Master of the college at the time of my arrival, A.B. Ramsay. Ramsay had come to Magdalene in 1926 after thirty-five years of teaching classics at Eton (where he had previously been a scholar). When I knew him, the Ram was a kindly old gentleman who had the interests of the college and all its people very much to heart, but, with the best of intentions, he could not deal with undergraduates other than as though they were schoolboys. But with other members of the High Table, the family ethos of Magdalene was a liberation. They would have been upset if undergraduates had not called them by their Christian names, they entertained them in their homes as well as in their college rooms, would engage with them in bridge or party games, and would invite them to vacation reading parties at the seaside in which academic study and discussion would be enlightened by afternoon excursions or games on the beach. The family atmosphere was in some degree heightened by the war because the population of the college had become much smaller. In 1938 there had been in residence 187 junior members (undergraduates and B.A.s) and – if one excludes the two professorial fellows because they were neither involved in college teaching nor eligible to hold college offices – eleven Fellows. By 1940, the junior members were down to 86, while five fellows, elected in the 1920s and 1930s and so amongst the most active of their kind, had gone off on various kinds of war service.

In this situation it was perfectly possible to know every member of the college, and by my second year I probably did. Initially, however, I was at a disadvantage since I was a "by-termer", i.e. someone who had arrived in the college after the first term of the academic year had passed. The great social focus of each day was dinner in hall, and here a newcomer found virtually every section of each long table inhabited by a particular group of established friends. Some of these would be rowing men, others might be sitting together because they were all scientists, or would-be medical men, or beaglers. One very distinctive college group was composed of Old Etonians: about a third of Magdalene's undergraduates had come from Eton – because they had failed to get into King's, or because the Ram had persuaded their parents that their sons would be safer or happier in his college. This group might have been balanced by those who had come as scholars from northern grammar schools with which Magdalene had particular connections, but these men were appreciably fewer than the Old Etonians, and they lacked the effortless self-confidence which was their distinctive hallmark.

The clumping tendency meant that time was needed to experiment before a newcomer could discover a group with similar interests and background to his own, and before he had gained acceptance in it. I suppose there might have been a group of by-termers, but in retrospect I can remember only one other man who had arrived in the college when I had done. This was Charles Curran, whom I remember not because his career culminated in his becoming Director General of the B.B.C., but because he too had entered Magdalene with a scholarship in history, so that once a week we went together to be supervised by Frank Salter in a class of two. Initially we were rather shy of each other, partly I think because we were both shy young men, but also because we came from very different backgrounds, for Charles was the son of a warrant officer in the army, and it was from a Yorkshire grammar school that he had won his scholarship. I think we may not have got to know each other really well until we came together again in 1945 when we returned from the war. In 1940-41 our friendship might perhaps be described as an intellectual one, one that derived from studying history first with Frank Salter and then with Philip Grierson; in this respect it may well have been as stimulating as my friendship with Sidney Keyes, but its range was narrower.

Frank Salter had been enticed to Magdalene in 1910 as a bright young graduate from Trinity College with the idea of establishing history as a college staple alongside the traditional subjects of the classics and mathematics. In this he was very successful, so that by 1938 the college found it necessary to elect a second history fellow, the medievalist Ralph Bennett. Frank was a man of compelling energy in any number of fields. As a historian he wrote relatively little; here his energies went into teaching. I never heard him lecture – in his field of modern economic and social history, he did not wish to appear as a sole authority – but as a supervisor he was marvellous. Charles and I would provide him in advance with our weekly essays; they would be handed back to us with copious annotations written all over them, and these would provide the spurs with which he would challenge and tease us. In no time at all a lively three-sided discussion would develop, during the course of which he would leap round his room pulling out from their shelves books which he thought we should know about. But, however important to us, this was only one aspect of his energy; there seemed to be no end to the number of jobs he had done for the college, for the university, for the town, and for a variety of extramural and social organisations. During 1939-45, besides his teaching, he was tutor to at least a third of the undergraduates and also a part-time Lieutenant-Colonel in charge of Army Welfare in Cambridgeshire. Charles and I were not at all happy when he told us that he would not be supervising our work in our second year because we would then need to concentrate on medieval history. Since Ralph Bennett had gone away to war, our supervisor would be Philip Grierson at Caius College. We need not have worried; Philip, though much less rumbustious and with a knack of giving us essay titles which involved quite a bit of work before they were readily comprehensible, was in his subtle way as good as Frank at inspiring us with his learning. Some of this has stuck with me to this day, so that occasionally I still think it right to send him offprints of articles I have written.

Having missed the first term of 1939-40, and doubtless too because I felt a need to justify the temporary deferment of my military service, I do not seem to have done very much at Cambridge during my first two terms except work. I was certainly a conscientious attender at the lectures provided for the first year of the History Tripos, but I can now remember only three of the lecturers: Kitson Clark, who lectured very positively on modern English constitutional history, Kenneth Pickthorn, and E.E. Rich – and the last two only because Pickthorn was so rude to women who came to listen to him, and Rich because in his lectures on English economic history he told us about legging his way through the long canal tunnel running under the town of Dudley. Outside work, I cannot now remember much more than joining the Cambridge Union – which I think I valued more for its restaurant than for its debates – and the Cambridge University Socialist Club. At this time C.U.S.C. was thought to be very left wing or even crypto-Communist; I believe indeed that it had been disaffiliated from the Labour Party. But for me the later 1930s had been overshadowed by the civil war in Spain and the pan-European advance of fascism; I remember that the subjects of two of my entries for literary or poetry competitions at Tonbridge had been "The Streets of Teruel" and "The Refugees". So when

I got to Cambridge and was free from the bondage of school, joining C.U.S.C. seemed as natural a thing to do as buying the publications of Victor Gollancz's Left Book Club. But I think I may not have found its political activities all that compelling. The chief memories that survive are of the film shows given in its clubroom on Sunday afternoons by Michael Orrom, a physics student from Trinity College, casually dressed, tall and voluble, with a cheerful puckish face topped with thinnish curly hair. Michael was a film enthusiast who had planned to set up a film society operating through one of the Cambridge cinemas. When this had been thwarted by the outbreak of war, he had organised the purchase of a second-hand 16mm projector which he used in the cramped conditions of the C.U.S.C. clubroom to show many of the great classic foreign films, mainly from Russia and Germany, which were rarely shown in British cinemas. I do not think I missed a single one of them, and out of our common obsession with the cinema a quick and easy friendship was to develop. It must have been through Michael that I first met Raymond Williams, also from Trinity, reading English, a less flamboyant figure, tall and darkly handsome, but so quietly spoken that neither his Welshness nor his self-confident authority were immediately apparent. He was then editing the sole surviving undergraduate newspaper, *The Cambridge University Journal,* the *Varsity* of its day, but put together in a garret and scruffily printed on a shoestring, and was glad of any volunteer hack labour he could find. It is possible that it was in this paper that my first film reviews appeared in print (but, if so, I can only have been a number two to Michael Orrom); however I think my main contribution to the paper was helping to cut items from the galley proofs and to stick these onto appropriate places on the page paste-ups.

But it was not until my second year at Cambridge that I became at all closely involved with Michael and Raymond. In my first two terms I was still feeling my way outside Magdalene, and in the college there was a great deal to savour and absorb. I suspect that Magdalene's cautious conservatism (Frank Salter was probably the only surviving representative of a radical strain which had once numbered such as Patrick Blackett, I.A. Richards, Kingsley Martin, Charles Madge and William Empson), meant that it may have been slower than some other colleges to adjust its customs to meet wartime stringencies. For example, no breakfast was served in Hall other than for the R.A.F. cadets who then occupied most of the rooms in First

Court. The college continued with the practice by which undergraduates who wanted a cooked breakfast selected it the previous evening from a number of available dishes, and it was then delivered to their rooms at an agreed time in the morning by the kitchen porter, a strange man-boy known to all as "Horace". If one could afford it, it was still possible to entertain a lunch or dinner party in one's rooms with food and wines provided by the college kitchen and buttery. Gyps, i.e. man-servants, had become scarce, but men still came round each morning to brush shoes and to deliver a scuttle of coal for the keeping-room fire. There was no shortage of "bedders" who came seven mornings a week and, as well as making one's bed, laid the fire, set the table, washed up whatever crockery and cutlery needed attention, and did some general cleaning. In 1940, the main change brought by war to the life of the College was probably the need to take part in Air Raid Precautions. For most undergraduates this involved no more than occasional fire-watching. I chose however to join the college's little fire brigade, and was trained by one of the college porters, a former naval man we knew as "Monty", to operate a trolley-mounted fire engine, to run out its fire-hoses, and to clamber all over the roofs of the college buildings. Since in my time there were no fires to put out, it was all rather a lark.

In my second year at Cambridge, 1940-41, I might have supposed that I should work even harder than I had in my first two terms, since the year would culminate in my taking Part I of the History Tripos examination on which my ultimate university degree would depend. In fact I think I did work hard, so that I did secure a First (as also did Charles Curran). But looking back on this year, what most impresses me is not how hard I worked, but how hard I played. I began the year by securing election to the Amateur Dramatic Club, the only one of the three major Cambridge undergraduate dramatic societies to remain active during the war – no doubt because it had its own delightful little theatre and clubroom in Park Street. So far as I am aware, the wartime A.D.C. never sought to carry on the role of the Marlowe Society as a purveyor of Elizabethan and Jacobean drama; in 1940-41 at least it seems to have been agreed that what was required for the darkness of wartime was entertainment of the kind associated with the Footlights Club. So in December I found myself participating in a topical pantomime, *The Sleeping Cutie,* and in June in a May Week revue, *Daffadown Silly.* In neither of these productions did I have more than what might euphemistically be styled "a supporting role". The stars were such as Donald McWhinnie and Walter Todds, later major producers for the B.B.C. of drama and music respectively, and Jimmy Edwards, already displaying a marvellous natural talent for broad comedy. I had little gift for the discipline of acting. What attracted me to the theatre was its ambiance, especially in rehearsals, sitting in the semi-darkness taking in what the producer, the stage manager, those in charge of the sets, the costumes, the music were up to, climbing up into the flies and scrambling along the catwalk which – in the A.D.C.'s theatre – ran between ceiling and roof from the flies to the projection box at the back of the theatre. There were rehearsals most evenings of the week, and part of the fun was the exhilaration of dashing back through the cold air of the streets to reach Magdalene before its gate was locked at midnight.

Another time-consuming activity occupied my Monday afternoons. Equipped with a card that promised a pair of free seats, I would go with a friend to whichever local cinema was showing a film that might be supposed worthy of notice, so that I could write a review of it for *The Cambridge Review,* the donnish local equivalent of *The Spectator* that was edited by the Rev. Canon Charles Smyth of Corpus Christi College. How I got this job, I cannot now think, but it was one that had to be done quickly because *The Cambridge Review* was published on Fridays, and there was no advantage to the cinema that had provided free seats if the film that I had reviewed was no longer on show.

The Cambridge University Journal disappeared at the end of 1940 or early in 1941; it had not been bringing in enough income to make it possible for its printer to continue to print it. It was agreed that undergraduate journalism needed to be subsidised, and people like Michael Orrom and Raymond Williams decided that they must find backers who possessed both good literary taste and funds to support it. One of these, possibly the only one, was John Lehmann. Because of wartime paper rationing, which included a prohibition on the establishment of new periodicals, the first result was an attempt to resurrect a one-off title of 1940, *Cambridge Front,* as a periodical. A beautifully printed new issue appeared in March 1941, a local *New Statesman* to rival Charles Smyth's local *Spectator.* But the government's Paper Controller was not fooled, and the undergraduate writers and journalists had to return to one-off publications, such as *Outlook; a selection of Cambridge writing,* a little sixpenny book in a yellow paper cover which was published in the summer of 1941. Michael and his friend Lionel

Cole edited the revived but stillborn *Cambridge Front;* the editors of *Outlook* were Raymond Williams, Michael Orrom, and the Magdalene poet Maurice James Craig. I was never a major player in these activities, but they meant a lot to me at the time. I contributed an article to *Cambridge Front,* and my translation of Hölderlin's "Hälfte des Lebens" was used to fill up a page of *Outlook* (albeit with a sad misprint in the second verse). I also had a hand in the distribution of *Outlook,* despatching parcels and invoices to W.H. Smith and other booksellers, and also copies to Sidney Keyes, then much involved in *The Cherwell,* who was able to get them placed on sale in two Oxford bookshops.

But by this time any literary aspirations I had were taking second place to my concern with the cinema. Through the A.D.C. I had become acquainted with Peter Price, who had been a flagrantly outrageous Fairy Queen in *The Sleeping Cutie.* An undergraduate at Trinity who lived in some luxury in rooms above Trinity Street, he had, I think, already had some connection with at least the documentary side of professional film production. In the autumn term of 1940 he set about establishing a Cambridge Film Society. Basil Wright, famous for directing *The Song of Ceylon,* one of the most poetic of the great British documentary films of the 1930s, was persuaded to become its president, and Peter secured two college fellows and the manager of Cambridge's Arts Theatre to serve on its committee, together with himself, as secretary, and three other undergraduates, Michael Orrom, Lionel Cole and myself. The society very soon had more than six hundred subscribers, and in the second and third terms of 1940-41 was able to launch a first season of six shows at the Arts Theatre. I cannot say that the first film we showed, *The Petrified Forest,* a somewhat pedestrian filming of a play by Robert Sherwood, was really film society material; either it was chosen because it was thought advisable not to frighten newcomers to the world of film societies (neither the London nor Oxford film society was active at this time), or because it was a film which Peter had missed on general release and which he wanted to see! But soon, for an annual subscription of only six shillings (30p), the members were entitled to view such classics as *The Cabinet of Dr Caligari* and *Zéro de Conduite,* and in addition to listen to talks by Basil Wright on the role of documentary films in wartime, by the conductor Muir Mathieson on film music, and by Bernard Miles on film acting.

By the summer Michael and I had decided to make a film of our own. It was to be called *Ivory Tower,* and it was intended to be an ironic look at the pleasures of student life in Cambridge in the midst of a world at war, a world which we knew was about to engulf us both. It was enormous fun, but we were miserably equipped for our task. We had so little money that, whereas someone like Peter Price setting out to make an equivalent film would have shot it on 16mm film stock, the next best thing to the 35mm stock used by professional film-makers, we had no choice but to use the 9.5mm film manufactured for amateurs by the French company Pathé simply because it was the cheapest film stock available and Michael already possessed a 9.5mm camera. Beyond this, we had virtually no equipment at all. But in retrospect I believe that our greatest weakness was that our script, in which I had a substantial share, did not measure up to the ambition of our intentions; it is not easy to make a good film from a weak script. I suppose that in the end we could not have shot more than half of what was needed to make a properly constructed short film, and I suppose that I would say that this was more pretty than meaningful. Many years later, Michael was to make use of some of it – and so give me my only screen credit – in a television programme about the life and attitudes of Cambridge students during 1938-41 which he called *Fragment of Memory* (Channel Four, 1984), and which does in its way reflect our original purpose rather well.

One of the reasons why in the summer of 1941 I was able to indulge in film-making in Cambridge was that by this time I had been released from my commitment to the army and had been accepted for R.A.F. aircrew training, the initial stage of which was to be with the Cambridge University Air Squadron. This was no sudden whim. I think I had originally chosen the army for my attestation for service mainly because at that time, when I was still a schoolboy, I was following the behest of my parents, who thought that the risk of losing their only son in war would be appreciably greater if he became an airman than if he became a soldier. However, I had been fascinated by aeroplanes and aviation from a very early age. I cannot have been more than about ten years old when I began making model aircraft, and hardly older than that when I used to cycle to Hanworth and Heston, the nearest aerodromes to Teddington, to watch aeroplanes taking off and landing. By about 1936, my father had twice paid for me to take joy-rides. Then when in the following year, the Officers' Training Corps at Tonbridge started an Air Section, I immediately joined it, thus exchanging a lot of dull O.T.C. routine for the joys of visiting R.A.F. stations and flying in their aircraft. On one occasion, I even had a short trip in a flying boat, which I immediately concluded was the most entrancing means of moving over the earth's surface ever devised by man. Had I arrived in Cambridge in peacetime, I would undoubtedly have sought to join the University Air Squadron. But the university air squadrons' tradition of light hearted cross-country flying all over Britain obviously did not appeal to serious men in the Air Ministry when they were faced with winning a real war in the air, and the university air squadrons were disbanded. However by 1941 someone must have realised that the R.A.F. had in this way deprived itself of a useful means of recruiting university trained men, and the university air squadrons were brought back to life, although this time there was to be no joyful flying about the country at public expense. Indeed, there was no flying at all; as a member of the Cambridge University Air Squadron I did the same six or so weeks of ground training that less privileged aircrew recruits did in Initial Training Wings; the main difference was that, when work had finished for the day, my colleagues and I returned to our colleges, removed our uniforms, and were again undergraduates.

By September I had completed my ground training with the C.U.A.S., passing at a level which meant that I was thought fit to be trained as a pilot or observer. I then went home to Teddington to await my R.A.F. calling up papers. With the impatience both of youth and civilians, I thought it an irksomely long wait, but I was not idle. Shortly after finishing my Tripos examination, I had begun writing a book which I called "The Cinema as a Social Art". This was an outline history of the cinema which attempted to trace the relation between the socio-political conditions in the major producing countries – the U.S.A., the Soviet Union, Germany, France and Britain – and the films they made. (The title was adapted from *The Cinema as a Graphic Art* by the pioneer Russian cameraman Vladimir Nilsen.) By the time I was summoned to present myself at the Aircrew Reception Centre in London on 15 November 1941, I had a virtually complete draft in typescript. I soon realised the truth of a remark my father had once made to me when, on a walk from my aunt's house at Kimberley, we had looked over the fence of the R.A.F. airfield at Hucknall, and had seen two or three ground crew standing or sitting around one of the graceful Hawker biplanes of the 1930s: "You know, John, there's a lot of waiting about in the Services". It was not until the middle of March 1942 that the R.A.F. shipped me off to Southern Rhodesia (the modern Zimbabwe) to begin my flying training. During the intervening four months there were only three weeks of work directly relevant to this. This was when I received ten hours dual instruction in Tiger Moth training aircraft at an Elementary Flying Training School in Oxfordshire, on a grading course to assess my suitability to be trained as a pilot. The rest of the time was spent in three different holding centres (where I think the most useful thing I learnt was how to wash a floor without flooding it). So from November to March I travelled round Britain – to Brighton, to Shellingford in Oxfordshire, to Heaton Park outside Manchester – carrying typewriter, notes and typescript as well as my kitbag, and trying gradually to improve the first draft of my book. Ultimately I arrived at Blackpool and embarkation leave, at which point I saw no alternative but to leave the typewriter at Teddington, and to send the top copy of my typescript to Michael Orrom. Michael, while awaiting the call to a war job appropriate to his science degree, was then working with Paul Rotha, who was one of the most socially conscious of the great documentary film directors who had emerged in Britain since the late 1920s. More than this, he had written some notable books on the cinema, such as *The Film Till Now,* a splendid pioneer history of the cinema which had been published in 1930, and an important study of the *Documentary Film* (1936). So I asked Michael not only to send me his comments on my book, but also to seek Rotha's opinion of it and, if this were favourable, to seek his advice as to a possible publisher.

In due course I received a marvellous 1500-word letter from Rotha which paid me the compliment of saying that my approach to cinema history was "the most important one you could have chosen" and that my book did "a great deal towards pulling off the job". But he then went on to say that "the book could be better even than it is". He added that he regretted that as a young man he had rushed into publication with his *The Film Till Now,* and strongly advised me to do more work on my book before offering it to a publisher. As he knew, it was virtually impossible for me to do what he thought necessary when I was engaged in a full time training programme in Rhodesia, and it was not until the last quarter of 1943, when my R.A.F. career was again marking time in a holding unit in England, that I had a chance of trying to do what Rotha thought needed to be done to my book. When I sent it back to him, he thought it "certainly improved", but still not as good as he would have liked. But by the time I had received this second opinion from Rotha, I was again very fully involved in active flying, and when finally, in the summer of 1945, my typescript was submitted to publishers backed by a recommendation from Rotha, it was not accepted. The publishers said, correctly, that this was a difficult time for publishing; more precisely, I suspect that they may have thought that the market had been cornered by the publication by Penguins in 1944 of Roger Manvell's book *Film*. Looking back on this episode in my life, I can see that Paul Rotha was right. What I was trying to do was well worth trying, but my knowledge and experience were inadequate to achieve anything approaching a definitive outcome. Rereading what I wrote fifty or more years ago, I am amazed at once by what I managed to do when I was so young, and by my temerity in even attempting it.

CHAPTER 3
WAR SERVICE I: LEARNING

On 15 March 1942, together with other successful members of the aircrew grading course we had taken at Shellingford, and with several thousand sundry other servicemen, I boarded the Union Castle liner *Arundel Castle* at the Liverpool pierhead. After casting off, the ship steamed out of the Mersey to anchor in Liverpool Bay. With a strong ebb tide running, we could soon see that it would be impossible for our vessel to avoid giving a glancing blow to another ship which had already moored close by the main channel; luckily there was no more than superficial damage to either vessel. Soon as far as eyes could see, vessels were anchored all over the bay. This was the Liverpool contingent of what ultimately developed into a large and magnificent convoy of some fifty vessels. It included a sizeable passenger ship which carried landing-craft in place of lifeboats and one of the new fleet aircraft carriers, and was guarded by a substantial number of destroyers and other escorts. We were later to realise that some of the ships and men in our convoy were destined for the invasion of Madagascar. We spent as much time as we could on deck watching what was going on in the convoy (which sometimes included aircraft taking off from, and landing on the carrier) because we were not exactly enamoured of our accommodation on the troop decks, large ill-lit and ill-ventilated spaces furnished with little more than mess tables and benches and hooks on which at night we hung the hammocks on which we were meant to sleep. If this was the everyday lot of seamen in the Royal Navy, at least they had done some real work before tumbling into their hammocks; we had little else to do other than to look at what was going on around us. The moods of the sea and the shapes of all our ships upon it were soon very familiar.

It was a great joy when the convoy put in at Freetown. Although no one went ashore, it was enough to see the rounded green hills of the land, and to smell it – which we could do quite a while before we could see it.

Moreover it was a strange new land, with vivid colours and new associations, inhabited by men and women whose outlook on the world was not the same as ours and who, I felt, may well have looked on us, cooped up behind our ships' railings, rather as strange animals in a fanciful zoo which had been brought across the sea for their amusement. By this time we knew for certain that our destination was Southern Rhodesia, and so we were considerably surprised that when we next smelt land, we were not approaching Cape Town. Instead the sea turned brown, and in due course we were steaming gently up the estuary of a great river which could only be the Congo. The ship anchored many miles up this estuary, and we were able to gaze at its long, low, remote, palm-covered northern shore sweltering steamily under a still sun. Nothing whatever appeared to be happening either on land or on the water; what we were doing on this threshold of Conrad's *Heart of Darkness* was a mystery, the first of many that war service was to bring. However eventually the ship stole away as unfussily as it had arrived and, some days later, early one bright and breezy morning, Table Mountain did appear above the horizon, and then we were ploughing through a choppy sea past Robben Island to tie up in the docks of the city it overshadows.

We had a day to savour Cape Town before boarding the train that was to take us to Rhodesia, and a jumble of memories remain. Coming from the Britain of blackout and rationing, and after five weeks in a crowded and uncomfortable ship, it was a pleasure just to walk the streets. From the docks we came first to a quite small grid of modern offices and shops, pubs, restaurants and cinemas, which might almost have been part of some British city, and here we feasted on the plenty of street lighting, cheap fresh food and fruits, wines and tobaccos. But beyond this we found a little Government House and Parliament standing beside a little park with architecture and vegetation that were less British, and when one penetrated inland on a trolley bus the more the exotic elements increased, with Coloured citizens, stucco houses, Dutch gables, overhead cables, and roads ending in undeveloped country. But Cape Town is the most European, if not perhaps the most British, of South African towns, and it was not until we were on the train to the north that we began to appreciate that we were in Africa. This appreciation was not immediate; for the first six hours or so the train travelled through lands which had long been developed by European farmers for vineyards and orchards and fields for the cultivation of other temperate fruits and cereals, and their valleys and the surrounding mountains might not have been out of place in Alpine Europe. But then the railway climbed onto the high veldt, the great central plateau of southern Africa, three to four thousand feet above sea level, and this seemed to go on forever. After passing through Kimberley and seeing the great hole in the ground which was the De Beers diamond mine, a day's travel from Cape Town, we began to realise not only that we were in a very large continent, but also that it was not one wholly dominated by Europeans. At towns like Vryburg and Mafeking, white women would turn out in considerable numbers to greet us and to present us with refreshments, but thereafter, in the Bechuanaland Protectorate, the modern Botswana, when the train stopped at the places where there was a passing loop on the single track railway, the people who came to see us, and who might offer us little things to buy, were black. Eventually, after we had spent our third night on the train, we could see smoke in the distance before us, and shortly afterwards the train reached its destination, Bulawayo, the capital of Matabeleland, the southern province of Southern Rhodesia.

We saw nothing of Bulawayo on our arrival, for the railway station was on its southern edge and we were immediately marched a mile or two further south into open country to the Royal Air Force station at Hillside. Here we met with a big disappointment. The R.A.F. Group training aircrew in Rhodesia had been set up on the assumption that it would conduct all their training; the primary function of its Hillside station was to serve as an Initial Training Wing. But our batch of cadets had already done their initial training in Britain; indeed they had already embarked on flying training by passing their E.F.T.S. grading course. The idea of doing the I.T.W. course for a second time did not strike us as sensible. Eventually authority agreed with us. However it also pointed out that there would be no room for us at the E.F.T.S stations until recent I.T.W. courses had passed through them in three months' time. So for the time being we would have to stay at Hillside, and a "refresher" course would be organised for us. As a result of this, we had a good opportunity of getting to know Bulawayo, and some of the surrounding country.

In 1942 the population of Bulawayo was about thirty thousand, divided more or less equally between whites and blacks. But the equality was no more than numerical. I cannot say that one never *saw* black people in the rectangular grid of streets surrounding the domed town hall and containing the shops, hotels, cinemas and other paraphernalia of western civilisation, as well as the homes of those white inhabitants who had not been successful enough to move out to pleasanter suburbs. But one never *noticed* them; they did not belong to the Bulawayo – or to the Rhodesia – to which the R.A.F. had brought us. Blacks were a kind of transient scenery; their home life was elsewhere, in the municipality's "native location" a few miles away to the north-west, which we never saw, or in lesser locations on white owned farms and mines, and in the rural "native reserves", to none of which we – like most settled whites – ever penetrated. But without this background, without a lower layer of inhabitants providing menial supporting services, the whites would have found it difficult if not impossible to maintain a standard and style of living which was universally higher (there were virtually no poor whites) than that of the inhabitants of a town of similar size in Britain. Thus although there were roughnesses in Bulawayo, for example some unmade streets, which one would not expect to find in a British town, in my letters home I commented favourably on Bulawayo's daily newspaper, bookshops, public library, and even the concerts given by its amateur municipal orchestra. But it did not take me long to realise how important the black substructure was for the maintenance of such things and, indeed, of much more material comforts. As early as 8 June, I wrote (using terms which now seem crude and impolitic):

> The high standard of living of Europeans living out here is due in a great measure to the extent and cheapness of native labour. For example, the minimum wage of a native conscripted for war work is 12s. 6d. [62.5p] per month. Though this is the minimum, native wages don't go very high since there are no really intelligent {sic} jobs open to them and they thus have no means of raising their social {sic} status.

It was not until later that I first saw Salisbury (the modern Harare), the capital of the colony and the chief town in the northern province of Mashonaland, and I never knew it as well as I knew Bulawayo, which was my local town throughout my time in Southern Rhodesia. But despite (or even because of) Salisbury's white inhabitants' higher pretensions – they had the colony's parliament and rather impressive government buildings and somewhat more opulent or graceful shops, hotels, streets and suburbs – what I wrote of Bulawayo would do for Salisbury or, indeed, for the whole of a colony in which 70,000 whites ruled, and were supported by the labour of, 1,400,000 blacks.

I was able to see something of the country around Bulawayo largely because petrol rationing was not introduced in Southern Rhodesia until after our arrival, and if four or five cadets banded together we could afford to hire a car. In my letters home I find that I thought the Rhodesian countryside rather fine, comparing it for example to southern English parkland. I think that this was somewhat flattering, at least for Matabeleland, where the uncultivated bush, or *bundu,* was a pretty tough environment. Its scratchy and tick- and insect-ridden grasses could easily be waist high; a hot sun burnt down remorselessly, so that it would be a cool day if the midday shade temperature were as low as 80°F; and the scattered trees would be for the most part small thorn trees, *mopani,* which afforded hardly any shade. (The main value of the *mopani* was that it was proof against attack by termites, and so good for building.) I suppose my good opinion of the landscape was influenced by the fact that we would go in our cars to acknowledged beauty spots, particularly places where men had built dams which created attractive stretches of water to enliven a generally very dry land, for example in the wild, boulder strewn Matopo hills, or at Khami with its ancient stone ruins. The much more splendid ruins of Old Zimbabwe were out of our motoring range, and were not as readily reached by train as the greatest natural splendour in all southern Africa, the Victoria Falls, which we went to gaze at on a short leave.

At length, at the beginning of August, I was posted to 27 E.F.T.S. at Induna, a small grass airfield about nine miles north-east of Bulawayo, and my love affair with the aeroplane could at last begin to be consummated. This was facilitated by the Rhodesian climate and by the personality of my instructor. The aircraft on which I learnt how to begin to master the art of flight was the de Haviland Tiger Moth, a light and skittish little open cockpit two-seater biplane which could easily take things out of the hands of its pilot, and yet required a light touch if it were to be mastered. As I knew from my grading course, it was not easy to achieve this in an English winter. Wind, precipitation and visibility could easily be such as to make flying impracticable, at least for learners, for days at a time. When a pupil did take to the air, his body and limbs were encumbered by a heavy flying suit, boots and gloves, which made it difficult to master the continual jostling from winds and currents which always wanted to blow the aircraft into an unwanted direction or attitude (especially when one was trying to land), and which still left the face open to attack from the elements and which could never keep the body even moderately warm for more than an hour at most. When we were at Induna we were in what passed for winter in Rhodesia. But this meant that we were unlucky if we saw rain on more than one day in a month; for the rest of the time each day offered us at least nine hours of sunshine and a midday temperature reaching to about 80°F. So, besides flying-helmet and goggles, we could go flying in no more than shirt, shorts and stockings; in this way a pilot became at once beneficially almost part of the aeroplane and delightfully close to the air through which it moved. It was as though the air had become our natural element. I see from my logbook that there was one day at Induna on which I made as many as six flights, spending altogether nearly six hours in the air, only one hour of which was with an instructor. But this was rather exceptional, because in the heat of the day the sun's heat could create convection currents which made the air too bumpy for comfortable flying or for safe landings in a light plane like the Tiger Moth. But starting at 6.30 soon after daybreak, engaging in ground instruction from 10.30 to 1.30 p.m., and then resuming flying about 3.30, it was easily possible to get in at least three flights before darkness fell about 6 p.m.

The instructor to whom I was allocated was "Daddy" Wright, so called because, unlike most of the other instructors, who were young men who had often themselves only learnt to fly in the wartime R.A.F., he was a mature man with great experience of his trade. He was a graduate of the famous de Haviland Technical School, so as well as knowing everything there was to know about how a Tiger Moth behaved in the air and how it should be handled, he could probably also have built one. He radiated a calm confidence which overcame my fear of making a fool of myself by being airsick, so that ultimately, although always a cautious pilot, I also gained the confidence to enjoy every moment in the air. But I was much happier flying solo cross country exercises than performing aerobatics and, when we were asked to say what kind of service flying we would prefer to do, I opted for flying multi-engined aircraft, preferably with Coastal Command, and if possible in flying boats.

In due course all these wishes came true but, ironically, as a result of a silly plotting error, I failed the navigation paper in the end-of-course examination at Induna, and so incurred the penalty of spending six weeks at Hillside revising navigation before I could retake it. This time I passed it with high marks, and I was then posted to 21 Service Flying Training School at Kumalo as an A.S.U. i.e. an Acting Sergeant (unpaid). In peacetime, Kumalo, not much more than a mile from the centre of Bulawayo, had been the town's airport, and it was equipped with two parallel tarmac runways. With the S.F.T.S. in residence, these were in more or less continual use during daylight, one for Oxford training aircraft taking off and the other for Oxfords landing, in each case at intervals of only one or two minutes. The Oxford was a twin-engined low wing monoplane which was an adaptation of a small pre-war airliner designed to carry six to eight passengers. It was therefore quite a step up from the Tiger Moth, four times heavier and with nearly six times as much power, and with such mod cons as flaps and a retractable undercarriage. Pupil and instructor sat side by side in comfort at the front of the enclosed cabin, facing, I suppose, something like five times as many knobs, switches and dials as might be found in a Tiger Moth. I must confess that I quickly forgot all about the joys of flying in an open cockpit, and decided that it was much more purposeful to be at the controls of such a businesslike machine. I loved the surge of power when I opened the throttles and the Oxford sped down the runway to take off, and I liked the way in which, when the aircraft was pointed in the direction I wanted to go, it would go in that direction without fuss and without any of the yawing and pitching beloved by Tiger Moths. When, after only six hours of dual instruction on the Oxford, my instructor told me that I could make my first flight without his rather bulky figure sitting by my side, I was somewhat surprised, because I had flown Tiger Moths for ten hours at Shellingford and nine at Induna before I was thought safe to fly one solo, but not for a moment did I doubt my ability to control this much larger and more complex machine.

The S.F.T.S. course lasted twice as long as that at E.F.T.S. The first three months were in principle little different from what we had done at Induna, except of course that we were learning to fly, and gaining experience of handling, not the Tiger Moth but the Oxford. After these three months, with a total flying experience of 173 hours, I became qualified to wear the wings of an R.A.F. pilot, to carry "authorised passengers", and to do one or two other, more technical things. I was also one of the members or our course selected as a candidate for a commission and, as such, I moved from the somewhat bleak sergeants' mess to the much more comfortable, club-like ambiance of the officers' mess (so it could be seen whether or not I was the sort of man who used a knife to eat his peas). The second three months were devoted to the "S" in S.F.T.S., i.e. "service" flying, which meant becoming acquainted with the basics of how an aeroplane might be used in war. For this purpose each of us paired with another cadet, taking it in turns to be the pilot and captain of the aircraft, or its second pilot, navigator, bomb aimer and so forth. I paired with Douglas Hodge, a large and cheerful Yorkshire policeman, very fond of his calabash pipe. Together Douglas and I engaged in various kinds of navigation and bombing, flying on instruments, formation flying, low level flying, air photography, sundry combinations of these things, and much else besides. I began to think that I might become a useful member of the R.A.F., especially perhaps when I was used to fly with passengers to other parts of Rhodesia – once to Salisbury, where I was able to spend a night with friends.

At the end of April 1943 Douglas and I completed the course at Kumalo, were commissioned as Pilot Officers and, with some three hundred hours in our logbooks, were sent, together with another Kumalo pair who were Australians, for more specialised training, to fit us for maritime flying, at the School of General Reconnaissance at George on the beautiful south coast of South Africa. Except for a Sunday when we Kumalo graduates scrambled up the 5000 ft high Outeniqua Mountains behind this sleepy little rural town, and a weekend leave when the same group stayed at a hotel at the lovely beach resort called The Wilderness, about nine miles from George, we had little time to admire the scenery except from the air. Our flying was done in Ansons – aircraft not unlike a larger and more antique version of the Oxford – which were piloted by young lieutenants of the South African Air Force while pairs of trainees practised what they were being taught in a very intensive ground course. We learnt how to distinguish between our ships and those of our German and Japanese foes, and how to use codes to communicate with the former and to report the latter; we learnt about the secret weapon which we knew as A.S.V. and which is now embraced under the generic term Radar; and we learnt a variety of essential skills to help us find our way over featureless oceans, including that most recondite of skills called "astro-navigation" – measuring the altitudes of stars, sun or moon with a sextant and converting these into positions of latitude and longitude by the use of tables which made use of the principles of spherical trigonometry. This last seemed a bit rash to me, who at school had been frightened by even "ordinary" trigonometry. However, since it was now an essential part of an R.A.F. activity which I found completely fascinating, I ended with a mark of 100% (!) for astro-navigation, and an overall mark of just under 90% for the course as a whole (ten percent better than the course average). Whereas assessments of my flying had previously been routinely "Average", my air exercises at George were now marked as "Above Average", and my logbook was endorsed with the encouraging report that I was "A sound navigator, who should develop into an excellent G[eneral] R[econnaissance] pilot".

To achieve this destiny it was necessary that I should be posted either to an operational G.R. squadron, or to an Operational Training Unit which trained crews for such squadrons. But what came next was a typical R.A.F. hiatus. First of all my colleagues and I were sent to Cape Town to be put on a ship to return to the U.K. But passages to Britain were in short supply, and we were told that we might have weeks to wait in the transit camp at Retreat, nine miles south of Cape Town on the suburban electric railway line to Simonstown. So I settled down to a routine by which, after checking that my name was not on the lists posted every morning detailing movements for the following day, I would take the train into Cape Town, do some reading in the South African Library (the local equivalent of the British Museum Library), and then see a film or perhaps attend one of the concerts of the Municipal Symphony Orchestra. However there was one glorious occasion when this routine was broken. Our continual badgering of the movement control officer at Retreat induced him to think that we might take up the empty space on an American military transport which was returning to the U.S.A. half full of U.S. army nurses. He cheerfully told us that when we arrived in the U.S.A., movement controllers there would be bound to find us passages to the U.K. We actually spent some hours on the American vessel before some higher or American authority intervened and sent us back to Retreat. Eventually we learnt that, although as officers we could expect accommodation in cabins, space would be found for us in the troop decks of the *Aorangi,* a New Zealand Line vessel, which would be sailing in convoy from Cape Town for the U.K. on 4 August. In practice this time we escaped the troop decks: the R.A.F. aircrew travelling on the *Aorangi* were given the job of manning the eight Oerlikon 20mm anti-aircraft cannon which were mounted on the topmost deck above the lifeboats. Since the weather in both South and North Atlantic in the August and September of 1943 was superb, we slung our hammocks from whatever suitable supports we could find on *Aorangi's* topmost deck, and then, if we were slow to sleep, we could feast our eyes on the stars, or watch the little red sparks that from time to time escaped from the ship's funnel. It turned out to be one of the pleasantest ocean voyages I have ever experienced.

There was more waiting to be done in Britain, where from early September onwards I spent three months in the aircrew reception centre which occupied a number of the hotels in Harrogate. In retrospect I think that towards the end of 1943 the R.A.F. must have been experiencing a glut of newly trained aircrew – at least in my maritime speciality. Things were different for our two former colleagues who were Australians. Royal Australian Air Force pilots trained in maritime work must have been rare birds in the U.K., and by October our two friends had been slotted into place as second pilots on the Sunderland flying boats operated by 10 Squadron R.A.A.F. from Pembroke Dock; I was very envious. However at the beginning of December I was posted to 131 Operational Training Unit at Killadeas in County Fermanagh in Northern Ireland. This was one of the two flying boat stations which had been set up on Lough Erne in Northern Ireland, the other being Castle Archdale, further to the west, where Sunderland squadrons were based. Lough Erne, providing a substantial expanse of sheltered water free from tides, currents and corrosive salt water, yet close to the sea, was well suited for flying boat operations. But it did have the interesting peculiarity that R.A.F. flying boats from it had to fly for about ten miles over the neutral territory of the Irish Republic before they could reach the sea and their operational area in the western approaches to the British Isles. I believe that a corridor had been agreed by the two governments for this purpose.

My abiding memories of Northern Ireland in the winter of 1943-44 are that it seemed strangely foreign – I was particularly struck by the regular alternation of chapels and bars, and by the armed policemen who always patrolled in pairs – and very wet and cold. Killadeas in summer must, I think, be very beautiful, because thereabouts the Lough is embellished by many attractive small tree-covered islands. The only permanent building that I can remember on the station was the country house in which the officers ate, drank and relaxed. Almost all the other buildings, including the officers' sleeping accommodation, were Nissen huts. Although these were lined and were equipped with patent American oil burning stoves, they suffered from condensation, and every time one went from one hut to another one it seemed impossible to avoid wading in the rain through inches of mud. These conditions were not conducive to robust health. I vividly remember one morning a few days before Christmas when I and another member of my hut each woke up with such splitting headaches and high temperatures that the station medical officer feared we might have meningitis, and had us whisked away in an ambulance to a nearby U.S. Army hospital. We were both comatose when we got there, but luckily his fear proved groundless; we must have been victims of an unusually virulent type of flu. After some forty-eight very unpleasant hours, we began to recover with the hospital's marvellous comfort, food and warmth – a warmth that was human as well as physical, so that shortly after Christmas we were able to return to Killadeas thoroughly set up for the remainder of our course.

I found that I had not missed much; the weather during our absence had been so filthy that little flying had been possible. Killadeas in 1943-44 was training crews for operations on the Catalina. This was a twin-engined flying boat, designed and built by the Consolidated Aircraft Corporation in the U.S.A., which had been delivered to the R.A.F. in some numbers from 1941 onwards when the Air Ministry had realised that it did not have enough of the British equivalent, the Sunderland, to meet growing demands for maritime reconnaissance, the protection of convoys, and the war against submarines. I was initially more than a little disappointed that I was to be trained in the operation of the Catalina and not of the more modern Sunderland, a larger and more impressive four-engined aircraft developed from the commodious passenger and mail carrying "Empire" boats designed for Imperial Airways' routes to Australia and South Africa. But quite soon I began to see that, although the developing technology of warfare – radar and so forth – had made the Catalina a rather crowded and overweight vehicle in which to go to war, it had certain advantages over the Sunderland. It was stronger and so able to operate in rougher waters, it had a longer range, and above all, although it had only two engines, these were much more reliable than the four in the Sunderland. When I was serving at Kogala in Ceylon, it was by no means unusual to see a Sunderland returning from an uncompleted mission because one of its engines had failed. On the other hand, an engine failure on a Catalina was almost unknown.

An operational flight in a Catalina could well last sixteen or seventeen hours, so its equipment included a hot plate and cooking stove, and bunks for off duty crew. To enable an adequate watch to be kept on patrol, a minimum of nine airmen was needed to crew a Catalina: a first pilot and captain; a second pilot; a navigator; two flight engineers; three wireless and radar operators or mechanics, who doubled as air gunners; and an air gunner who was also responsible for mooring and anchoring the boat on the water. Our crew were all N.C.O.s except for the captain, Lance Emerson, and the air gunner, Walter Copeland, who were both Canadians, and myself. None of us had had any experience of Catalinas or of operational flying except our captain, who had earned his chance to become a captain from many hours experience as a second pilot on Catalinas operating from the rough seas of Gibraltar. Laconic and imperturbable, Lance proved to be an excellent man to work with. However at first I found there was little opportunity for me to serve alongside him as his second pilot. This was because our early flying from Killadeas was done with instructors on board, engineering, electronic and gunnery instructors as well as flying instructors. Sometimes too there might be another trainee captain occupying the cockpit alongside Lance, the two of them taking it in turns to practise taking off and alighting and the special skills of handling a flying boat on the water. So the aircraft would be pretty crowded, and it was as much as I could do to keep out of the way and at the same time try to follow what was going on. I can remember, after we had tied up to the buoy after my first Catalina flight, the eerie sensation of suddenly realising that all my companions had vanished, and that I was apparently alone on board what had a few moments earlier been a crowded boat. Very tentatively I peered out from the entrance blister to discover that everybody else had climbed out onto the wing high above the hull, where they were waiting for a dinghy to take them back to shore. Standing on the wings was an idiosyncrasy of flying boat crews which was new to me. So I then had gingerly to set out to find how to get onto the wing of a Catalina without falling into the water – which looked so lovely when white masses of it were flashing past (and sometimes over) the cockpit when taking off, but which otherwise could be dark, cold and treacherous.

By the end of January, all the instructors had long since disappeared, I was beginning to be used to sitting beside Lance doing whatever he needed me to do to supplement his own hands, feet and eyes, and the crew had successfully learnt to work as a team on exercises over the Atlantic of up to about six hours' duration. We were then allowed a short leave before being posted to the Ferry Training Unit at Oban on the west coast of Scotland, where a new Catalina would be allocated for our crew to prepare and prove for service overseas. After the wilds of Fermanagh, Oban seemed very civilised. The R.A.F. occupied a series of hotels along the sea front north of the trim little harbour. When we needed to go flying, we could almost step out of our hotel into the dinghy to take us to our Catalina moored in the Sound of Kerrera; when there was no flying to be done, a short walk would take us to excellent shops and cafes. What is more, by some quirk of the climate, in that winter the west coast of Scotland seemed to be enjoying much more sunshine than ever came our way in north-western Ireland, and whether ashore or in the air we could gaze upon the most magnificent scenery. But perhaps the contrast was at least partly in the imagination. Thus going on leave from Killadeas, I remember that when, after a dreadfully slow and cold train journey across Ireland, we eventually reached Larne, we found that the sea in the North Channel was so rough that the scheduled ferry to Stranraer was indefinitely delayed. When eventually, in the early hours of the following morning, the steamer did sail, it was the roughest channel crossing I have ever experienced. When we arrived at Stranraer, Lance, Walter and I were so tired that we went to sleep before the train had even left the station, and did not wake up again until eight hours later when it arrived in Euston. On the other hand, the journey from Euston to Oban not much more than a week later was marvellously smooth, travelling up to Scotland in a first class railway sleeper, and there waking up to the splendour of the scenery from Crianlarich past Ben Cruachan and Loch Awe and through the Pass of Brander to Oban. There could be no better introduction to the Scottish Highlands.

CHAPTER 4
WAR SERVICE II: DOING

Not long after arriving in Oban, Lance Emerson and his crew became the proud possessors of a bright new Catalina, something I do not think any of us had seen before. Certainly Killadeas's aircraft had been well past their prime. But JX276 was resplendent in unsullied and unscarred paintwork, and we had very soon cleared up any debris or dirt left over from her trans-Atlantic delivery flight and her subsequent adaptation to R.A.F. requirements. We took about a fortnight to establish that she was thoroughly serviceable and to master some items of equipment, such as guns, radio and radar, which were different from those in earlier Catalinas, and we were then instructed to fly our boat out to the R.A.F.'s South-East Asia Air Command.

This great adventure began on 15 March 1944 with the short flight to Mount Batten, the flying boat base in Plymouth Harbour, which was to be the starting point for the long haul across the Bay of Biscay to Gibraltar. Here we found that JX276 was not quite the beauty we had supposed. The white paint on the underside of both wings behind the engines had become disfigured by nasty green stains. Engineer officers were called to inspect these and to see whether they could do anything about them; we took the aircraft up on a couple of air tests to see whether the stains were still appearing. They were. There was no question but that the petrol tanks which were an integral part of the structure of the wings were leaking. (Later we were to learn that this fault was not unusual in the batch of Catalinas which included our JX276, a batch which had been been built not by the Consolidated Corporation in San Diego, but by the Boeing Company in a Canadian factory.) Higher authority was consulted, and eventually, after spending eight days at Mount Batten, we were instructed to continue with our journey.

We set off for Gibraltar at dusk, so that the Bay of Biscay, with its risk of attack from German fighters, would be crossed at night. Our landfall was not far north of the bright lights of Lisbon, a very welcome sight; and we arrived at Gibraltar, after twelve and a half hours flying, shortly after daybreak. Here Lance looked up old friends and I made contact with a Royal Engineer cousin who showed me something of the network of tunnels which had been constructed in the Rock. We resumed our journey on 28 March, taking sixteen hours to fly to Cairo with an overnight stop at the island of Djerba, the "land of the lotus eaters" of the ancients, in southeastern Tunisia. At both places we used the facility maintained by B.O.A.C. for their flying boat services to India and South Africa, that at Cairo being on the Nile at Rod el-Faraq, south of Gezira Island. At Cairo there was a second delay to our journey; our navigator, Flight Sergeant Willington, a robust Australian, went down with flu. However the rest of us rather welcomed the chance of seeing something of the crowded, smelly, noisy, and dusty city; in my memory the dominant smell was of petrol fumes, and the characteristic noise that of the grinding differentials of the three-ton trucks which the R.A.F. employed to transport us between our billets in Heliopolis, close to Almaza airfield, and our aircraft moored almost in the middle of the city on the Nile nearly ten miles distant — too far away for Lance's peace of mind.

We did not get away from Cairo until April 11. Then six hours flying took us into Palestine, past the Dead Sea and across the Syrian Desert along the line of the oil pipeline to alight on the little lake alongside the R.A.F. station at Habbaniya, about eighty miles west of Baghdad, which in 1941 had been besieged by the Iraqi army. On the following day, five hours flying brought us to our next night stop at the island of Bahrain, half way down the Persian Gulf. From Bahrain we took just under eight hours to fly across what are now the United Arab Emirates and then parallel to the forbidding mountainous coastlines of southern Iran and Baluchistan to Karachi, where we alighted at the flying boat station at Korangi Creek. Technically this was the end of our mission; we had arrived within the sphere of Air Command, South-East Asia, and this had now to decide what should be done with us and our aircraft. The journey from Mount Batten had occupied twenty-one days — which must place it among the slowest flights from England to India. But we had had only six flying days, and had covered some 6000 miles in just over 47 hours flying.

After a fortnight we received orders to take JX276 to 205 Squadron at the flying boat base at Kogala in Ceylon (now Sri Lanka), some 1600 miles from Karachi. This we did on 19 and 20 April, taking off in the evening and flying through the night so as to arrive at Kogala in the early light of morning thirteen hours later. We were not received with great enthusiasm by 205 Squadron. We were told in effect that, although they welcomed the gift of a new aeroplane (perhaps they had not yet taken in that its petrol tanks were leaking), they already had quite enough aircrew for the amount of flying they then had to do. However 205 was not the only Catalina squadron at Kogala; there was also 413 Squadron of the Royal Canadian Air Force and, as a Canadian with another Canadian in his crew, Lance set to work to get us all put on its strength. Before the end of May, this had been done.

Kogala is on the main road and railway line from Colombo to the historic town and seaport of Galle at the south-western corner of Ceylon where the coast begins to turn to the east; Galle is about twelve miles to the south. The land is flat and typically covered with palm trees tended by the people of small villages along the line of the road and railway. About 1200 yards inland from the shore, where white sands and coral reefs are incessantly pounded by breakers from the Indian Ocean, there is a brackish lake four or five miles long and shaped rather like a banana. This was where the R.A.F. had chosen to put its main Indian Ocean flying boat base after Singapore had fallen to the Japanese. When we arrived at Kogala, a runway for landplanes had been added, running between the lake and the sea, with traffic lights and railway signals to stop road and rail traffic when aircraft were taking off and landing. In the corners between this runway and the lake, a multitude of buildings had been erected to house the people, offices and workshops of a substantial R.A.F. station. The roofs and walls of the living accommodation were clad with palm-thatch, *cadjan*, which was remarkably successful in keeping out torrential monsoon rains, but which was home to a multitude of small creatures – insects, spiders and scorpions. Kogala's first occupants were 205 Squadron, the pioneer of R.A.F. flying boat operations in the Indian Ocean area, which had ended up at Kogala following the loss of its original base at Singapore, and 413 Squadron, the first aircraft of which had arrived just in time to provide warning of the Japanese naval sally into the Indian Ocean at Easter 1942 which, as well as sinking four substantial Royal Naval vessels and many merchant ships, brought carrier-borne air raids to Ceylon. These squadrons were reinforced early in 1944 by the arrival of 230 Squadron with its Sunderlands. When we arrived at Kogala later in that year, there could well be forty or more flying boats moored in the lake close by the eastern end of the runway.

My first three operational flights were anti-submarine sorties undertaken towards the end of May when Emerson's crew were still on the strength of 205 Squadron, and when there was some evidence of Japanese submarine activity in waters not too far from Ceylon. Not long before, there had been a tragic sinking of a troopship in a passage through the Maldive Islands, and our second and third sorties involved use of the advanced base at Addu Atoll in these islands. The first sortie was unusual only in the way it began. The plan was that three Catalinas should take off before dawn so that by daybreak they would be making concerted searches of an area in which it was thought a submarine might be found. Our aircraft was not one of these, but we were required to be standing by on board at its mooring in case something went wrong with any of the others, and it did. We saw and heard the first Catalina roar down the flarepath, the noise softening as the engines were throttled back after take-off. Then there was the gradual fading of noise and the disappearance of its lights as the aircraft climbed away towards its search area. Some minutes later there was a repeat performance by the second Catalina. But for the third aircraft we heard only the roar of taking off; then suddenly there was complete silence and nowhere were its lights to be seen. I think Flying Control must have been as puzzled as we were as to what had happened; surely if the aircraft had crashed, we would have heard the noise of the impact? The explanation of what had happened lay in the fact that, if a Catalina was heavily loaded, and if there was no wind and the water was mirror smooth, it was not always easy to get it into the air within the space available at Kogala. The captain of the third Catalina was, I believe, new to Kogala and, taking off in the dark and anxious to get airborne, it seems he must have pulled his aircraft off the water before it was really ready to fly, with the result that, semi-stalled, it had come down on the waterlogged land just beyond the shore of the lake. Luckily there was little or no damage to crew or aircraft, so the engines were switched off, and in due course the aircraft's predicament was reported to Flying Control. This then of course ordered us to take off and undertake that part of the search which otherwise would not have been done. All this took some time, and by the time we became airborne it was already becoming light.

Anti-submarine patrols and searches took place at irregular intervals throughout my time at Kogala but for the most part they were hardly worth remarking since, at least so far as I was aware, it was quite unusual for any submarines to be found, let alone attacked. I think that by this time I was beginning to see, for the first time, that we were on the winning side in the war. I said as much in a letter written to my parents in the middle of June. I added that, so far as the Japanese were concerned, "perhaps it isn't possible for them to recognise it yet". Although we now know that the Japanese had reached the limits of their resources, so that it had become impossible for them to maintain an offensive in the Indian Ocean even with submarines, I think it possible that at the time my optimism may have had something to do with a visit to Kogala in mid-May by Admiral Lord Louis Mountbatten, the Supreme Commander in South-East Asia. I cannot now remember his speech to us, but I do recall that his visit was very welcome, because – as I wrote in a letter – "few men ever see their C. in C. at all, and fewer have such an acceptable one". He seemed to be genuinely interested in people, having a word with every officer on the station and with a high proportion of the other ranks.

I did no operational flying between the beginning of June and the middle of October. The first reason for this was that, shortly after I had joined 413 Squadron, the maritime reconnaissance squadrons around the Indian Ocean were each asked to nominate someone to take an advanced astronavigation course at the Indian Ocean General Reconnaissance and Astro-Navigation School whose Ansons flew from the Kogala runway. My new squadron chose to send me, I would guess on the ground that I was its newest second pilot, and so the one who would be least missed, rather than because I had done well in astro-navigation during my G.R. course at George. The course ran for a month in the same way as that at George, with trips in Ansons to put into practice what we had been taught in ground school, but the astro-navigation was now at a much higher level than the astro-navigation which had been taught at George as only one of many subjects. This time, for example, I could not take the spherical trigonometry for granted – we were actually required to do some calculations in it – and the air exercises were much more sophisticated. So far as I can remember, seven of those on the course were navigators by training and only four were pilots, and I was very bucked when I passed out fourth, with a mark three percent above the course average of 87%, first of the pilots and ahead of four of the navigators.

Secondly, just before I started on the astro-navigation course, I was one of those who, while bathing in a pool between the coral reef and the beach at Kogala, had been knocked over by an unusually large wave and had cut his leg on the coral. Lance Emerson was another of these, and as a consequence had spent a few days in the station sick bay. My little wound was thought to require no more than a stitch and a bandage, but it was reluctant to heal properly, and shortly after I had returned to the squadron, the medical officer decided that more active measures were needed. After some time in his sick bay, the wound was healed, but a skin infection had developed, as a consequence of which he sent me off to an Indian Army hospital in Colombo. After about a week there, the medical opinion was that it would be difficult to deal with the infection in the hot and humid climate of Ceylon's coastlands, so that I was transferred to another Indian Army hospital in the more pleasant climate of Kandy, the old Sinhalese capital in the interior where Mountbatten had chosen to place his headquarters in beautiful botanic gardens. Here eventually medicine did triumph, but I had then been in medical hands for two months, and to complete my recovery I was sent off to spend a fortnight in a convalescent camp at Diyatalawa, about 4000 ft above sea level. Although I became inclined to think that at least part of my medical problem may have been not wholly unconnected with some of the medicaments used on my leg, I have nothing but praise for the Indian Army hospitals that looked after me, that in Kandy in particular, where the sister, nurses and orderlies were all delightful people. But I also remember my hospitalisation for the opportunity it gave me to extend my knowledge of Ceylon beyond what was readily visible from Kogala. Galle, the nearest town to Kogala, I had thought was most attractive, with its magnificent fort and walled town remaining from the days in the sixteenth and seventeenth centuries when it was the chief town and port for the Portuguese and Dutch colonies in Ceylon, and the numerous little shops and jewelry manufactories clustered outside the walls. Colombo, viewed on leave from Kogala, had struck me as rather splendid, especially perhaps its Galle Face seafront – but less attractive, in part because, as the current capital and major seaport, it was so much larger that exploring it was so much more tiresome in such a hot and sticky climate.

While convalescing, I was then briefly privileged to view the splendours of Kandy's palace, temples and artificial lake, and then to experience the cool grassed highlands in the centre of Ceylon above the highest tea plantations, rolling country somewhat reminiscent of Salisbury Plain, except that the grass was much lusher and – as one soon found when walking through it – infested with voracious leeches.

Shortly after my return to 413 Squadron, our C.O. called a meeting of all his non-Canadian aircrew to tell them, most apologetically, that his political masters in Ottawa had decreed that, so far as possible, Royal Canadian Air Force squadrons should be manned exclusively by Canadians. His non-Canadian aircrew were therefore being put together to make up three crews which would in due course be transferred to R.A.F. squadrons. I therefore became second pilot in a new crew captained by Ken Draycott, a neat and dapper little Englishman, a bank clerk in civilian life. In the short period of three weeks in which this crew had with 413 Squadron before it was transferred elsewhere, it was kept pretty busy. Two jobs we did were rather out of the ordinary. The first was to ferry one of the JX series Catalinas to Bangalore so that its leaking petrol tanks could be dealt with at the Hindustan Aircraft Factory. We then went north again to Redhills Lake at Madras, a base from which Catalinas were used to fly agents and equipment into and out of Japanese-occupied territory in the Andaman Islands, Burma and Thailand. One of these aircraft (whose second pilot I had known since Cambridge University Air Squadron days) had not returned from such an operation, and our job was to conduct a search to just short of the Andaman Islands to see if we could find any trace of it; unfortunately we found nothing.

In mid-November, an unusual and magnificent four-engined flying boat alighted on our lake at Kogala. This was B.O.A.C.'s *Golden Hind*, the only survivor of three enlarged developments of the Empire boats, which had been built in 1939 for a trans-Atlantic passenger service which the outbreak of war prevented from starting. She had come to take us and the other two non-Canadian crews from 413 Squadron to East Africa to serve with one or other of the three Catalina squadrons based there. To our great joy we found that, whereas in wartime the ordinary Empire boats had been fitted out with very utilitarian seating, *Golden Hind* was equipped to full pre-war airline standards for 38 passengers, so on 15-17 November it was in the greatest luxury that we were flown across the western Indian Ocean by way of Addu Atoll and the Seychelles Islands to Mombasa. From Mombasa, Ken Draycott's crew went by train right across Kenya to the eastern shore of Lake Victoria, to collect a Catalina from the R.A.F. Maintenance Unit at Kisumu. While we were occupied in testing this boat, we were asked to search the slopes of Mount Elgon in Uganda to see if we could find any trace of a B.O.A.C. landplane which had disappeared on a flight from Nairobi to Juba in the Sudan. This was a somewhat unusual task for a maritime reconnaissance flying boat to undertake, but Mount Elgon was less than an hour's flying time from Kisumu and, at over 14,000 ft, was the highest point on the airliner's route. We did not find anything for, as was discovered some time later, the missing plane had crashed in Kenya on the 8000 ft Mau Summit.

Early in December we were able to complete our acquaintance with the three major mountains of British East Africa when we flew past Mt Kenya (over 17,000 ft) and then Mt Kilimanjaro (over 19,000 ft) in the Catalina we had collected at Kisumu, on our way first to Mombasa, and then to Dar es Salaam, where we picked up another crew. Like ourselves, this had instructions to join 265 Squadron at Diego Suarez. Now called Antsirane, Diego Suarez was the French naval base at the northern end of Madagascar which British forces had captured in 1942; it has one of the finest natural harbours in the world, but otherwise we found little to recommend it. The R.A.F. camp was situated on an exposed sandy waste; the town, ten or so miles away, was a crude replica of a small provincial town in France to which had accreted an extensive suburb of hovels to shelter a black population, and had little to attract us. It was even difficult to find a good place for swimming; the only highlights of my time at Diego Suarez that I can remember were the visit of a French naval vessel on which we were entertained to a marvellous lunch of roast sucking pig, and one or two games of cricket – remarkable only in that there cannot be many people who can claim to have played cricket in Madagascar! Luckily much of my time with 265 Squadron was spent away from base.

First of all, at Christmas 1944 Ken Draycott's crew was detached to Tulear, nearly a thousand miles away on the green and pleasant south-western coast of the *Grande Ile*. Our job was to provide an escort for the battleship H.M.S. *Valiant* on her way up the Mozambique Channel. We were originally instructed to fly south to Tulear on Christmas Day itself. When we asked whether it was absolutely essential to spend Christmas Day in this fashion, we were told that we could choose to delay our take-off until after midnight. This we did, with the consequence that just as day broke we found ourselves face to face with the Inter-Tropical Front, a frightening line of thick black cloud stretching right across our path from less than 500 feet above a storm-tossed ocean to as high as we could see. We turned the aircraft first one way and then the other but could find no gap; we tried climbing, but quickly found that a laden Catalina could never get high enough to pass over the cloud. We then began to realise that if we continued in this sort of way, we would quite soon not have enough petrol left to reach Tulear. So there was nothing for it but to fly under the Front through the narrow gap between the cloud and the spume-streaked sea. This we did, but it was the most frightening experience of my flying career. The vertical gusts were such that there were some moments when, with the throttle levers back and the control yoke forward, our heavy aircraft was still being sucked up into turbulent cloud, and others when, with full throttle and the yoke hauled back to climb, we were descending towards the sea at the rate of 500 feet a minute.

Virtually the whole of January was spent on detachment to Port Victoria, the capital of the Seychelles, the group of volcanic and coralline islands about 1200 miles east of Kenya which General Gordon had thought were such a tropical paradise that they must have been the Garden of Eden, and which nowadays, since the building of an airport, have become a considerable attraction for tourists. Our aircraft was one of three sent to engage in a number of training exercises of various kinds; among other things, I was given the opportunity to practise Catalina take-offs and landings, and to act as the navigator of our aircraft on a five-hour flight. We also had time to enjoy the pleasant little town of Victoria and the beautiful beaches and mountains of Mahé Island. But after a week, things began to go awry. One of our Catalina's engines started misfiring, and it was eventually decided that the wisest course would be to replace it with a spare engine that was held by the small R.A.F. establishment at Victoria. So our aircraft was brought up the slipway, our two engineers set to work, and with the help of a little unskilled labour from the rest of the crew, within a couple of days or so the not inconsiderable job of taking one heavy engine off the high wing of a Catalina and replacing it with another when away from proper maintenance facilities was successfully accomplished. The aircraft was then put back in the water, whereupon two disasters occurred. First, when early in the following morning the time came to relieve our crew member, F/Sgt Williams, who had been on board as boat-guard during the hours of darkness, he was nowhere to be seen. It was not until two days later that his body was found floating in the harbour and we could embark on the sad businesses of his funeral and an official enquiry. Secondly, on the day when Williams's disappearance was discovered, there was a severe squall which caused a fishing boat to break loose from its mooring and crash into the port wingtip and float of our aircraft. So once again we had to take her out of the water so that the damage could be repaired. All in all there were two weeks of our stay in the Seychelles during which our aircraft was unserviceable. I became increasingly inclined to believe in the existence of Black Magic and to wonder if I would ever return to enjoy an ordinary, normal existence. I also came to understand why young Seychellois often longed to escape from their island paradise; the community was so small that in our short stay it seemed possible to meet everybody of substance, even the Governor!

Our next break from routine and Diego Suarez came the following month, when Ken Draycott's crew was chosen to operate one of the regular "Courier" flights by which R.A.F. Catalinas carried service mail and passengers to and fro across the 3,400 miles of the western Indian Ocean between Mombasa and Kogala. Our outward bound service from Mombasa was somewhat special. Because our passengers were V.I.P.s – Lieutenant-General Sir Kenneth Anderson, G.O.C. East Africa, and four of his staff on their way to visit African troops fighting in Burma – the R.A.F. did the best it could to turn the Catalina selected for the flight into the semblance of an airliner. The guns were removed and airline seats fitted in the blisters in their place, bed linen was provided for the bunks, and for the two long legs of the journey, Mombasa-Seychelles and Seychelles-Addu Atoll, each of eight or so hours flying, we were provided with the provisions needed to prepare three-course meals! The return journey was more ordinary: the few passengers we had were R.A.F. groundcrew.

When in mid-February we arrived back at Mombasa, all the crew except Ken Draycott, who had had the misfortune to pick up a skin infection which required hospital treatment, were given a fortnight's leave. I took the train to Nairobi, which bore comparison with Rhodesia's Salisbury, although I thought its transported European society more artificial and brittle. I did not feel at ease there, and after a few days departed for the White Highlands, where, through the Kenyan equivalent of the W.V.S., I had secured an offer of hospitality from a retired naval officer and his wife. Captain and Mrs Rawson had a small-holding of about 200 acres some twenty miles from the little town of Naivasha on the shore of the lake of the same name. Here they were cultivating the rich lakeside soil to produce an intriguing mixture of temperate and tropical vegetables and fruits for consumption by Kenya's European population, then swollen by wartime circumstances. The three military services had brought appreciable numbers of their men to Kenya, and there was also an even more evident influx of Italians. These were men who had been captured in the African campaigns and who, in the circumstances of 1945, were perhaps as much – or as little – allies as they were prisoners of war. Substantial numbers of them were usefully employed on the farms and estates of the settlers in the Highlands; the Rawsons had a couple who were essential to their agricultural activities.

The Rawsons were in every respect perfect hosts, providing excellent accommodation in a custom built visitors' chalet with its own hot water, good meals, conversation and books, and quite a bit of tennis, and early in March I returned to Mombasa greatly refreshed. I found that Ken Draycott had come out of hospital and had gone off on his leave. Since there was not much point in his crew returning to Diego Suarez without him, the rest of us secured permission to go off for a second period of leave. So once again I took the train to Nairobi, and then on to Naivasha for another delightful stay with the Rawsons. It was the end of March before we were all back in Madagascar, and within a few days I was told that I was to go back to the U.K. to go to O.T.U. to train to be a flying boat captain. On 12 April I embarked for a second time on *Golden Hind*, which was meant to take me and other members of the R.A.F. from Madagascar and East Africa to Cairo en route for the U.K. However, when taking off from Kisumu, *Golden Hind* developed serious engine trouble, and her passengers were disembarked to wait impatiently until passing Empire flying boats on the regular service between South Africa and Egypt had space available to take one or two of them on to Cairo. So it was on the hard wartime seats of *Caledonia* – the second Empire boat to be built, the first to fly the Atlantic, and now a nine year old veteran – that I had the privilege of flying along the historic Nile route to Cairo. This involved two night stops, at Port Bell in Uganda and at Khartoum, the stupefyingly hot and humid capital of the Sudan. When flying over Uganda and the southern Sudan, Capt. Wood would take us low to admire sights like the Murchison Falls or herds of elephants, and every two or three hours we would alight on the Nile to pick up fuel or passengers. Sometimes this would be at now-forgotten little places like Laropi and Malakal, sometimes we would briefly visit places of some consequence, such as Wadi Halfa with its cataract, or Luxor, from which we could tantalisingly glimpse some of the grandeurs of ancient Thebes.

I arrived at Cairo on 24 April; a week later I was a passenger in a R.A.F. Dakota flying from Tripoli to the U.K. when its captain made an announcement over the cabin loudspeaker which made it plain that the German surrender could be expected within a day or two. If the war against Germany was about to end, it was easy to see that the R.A.F. would have quite enough experienced captains of flying boats to make it unnecessary to train any new ones just for the war against Japan. There would be precious little chance of my getting to O.T.U.; indeed there might be no need at all for any flying boat training in the R.A.F. All the R.A.F. could immediately offer me was another three month spell at Harrogate followed by a posting to what was called an "Advanced Flying Unit" which was equipped with Oxfords. This was a ploy to try and ensure that surplus pilots kept their hand in. I did not enjoy it much. It was not simply that I did not fancy the idea of putting the aeroplane down on a narrow little runway instead of one of the broad expanses of water that flying boats were accustomed to use. I missed flying over the sea, with its ever changing textures and colours: the smooth dark rolling swells, the whites of breaking waves and of the streaky lanes blown on it by the wind, the sometimes subtle and sometimes brilliant light green-blues of the water seen as the aircraft flew over reefs and shallows before coming to black cliffs or dazzling white sands. And I felt how dull it was just to motor the aircraft to the runway and take off or, after landing, to park it on the tarmac, step out and walk away. How much better and more alive was the business of unshackling from the buoy, singling up and casting off; or ploughing through the waves to the take off point, and then the great curving sheets of water coming up from the hull bottom as the aircraft accelerated until eventually the water was behind and below; or, after alighting, all the fussy, tricky business of manoeuvring with the aid of drogues through wind and tide to moor up to the buoy, followed by the tossing little sprayswept dinghy trip to shore.

I was therefore glad that, as one whose time at university had been interrupted by the war, I was eligible for early release from military service.

During September the formalities of my demobilisation were completed, and I became a civilian again just in time to return to Cambridge for the beginning of the new university year in October.

*

Two postscripts should perhaps be added to the narrative of my experiences in the R.A.F. The first is to say how very kind civilians could be to young men like myself who had been temporarily removed from their homes and families. I have already paid tribute to the hospitality I received from the Rawsons at Naivasha, but this was unusual only in the length of time that I enjoyed it. During my time in Southern Rhodesia, I can remember no less than three very hospitable Bulawayo families, the Edgecombes, the Ibbotsons and the Shaws – the latter two families, who were friends, inter alia entertaining me and another cadet for Christmas and Boxing Day, while when Douglas Hodge and I were on leave in Salisbury a home was provided for us by the McBean family – who also put me up for the night when I descended upon them out of the blue after a ferry flight from Kumalo.

Secondly, from time to time my life in the R.A.F. would produce strange encounters of a kind which occur by no means unfrequently in the early novels of Evelyn Waugh and throughout Anthony Powell's "A Dance to the Music of Time" series. Two of the best examples of this occurred during my short stay in Kandy. First the man in the next bed to me in hospital turned out to have worked in civilian life in Bulawayo in what was then called "Native Affairs", as a result of which he knew the Ibbotsons. Secondly, when I was convalescent, I would walk into Kandy with another patient from our ward, and we would take tea in the Officers' Club. One afternoon I heard a voice from a chair behind us saying "Surely you're John Fage?" The speaker was Brian Hutton, a contemporary and friend of Sidney Keyes at Hill Side, who was now an officer in the Indian Army on leave visiting tea-planter relations in Ceylon. Brian and I naturally started talking about people we had known at Tonbridge, whereupon we discovered that many of these were also known to my companion, who had been a teacher at Yardley Court, the preparatory school in Tonbridge.

The author

John at the Isle of Wight, 1933

John at The Wilderness, Cape Province, in 1943

John with Draycott crew, 413 squadron, which flew a Catalina
flying boat from Oban to Ceylon

John with members of No 12 Short Astro-Navigation Course,
Ceylon, in 1944

On leave at Lake Naivasha, 1944

CHAPTER 5
CROSSROADS

When I returned to Cambridge at the beginning of the autumn term of 1945, my previous period of residence and my success in Part I of the History Tripos were sufficient, under the emergency special regulations which Cambridge University had made for students with war service, to qualify me to take a B.A. Degree without further residence and study. But I was quite clear in my own mind that I did not want a "war degree", but should complete my undergraduate studies properly by taking Part II of the Tripos. I therefore applied to the Ministry of Education for an award under the Further Education and Training Scheme for those who had served in the war. In the event I was to hold such an award for four years. As well as paying all my university fees, it provided an annual sum for maintenance which, together with what I received in scholarships, R.A.F. gratuity and post-war income tax credits, gave me about £300 to live on during 1945-46. In the following three years my basic income was much the same, but the Ministry of Education allowed me to supplement it without any reduction of its grant by what I could earn from up to six hours a week supervising the work of undergraduates. So far as I can now remember, this made my total income up to about £360 a year, on which in those days a single man could live happily and comfortably.

I decided to take advantage of the History Faculty Board's special regulations for wartime students to make a somewhat eclectic choice of subjects for Part II of its Tripos. I had no wish to return to the standard, Eurocentric, fare of Tripos subjects and preferred to concentrate on two newly introduced subjects. One of these was "The History of the United States of America", which had come into the syllabus when the Faculty of History had recently received the funds to enable it each year to appoint a distinguished visiting professor from the United States. In 1945-46 this was Dexter Perkins, a historian of the western U.S. states, whose outline lectures on American history proved to be marvellously entertaining and informative. Then there was a subject introduced for the first time for 1945-46 when, as a result of the worldwide nature of the war of 1939-45, the Cambridge Faculty Board had accepted that European students should be offered the opportunity to take some account of the history of the vast world outside their own continent. Called "The Expansion of Europe", this was a subject naturally interesting to someone who had spent a substantial part of his war in non-European lands. But it was a bold decision for members of the Faculty Board to have taken. Except for North American history and a few specialised courses in Middle Eastern and South Asian history which attracted students only in ones and twos, there was hardly any tradition or experience of teaching extra-European history in the United Kingdom universities. Cambridge's "Expansion of Europe" course was thus a virtually unique pioneer venture, and it was by no means easy to see how it might be effectively taught. Teddy Rich, who had edited the papers of the Hudson's Bay Company, was brave enough to essay to give an outline course which – in its first year at least – was of very uneven quality. As one who had actually been there only a few months earlier, I remember during one of his lectures watching in exasperation as he tried vainly to find Mombasa on his wall map. But it was generally accepted that students were not expected to cover all parts of such a vast subject, and a number of area specialists, some of whom – for example Sir John Pratt, a retired member of the consular administration in China – were not members of the University, had been found to give short courses of supplementary lectures. Since there was a marked lack of college fellows able and willing to provide appropriate supervision, some of the supplementary lecturers also held essay classes. I chose to concentrate on Africa and, more adventurously, on Latin America. This second choice was not because I had already seen the slave trading link between African and American history; after all, at that time, I had hardly set eyes on West Africa. I think that my interest in Latin America derived from the quite excellent lectures and classes on it given by John Parry – later, of course, to be Principal of University College, Ibadan, and much else besides – but then a fellow of Clare College lecturing in uniform since he was still not finally released from the Royal Navy. There were two other "specialists" whom I remember with affection as well as admiration. One was Jim Davidson, a New Zealander renowned for his work in Pacific history. In 1945-46, however, he was Cambridge's Lecturer in Colonial History and a fellow of St John's, writing a book on North-

ern Rhodesia for the series on colonial Legislative Councils edited by
Margery Perham; very daringly for those days, he lectured in a roll-necked
sweater. The other was Jack Plumb, then a research fellow at King's College. In view of his later eminence as a historian of eighteenth century
England, he might be thought an unlikely member of the "Expansion"
team, but in his younger days he had an interest in the European exploration of Africa and, surrounded by a splendid collection of first editions of
the explorers' works, he held a few classes in his rooms to which a handful
of students were invited to contribute papers on this exploration.

My third Tripos subject was much more conventional, "The Theory of
the Modern State", for which the lecturer was F.A.Simpson. For this subject I enjoyed the college supervision of Francis Turner, newly returned from
service with the R.A.F. (in which he had first served, with great distinction, in the war of 1914-18). Simpson is best known for his biography of
Napoleon III, but he had been giving his very lively "Modern State" lectures for twenty years or more. I remember one supervision with Francis
Turner when he asked what the topic had been of the last of Simpson's
lectures that I had heard. I told him this, whereupon Francis asked "In the
middle of the lecture, did Simpson go to the left hand wall of the lecture
theatre, lean his head and arm on it, and appear to be thinking?" My answer being "Yes", Francis then said "Do you know, he did just that when I
was an undergraduate attending his lectures"!

I cannot remember doing very much in that first post-war year outside
academic work and renewing acquaintance with other survivors of the war
who had returned to Cambridge. I think the enormous loss of life in 1914-
18 may tend to undervalue the extent of the loss in 1939-45: as many as
one in five – 22 out of 107 – of my Magdalene contemporaries who matriculated in 1939 or 1940, were killed in our war.

I did not go back to the A.D.C., nor did I do anything serious in the
Cambridge Union. I did however rejoin the Cambridge Film Society, and
almost immediately began to take an active part in its affairs. Thus I wrote
half the programme notes for the Society's 1945-46 season of 35mm shows
at the Arts Theatre, and for the following year I was styled "vice-presi-
dent". In this capacity I think my greatest achievement was to commission two Magdalene friends to provide a musical accompaniment to the
Society's showing of Fritz Lang's 1923 silent classic, *Siegfried*. Since the
Film Society could not afford to give them any significant remuneration,

and the film ran for two hours, it is fitting that they should be commemorated in these memoirs. The music was composed by William Mann (later for many years music critic of *The Times*), and was performed on two pianos by him and by John Stevens (later a very distinguished Cambridge professor and a foremost authority on the music of the Tudors). I gradually found myself assuming the role of elder statesman in the affairs of the Cambridge Film Society and, after I had taken my M.A., I ended up in 1948-49 by being elected its Senior Treasurer – that is, the senior member of the University required by it to ensure that an undergraduate society's business was respectably conducted.

In 1945 I also joined the New London Film Society, launched in December of that year to mark the fiftieth anniversary of the birth of the film and to continue the work of the pioneering original Film Society, which had died in 1939. This provided me with the opportunity to see many of the greatest films in cinema history, many of which had virtually disappeared from general circulation. For the next two years I regularly spent every other Sunday afternoon in London watching the film shows at the Scala Theatre in Charlotte Street.

While I certainly enjoyed and profited from my return to the once familiar routine of lecture-going, reading and essay-writing, the prospect of being formally examined on what I was learning became increasingly distressing, so that by the time that the examinations began I felt mentally and morally quite exhausted. I could not recapture the confident form that seemed to be natural to me in my last years at school and in my first two years at Cambridge and, when the Tripos results were published, I was almost relieved to find that I had sunk no lower than the upper division of the Second Class. However other people seemed to have more confidence in me. Frank Salter, Francis Turner and Philip Grierson all sent me sympathetic and encouraging notes, and Magdalene awarded me a research studentship for 1946-47. In addition, the University awarded me its 1946-47 Bartle Frere Exhibition, the lesser of its two awards for the support of postgraduate work in what was then known as "imperial history". But for the immediate future, all I wanted to do was to get away from Cambridge and academic work and to do something useful.

Since this desire coincided with a considerable shortage of men and women to undertake the harvest of 1946, it was not difficult for me to spend three weeks of the university vacation as an agricultural labourer. I have very little recollection of the wet week in September during which I helped to gather and dry wheat on a large farm in Wiltshire belonging to the family of a Magdalene friend, but I am unlikely ever to forget my earlier agricultural experience in July at a Ministry of Agriculture Volunteer Camp near Mildenhall, about twenty miles from Cambridge. This was not because I found picking strawberries under a hot sun – or even hoeing between their lines – quite the most tiring manual labour I have ever tried to do. It was because it was at this camp that I first set eyes on, and began to get to know, the attractive young lady who in due course was to become my wife. She was then Miss Jean Banister, about to become a student at the L.S.E., who incidentally had an uncle and aunt living at Grantchester just outside Cambridge, where he had a post in the Department of Psychology. Jean spent longer at the Mildenhall camp than I did and, after I had left, I remember her cycling to visit me at Magdalene. Before long we were arranging to meet in London to attend Promenade concerts and New London Film Society showings. This early stage of our relations culminated in our attendance at Magdalene's first post-war May Ball in 1947.

When in the autumn of 1946 I embarked on postgraduate work, I already had a clear idea of what I wanted to do. I wanted to try and discover how it had come about that in 1923 Britain had granted self-government to its Colony of Southern Rhodesia. This question interested me for two reasons. The first was that in 1923, the colony's political franchise was for all practical purposes restricted to its 35,000 or so white settlers, so that this small population (smaller, I said, than the population of the town of Cambridge) received all the full and elaborate machinery of parliamentary government to manage not only its own affairs, but also those of some twenty-five times as many black Africans. Secondly I wanted to know how it came about that, if the Colonial Office chose to divest itself of responsibility for this settler colony, it did not then join with the much larger and stronger white-dominated Union of South Africa across its southern border.

The obvious person in Cambridge to supervise research on Southern Rhodesian history was Professor E.A. Walker, who had spent many years as Professor of History at the University of Cape Town before he came to Cambridge as its Vere Harmsworth Professor of Imperial and Naval History. But Eric Walker was ill when I started my researches, and for the first few months I was entrusted to the care of E.A.Benians, the Master of St John's College, who had been one of the three General Editors of the *Cam-*

bridge History of the British Empire. Neither saw any objection to what I proposed to do, and I very soon demonstrated to Benians's satisfaction that my work would be original in that hitherto there had been no serious scholarly examination of my subject. Thereafter he, and Walker after he had taken over from Benians, did nothing but encourage me in my work – and, in Walker's case, improve my punctuation and talk to me about Cambridge rowing.

I think, indeed, that in the sizeable preliminary bibliography that I compiled for my thesis the only substantial published work providing any answer to the questions I had asked myself was *The Real Rhodesia* (1924) by Mrs Ethel Tawse Jollie. But she was *parti pris* to these questions, since she was one of the politicians who had actively worked to bring about responsible government for the Rhodesian settlers (she prided herself – justly – on being the first woman elected to a legislative assembly in the British Commonwealth). Of scholarly work, I think there was hardly anything other than an excellent but not very long or detailed section in the second volume of W.K.Hancock's *Survey of British Commonwealth Affairs* (1942), and the London Ph.D. thesis by Roy McGregor, "Native Segregation in Southern Rhodesia" (1940) which, though valuable to have was – as its title indicates – peripheral to my particular enquiry. Therefore there could be no real question as to the originality of my study of the history of the European community in Southern Rhodesia in the quarter of a century leading up to the receipt of a self-governing constitution in 1923. But my work could be open to criticism on other counts. In those days the original papers of British government departments preserved in the Public Record Office in London were subject not to the thirty year closed period known in recent years, but to a fifty year rule. So I was able to see the official Colonial Office papers relating to the administration of Southern Rhodesia only for the first three years of my period. Secondly, the British government's agent for the administration of Southern Rhodesia prior to 1923, the British South Africa Company, informed me that all its relevant records had been destroyed in one of the wartime air raids on London. The other end of its administrative correspondence was held in archives in Rhodesia but, thirdly, I was not in a position to visit Rhodesia when I was working on its history, for in those days there was very little in the way of funds available to support overseas research by British students. But here it may be added that, if I had been able to get to Rhodesia, it is unlikely that I would have been allowed to see the records of its administration; they counted as British official records, and so were subject to the same embargo as those in the P.R.O. The only positive response I received from enquiries to the Central African Archives in Salisbury was that V.W.Hiller, their Director, was so pleased to find someone working on Rhodesian history that he offered me a job. But what he wanted was someone to edit for publication the Portuguese records relating to the Rhodesian area from the fifteenth to the eighteenth centuries. Since I was then concerned with recent colonial history rather than the remoter reaches of African history; since the relevant Portuguese records for S.E.Africa were already being effectively worked on by a competent Lusophone historian, Eric Axelson; and since I could only attempt to rival him if I first learnt from scratch both the Portuguese language and the appropriate paleography, I did not think that Hiller's offer made much sense.

In practice I found I had quite enough to do to master the important sources that were available to me. In the excellent Library of the Royal Empire Society (later the Royal Commonwealth Society) there was a complete set of the debates in the Legislative Council of Southern Rhodesia under the British South Africa Company's administration, and for my convenience its Librarian, Mr James Packman, was kind enough to loan this temporarily to the Cambridge University Library (where it must now reside more permanently, since Cambridge now holds the books and manuscripts of what had been the Royal Commonwealth Society's library). Then there was a great collection of Rhodesian newspapers to be found by untying dusty brown paper parcels in what was then known as the British Museum's Newspaper Library at Colindale, while the Public Record Office and many libraries contained between them substantial numbers of relevant British blue books, and of Rhodesian political pamphlets and executive and legislative council papers. I was also able to contact living actors in the history I was studying. One of these, W.M.Leggate, who had emigrated to farm in Rhodesia, had gone into politics, and in 1923 became Southern Rhodesia's Minister of Agriculture, was quite extraordinarily helpful. In 1948 he had returned to live in his native Scotland, and he broke a journey to London to dine and stay the night in Magdalene, where we spent some hours talking Rhodesian history.

I was able to be hospitable to Leggate because at the end of my first postgraduate year, Magdalene elected me into a Bye-Fellowship for 1947-

48, and this was renewed for the following year. Although there was no increase in my income, the Fellows of the College had thought me worthy to join with them at their High Table and in their Combination Room. I thus became very much the youngest member of a very senior society. Including myself, there were I think effectively sixteen members of the Magdalene High Table in 1947-48, and no less than ten of these had been born in the nineteenth century. The eldest, the mathematician A.S.Ramsey (father of Michael Ramsey, before long to be Archbishop of Canterbury), who had been retired for ten years or more, was actually author of a text-book which my father had possessed when he was a student! There was only one Fellow, Derman Christopherson, shortly to become a professor at Leeds, who was less than ten years older than me. But looking back at these oldsters who had chosen such a youngster to join their little family, what strikes me is what nice people they were to live with, and how kind and considerate to me they all were. Nevertheless I was quite relieved when in the following year John Stevens was also elected into a Bye-Fellowship.

However in the immediately post-war years there was inevitably some jumbling of the old age-sets of university life. People like Charles Curran and I had been able to get release from military service as soon as the war with Germany had finished, so that by 1946-47 while Charles (who had got a First) was already embarking on the career that was to take him to be Director-General of the B.B.C., I was taking my first tentative steps towards becoming a university don. Francis Turner, who had now become my tutor, had argued very persuasively that I should "totally immerse" myself in my research, but Frank Salter, pointing out that there was no one else available, had persuaded me to supervise the essay work of undergraduates studying American History and the Expansion of Europe for the Tripos. Looking back on it, the result was really rather extraordinary. On the one hand, it was only the year before that I had been learning these subjects; on the other hand, some of the students I was supposed to guide had originally been my university contemporaries (or even, occasionally, my seniors) but had been unluckier than Charles or myself in that they not been able to secure immediate release from their war service. Two of these I got know particularly well, Braham Myers and John Challenor; the three of us made a daring expedition in a pre-war car to the south of France in the summer of 1947, and in 1949 I managed to secure Braham's services as best man for my wedding. Another pupil I will not easily forget was Freddie Mutesa, the Kabaka of Buganda, a shy and very polite young man.

By 1947-48 I was doing as many hours of supervision as the Ministry of Education would permit, and my pupils came from Caius as well as Magdalene. By this time too, I was beginning to be aware of graduate history research students working on African subjects from other colleges. These were Roland Oliver, with whom in due course I was to become closely associated, and Ronald Robinson and Jack Gallagher, the future authors of the classic *Africa and the Victorians* and ultimately the holders of chairs of imperial history at Oxford and at Cambridge (Gallagher holding both chairs in succession before his early death). In 1948-49 Oliver went off to the School of Oriental and African Studies in London and to fieldwork in East Africa, while Robinson was working at the Colonial Office and was not very often in Cambridge. So it was to Gallagher and me that the History Faculty turned in October 1948 with an invitation "to give some lectures on African history in the course of next term". In the event we shared equally in a course of eight lectures limited to tropical Africa, with Gallagher talking about West Africa and I on "European settlement and native problems in Central and East Africa". We must have done well enough, because for the following academic year the two of us were invited to give a longer course which was to be called "The History of the Dependent Empire". By the beginning of May 1949 we had begun to plan a course under this title which would have involved at least twenty-four lectures. However by the end of that month I knew that I was not going to be in Cambridge during 1949-50, so I had to turn the whole enterprise over to Gallagher.

What I was going to do after I had finished and submitted my thesis was a question of major importance during the whole of 1948-49. This was not least because in November Jean and I had become engaged and were thinking in terms of a wedding in July 1949, so that by that month or not much later, an income of somewhat more than my basic £300 a year seemed to be desirable. Neither of us can now remember exactly why it was we set our eyes on July for our wedding. But I think it must have been connected with the progress of my thesis. I know that by November 1948 I had a draft text with which I was reasonably happy except that it needed some pruning and some tying up of loose ends. It must have seemed reasonable therefore to have assumed that these things would not take more than six months to do, so that by July 1949 marriage could be my main priority. So in fact it proved – just! "The Achievement of Self-Government in Southern Rhodesia, 1898-1923" went to the typists in the second week of May, and it was submitted in time for my oral examination to be held on 6 July, eight days before that set for the wedding. The examiners were Keith Hancock and Teddy Rich, who were remarkably kind and did not seem to have thought up any of the kind of nasty questions that I used to try and invent later in my career on the occasions when it became my turn to examine candidates for the Ph.D. Degree.

When I was thinking what I should do after I had got my Ph.D., I did not think exclusively in terms of an academic career. It also crossed my mind that I might think of trying to get a permanent commission in the R.A.F. The idea arose because at the end of 1946 the Cambridge University Air Squadron had been reborn in something approaching its pre-war shape and habits. However as well as offering undergraduates the chance of learning to fly at public expense in the hope that this would attract at least some of them to become good candidates for R.A.F. commissions, it also offered an opportunity for wartime flyers like myself to join the R.A.F. Volunteer Reserve and keep our hands in as pilots. In November 1946 I applied for an R.A.F.V.R. commission and a place in the Air Squadron, and on 5 May 1947 I sat in the rear cockpit of a Tiger Moth for the first time since October 1942. The instructor in the front seat said "Taxi out and take off", and when I had done this he told me to do some turns, steep turns and spins, and then to do a landing. This turned out to be about the best landing I had ever done in a Tiger Moth, whereupon the instructor got out of the aircraft saying, "Right, off you go solo". So thereafter, once a week or so, when I had had enough of Rhodesia for the time being and the weather was not too bad, I would think of getting on my bicycle and pedalling the two miles along the Newmarket Road to Marshall's aerodrome to spend an hour so flying a Tiger Moth. Only very rarely would my instructor seek to check my competence, and from time to time I was allowed to use an aircraft for my own purposes, the only condition being that another qualified pilot from the Squadron should also come on the trip so that he too could build up his flying hours. Thus when I spent a week at Oxford, lodging at Magdalen College while reading Rhodesian law reports in the Codrington Library of All Souls College, I was able to avoid the tiresome cross-country train journey between the two university towns by flying to and fro. Later on two of us flew a Tiger Moth to Durham (which in Tiger Moth terms was so far away from Cambridge that there had to be refuelling stops en route at Doncaster!) so that I could visit my sister, who had recently moved to a job at Durham University.

Life with the C.U.A.S. and R.A.F.V.R. was not always so light hearted. Each summer we were required to undertake a fortnight's organised training, for which we received pay, at an airfield away from home. In 1947 and 1948 we camped at Shoreham Airport; in 1949 we went to the R.A.F. station at North Weald, near Epping. Here we would engage in things like night flying, formation flying and navigational exercises of various kinds. There would also be class work and the opportunity to do some flying in more advanced aircraft, like the Oxford or the Harvard, the Oxford's single-engined equivalent and quite a new experience for me. All this made me realise how much I missed flying boats, and in the summer of 1948 I asked whether, in addition to the regular fortnight's training, I might spend a fortnight with one of the R.A.F.'s two surviving flying boat squadrons. These were based at Calshot, at the south-western corner of Southampton Water, but by the time I got there both its Sunderland squadrons had gone to work on the Berlin airlift. So I was shipped off to Hamburg on the next Sunderland flight out. There I found there was a vacancy for a second pilot, so that I spent the next ten days engaged in the regular service between the Elbe at Hamburg and the Havelsee in Berlin. Every other day we would do two round trips. We would take off from Hamburg with a five ton load about 8.30 a.m. and land about an hour later at Berlin. Here the boat was speedily unloaded, so that within an hour we were on the way back to Hamburg. There we would be refuelled from one side and reloaded from the other while a hot lunch was brought to us. Then about 12.30 we would be off again to Berlin, where this time a return load (usually sacks of German Foreign Office files) was often put aboard. Then back again to Hamburg, where we would supervise the unloading of what we had brought out of Berlin and loading for the next day's flying. With any luck we would be ashore by about 5 p.m. We never went ashore at Berlin, so we could view its ruins only from the air. Those of Hamburg were relatively as great; except in the old quarter around the two Alster lakes, the predominant sight was of uncleared, dusty and smelly rubble. The best surviving hotels, cinemas and other amenities were reserved for the occupying forces; it was as though the Germans were on the wrong side of a colonial colour bar.

I was very quickly at home with the Sunderland crews; there were even one or two of their members who remembered me from my Catalina days. But I could not stay with them longer than the fortnight which had been arranged since early in September I was due at the C.U.A.S. summer camp at Shoreham. There I found I had been made "course commander" and was needed to give lectures on navigation. I enjoyed myself inventing an exercise by which nine or ten aircraft went off independently in different directions but in which, provided the pilots followed my instructions as to the courses they should steer for prescribed periods of time, each in turn joined a single snowballing formation coming back to the airfield. By the time of my last camp in 1949, it was apparent that I was regularly in line for responsible jobs in the C.U.A.S., so I would guess that I might have stood a good chance of returning to the R.A.F. had I applied for a regular commission. But it was too late; I was already committed to a university career.

It was in February 1949 that I began to explore what the chances were, once I had a Ph.D., of my making a successful academic career whether in Cambridge or elsewhere. Jean and I would both have liked to stay in Cambridge. Here Magdalene offered me the prospect of staying on in the College, supervising history undergraduates for twelve hours a week, for which I would receive £325 a year plus a rent-free room and free dining in hall three times a week. It would have been possible for me to increase this income by supervising students from other colleges, but it would have been hard work to boost it to a level adequate to support a married couple in any comfort, and it was not clear what acceptance of this offer might lead to. Frank Salter was due to retire in 1952, and I thought it quite likely that the College would seek to fill the vacated fellowship with another historian. But I knew it would only seek to elect someone with a University lectureship or assistant lectureship, and here there was a problem so far as I was concerned. Jack Gallagher and I were obviously in line for a History Faculty appointment in colonial history. But I could not see the Faculty wanting two lecturers in colonial history, both with African interests, and, if Jack and I were in competition, I thought the odds were likely to favour him; he was senior to me and already had his fellowship at Trinity. So Jean and I agreed that I should find out what the possibilities might be elsewhere than in Cambridge.

In February 1949 it seemed to me that the other universities in the United Kingdom were less inclined than Cambridge to be thinking of developing historical studies of parts of the world outside Europe, and this was also the view of Harry Kidd, a cousin of mine, who was then the First Assistant in the Cambridge University Registry, whose advice I sought. Harry suggested that the most likely place in which someone with my interests might find a post would be one of the new university colleges being set up in British colonies in Africa as a result of the British government's acceptance of the Asquith and Eliot Commissions' Reports of 1945 on Higher Education in the Colonies. The development of these colleges was being fostered by an Inter-University Council for Higher Education in the Colonies on which all the U.K. universities were represented, and whose Secretary was Walter Adams, until recently Secretary of the London School of Economics (a post shortly to be occupied by Harry Kidd). So I went to see Adams; nothing suitable for me was available in the central or eastern parts of Africa best known to me, but I was given particulars of a newly-established lectureship in history at the University College of the Gold Coast. This offered salaries one third higher than those in U.K. universities, partly furnished housing at rents not exceeding ten per cent of salary, and annual long vacation leave with free passages to and from the Gold Coast – for spouses and children as well as staff – all of which seemed sufficiently attractive.

Early in April, the Principal of the University College, David Balme – until 1948 Senior Tutor of Jesus College, Cambridge, and a wartime R.A.F. Wing Commander – was in Britain recruiting staff for an institution which had begun to operate hardly more than six months earlier, and he and Adams interviewed me for this new lectureship. The only detail of this interview that still sticks in my mind is that I was told that what I knew about Southern Rhodesia had no relevance to the Gold Coast. It was a black man's country, in which recent riots had forced the Colonial Office to think that the time for self-government might not be too far off. If black nationalists were to come to power in the not too distant future, it might be quite possible to envisage a white historian losing his job and being deported from the country. (There turned out to be a deep irony in this observation; the first university history teacher deported from a university college in British Africa, Terence Ranger, was on the staff of the college in Southern Rhodesia in the days when Walter Adams was its Principal.) Nevertheless at the end of the interview I was given to understand that the post was mine subject to passing a medical examination and to a vetting by the Chairman of London University's Board of Studies in History. This last came into the picture because the teaching at the colonial university colleges was for Degrees of the University of London under a scheme of "special relationship" which meant that the external (i.e. second) examiners were always recognised teachers of London University, but which allowed the London syllabuses followed by the colonial students to be adapted to meet local conditions and needs. In due course H.Hale Bellot, who was London's Professor of American History, invited me to lunch, and in no time at all I found myself in the extraordinary position for someone who had only given four university lectures in his life, and who had not yet taken up his post in the Gold Coast college, of negotiating with him for changes in London University's History Honours Degree syllabus so that in October the college could begin teaching for this degree. This came about because the College had only very recently agreed that it would no longer limit itself to the General Degree teaching with which it had started, and because the special interest of the only historian actually on its strength in the Gold Coast, Bernice Hamilton, was in the remote field of medieval political thought rather than colonial or African history. In the event six Gold Coast students had actually begun studying under the new syllabus which Bellot and I had negotiated before it had been formally accepted by the relevant committees in either the University of London or the University College of the Gold Coast!

About a month after my interview with Balme and Adams, and before I had received a formal letter of appointment for the Gold Coast college, Harry Kidd and I were shown to have been not wholly correct in our belief that Cambridge was in advance of other U.K. universities in its interest in extra-European history. Birmingham advertised a post in colonial history, while Glasgow declared its intention of appointing up to three lecturers in African Studies, one of whom might be an historian. In case anything went wrong with the Gold Coast appointment – it was not until 7 June that I knew I had passed the medical examination – I applied for both of these. A letter sent to me by the Principal of Glasgow after I had withdrawn these applications suggests that I might well have got a Glasgow lectureship. A few days after I had formally accepted the Gold Coast post, at a starting salary of £858 a year (which seemed a lot of money to us), Roland Oliver wrote to me from the School of Oriental and African Studies in London sounding me out as to whether I might be interested in a post there parallel to his own, but in the "tribal history" not of East Africa, but of West Africa. However Jean and I, and most of those we consulted, had already come to the conclusion that if I were to specialise in the history of Africa, it would be better if I were first to work from a base that was actually in the continent.[1]

---

[1] When in 1963 I ended up at the University of Birmingham, I was interested to find that W.B.Morgan, one of the two Africa-centred lecturers in its Department of Geography (and soon to become Professor of Geography at King's College, London), had made the same decision a little later but in circumstances very close to my own. In 1949 he did accept an appointment in Glasgow, but that university's attempt to set up a School of African Studies did not get very far because in the event it made only one other relevant appointment (in the social sciences). Therefore Morgan very soon came to the conclusion that, if he were to develop his African interests, it would be better if he were to have an African base, and secured a lectureship at the young Nigerian university college at Ibadan.

In 1949 there were two ways of going to the Gold Coast. The traditional way was to take a passage on one of the Elder Dempster mailboats which sailed once a fortnight from Liverpool, arriving at Takoradi after a twelve-day voyage with calls at Las Palmas and Freetown. But during all our time in the Gold Coast and Ghana, several months' notice were required to secure a cabin on one of the mailboats, so that Jean and I had no option but to make our first journey out by air. Shortly after the war, British Overseas Airways had launched a nearly daily service from Heathrow across the Sahara to Accra and Lagos with intermediate stops at Tripoli and Kano. If all went well, the journey took something like twenty hours, with the desert being crossed at night. But the York aircraft in service in 1949 were unpressurised, and so bumpy and noisy. They were also liable to break down, so that tired and fractious passengers could well arrive at their destination several hours or even, on occasions, a day or so later than scheduled. So we chose to make our first journey out in pressurised Constellation aircraft belonging to Pan American Airways and its Brazilian subsidiary, changing planes at Lisbon where at the airlines' expense we spent a comfortable evening and night in a good hotel. After brief stops at Dakar and at Robertsfield, the airport for the Liberian capital, Monrovia, we were decanted safe and sound at Accra airport shortly after midnight on 5 October. Here a posse of good ladies met us and others destined for the University College. Half asleep, we were whisked swiftly in their cars over the five miles to Achimota, and deposited in the beds that were awaiting us there.

My first real sense that we were in the land which was to be home to us for the first ten years of our married life was waking up in the soft cool of a sunlit early African morning as the first occupants of a newly built prefabricated house, hearing the pitter-patter sound of women breaking stones in a little quarry that lay below the western edge of Achimota hill close by the line of the railway to Kumasi. We learnt that such a house, a timber-framed structure clad with asbestos cement sheeting, was called a "Folly". Some two dozen of them had been hastily designed and erected since the previous June, the end of the University College's first academic year. Hith-erto it had been entirely accommodated in existing buildings of Achimota College, which had been designed to provide a complete residential educa-tion for both sexes from nursery school onwards. Alongside its main build-ings, a second, western, campus had been developed for pre-school and post-secondary work. During the war this campus had been taken over by the military, who had added a substantial number of temporary single sto-rey mud and thatch huts alongside the not unpleasing Achimota architec-ture in concrete. After the military had departed, all these buildings re-verted to post-secondary activities, some of them being used for a teacher training college, while the others were made available to the new Univer-sity College pending the construction of its own campus on Legon Hill, some three miles to the north-east.

Achimota College had been created in the 1920s by a far-sightedly de-velopment-minded Governor, Sir Gordon Guggisberg, as a model co-edu-cational secondary school which would provide the Gold Coast with the well-trained elite which he thought essential if it were to advance fully into the modern world. It had been extended by its first Principal, Rev. A.G.Fraser, to embrace nursery teaching at one end of the educational spec-trum and post-secondary schooling at the other. In one discipline, the very practical one of engineering, thanks to a very gifted teacher, Charles Deakin, Achimota had actually advanced so far as to produce students who had qualified for the external degrees of London University. Although teach-ing at this level did not survive the 1939-45 war (and Deakin's departure to a lectureship at Cambridge), teaching for the London Intermediate ex-amination had continued. It was becoming urgently necessary to provide degree courses for them because it could not be expected that all success-ful intermediate students would find university places outside the colony. So ninety first- and second-year pupils working at Achimota in 1948 for the external intermediate examinations of London were transformed into the first students of the new University College of the Gold Coast. Some of their teachers were also taken over from Achimota, and a few others were hastily recruited to supplement them. But towards the end of that first academic year, 1948-49, the decision was taken that in 1949-50 the College should begin to offer not only courses for the Intermediate and General Degrees of London University, but also Honours Degree courses. It therefore became necessary to find many more suitably qualified academic staff (and, of course, I was one of those swept up in the resultant recruiting drive). But the twenty or so staff who were already there knew that, in a general country-wide shortage of housing, they occupied all the available houses on the western campus, plus some in Accra up to seven miles away. In June they therefore asked their Principal how he proposed that recruits due in October could be housed; whereupon he said that temporary houses would be built for them. This was said to be "Balme's folly", with the result that the kind of house that we lived in for our first few weeks at Achimota became known as a Folly.

It was a well designed little house, with a sizeable living room with a verandah, a study, a screened area containing two bedrooms and a bathroom, and a pantry from which a covered path led to a kitchen containing a wood-burning stove, attached to which were a room for a servant and a garage. But while it proved relatively easy and quick to build Follies, and they proved much more durable than was intended (for some of them were still in use forty or more years later), there was an immediate problem in that they were intended to be provided with electricity and running water, and neither of these things were readily come by. Electricity was in short supply throughout the Gold Coast, so that eventually the College decided that it would have to generate its own power. So far as water was concerned, the problem was that western Achimota's distribution network had been greatly and hurriedly extended by the military; on the one hand, it could not readily take any further load, on the other hand nobody knew where the underground pipes lay that needed to be extended or enlarged.

So many of our earliest memories of living on the Gold Coast are of heat-producing pressure lamps and of carrying water over quite substantial distances by hand or by car. But initially we only had a few weeks in a Folly. David Balme's concept of a university was very much a collegiate one. Its teachers' responsibilities were to extend beyond the classrooms and laboratories to the moral care of their students, and for this reason he was always keen to recruit academic staff like myself accustomed to the tutorial systems of the older U.K. universities. I was to be a tutor to those of our students who lived in Aggrey Hall, a permanent Achimota building intended for a school boarding house which had little flats at either end to house masters to supervise the resident schoolboys. As soon as an earlier incumbent had moved out, Jean and I moved into one of these flats. Both the Hall and its attendant flats were ill shaped and too small for their new university purpose, and we felt oppressively cabinned and confined in our flat, but at least we could now enjoy running water and electricity (and so could exchange an icebox for a refrigerator). However by October 1950, we were back again in a Folly.

The reason for this was the continuing expansion of the University College. In 1949-50 there were just over a hundred undergraduates, and although by the end of that year the numbers of academic and administrative staff must have built up to something like forty, the College was still small enough for everybody to know everybody else, whether staff or student. It was in fact a very pleasant society to live in, and Jean and I made many friendships which only death could terminate. Many staff and their wives would lunch together in what passed for a senior common room, and when ten years later we left the country, we were still being invited to weddings or christenings by men and women we had first met as students in our first year in the Gold Coast. In our second year, the academic and administrative staff required to run a college with nineteen departments teaching three-year degree courses as well as intermediate or preliminary courses, must have built up to something like a hundred. The number of students was also increasing rapidly; for 1950-51 living space had to be found for over two hundred of them. This was appreciably more than could be accommodated in the buildings taken over from Achimota School. In the planning for the development of the Legon site, priority was given to the provision of living accommodation for both students and staff, but some time was yet to elapse before any buildings were to be completed at Legon. Indeed in March 1950 the College's tutors were being invited to comment on the architect's plans for the first permanent hall of residence there. So it was decided to build on the Achimota site a temporary student hall, a single storey quadrangle constructed with the methods and materials used to build Follies, and I became tutor to its students. This turned out to be very convenient, for South Hall, as it was called, was put up immediately south of the mud huts which housed the Department of History, while Jean and I, and the son and daughter who arrived in 1950 and 1953 respectively, inhabited a Folly only a few yards further on. Here we lived for four years until I became a fellow of Akuafo Hall, the second hall of residence built at Legon, and successfully entered a competition to reside in the permanent housing for university staff that was being built on the new campus at Legon.

This campus and the buildings on it were designed by Pearce Hubbard, an architect with Mediterranean experience, whose white-walled buildings all had pitched roofs clad with red tiles which contrasted strongly with the flat roofs and bright paintwork more commonly employed at the time in West Africa, for example by Maxwell Fry and Jane Drew at the Nigerian University College at Ibadan. Jean and I were to have experience of living in two of Pearce Hubbard's houses and could be critical of some of the details of his designs. This indeed was a common reaction not only to his domestic architecture, but to all his university buildings. But the general effect of them, especially as the trees and shrubs which had been planted around them began to grow, was superb. The University College at Legon – like Achimota in its early days – was not uncommonly criticised by some for being too splendid, and thus too expensive. It was expensive; by 1960 the cost of what had been built as a campus for a thousand students was some £10,000,000, which for that time and place was a lot of money, and 95% of it had come from the Gold Coast taxpayers. But the guiding ideal, of black politicians as well as of white planners (again this was parallel to the conception of Achimota), was "nothing but the best will do for Africa". Moreover sometimes it could be argued that the best might be the most economical in the long run: for example, building strongly enough to resist the earthquakes which may occur in this region of the Gold Coast, or insisting on the use of the best tropical hardwoods in preference to cheaper woods that would need to be regularly painted, or even specifying mattresses for the students' beds that would be more hygienic and durable than the local ones of straw. Furthermore, in the circumstances of an African colony, much had to be done that would have been unnecessary in Britain, such as providing a power house and sewage works, a hospital and a police station, and houses – not simply as residences for teachers and researchers and administrators – but also a whole village where clerks and cleaners and the like could find places in which to live and bring up their families.

A not unrelated, and perhaps more serious criticism of the University College was that it was an ivory tower whose people had too little contact with the rest of Gold Coast society. To some extent this was both true and inevitable. It was hardly surprising that, so far as I can remember, only eight of the first hundred or so senior appointments to the College staff were Africans, and that as staff was rapidly built up to the strengths necessary to enable nineteen departments each to teach honours degree courses, the proportion actually declined. It was not until about 1958, when it began to be possible to recruit from among those of the African colleges' own products who had gone on to do postgraduate work, that "Africanisation" could really begin. Before then there was no alternative but to import most of the academics, for the most part from the lands of the white peoples of Europe, America and Australasia. Since the professional future and advancement of the imports were more likely to lie in these lands than in Africa, very few of them could ever totally commit themselves to the African society in which they were currently living.

This consciousness was enhanced by practical circumstances. The College was situated some seven miles from Accra, so that it tended to be rather self-sufficient. There was little necessity to visit Accra other than for a weekly shopping trip. If one wanted good conversation, music or theatre or sport or a bookshop, what Achimota and Legon could provide could be just as good, or even better than might be found in Accra. Moreover, it was not only with Africans that many of us did not mix as much as perhaps we should have. In some respects we felt alienated from the European community in Accra, and this feeling was mutual. Few of its members had any academic pretensions, and they were inclined to regard us as unrealistic and dangerous liberals who thought themselves superior to the real workers on whom the Empire depended. Conversely we were inclined to think of the ordinary run of the mill expatriates, with their Accra Club, which admitted only Europeans, as narrow-minded and outdated philistines. Not to put too fine a point on it, we were different from other inhabitants of the Gold Coast, white as well as black, for in those early days of the University College we were unique. We were the only group of people in the country whose sole purpose and justification was the pursuit of knowledge.

However in our first few months on the Gold Coast, it was hardly possible to ignore what was going on in the country, especially in Accra, its capital. Riots in 1948, a quite unusual event in the history of the Colony, had led to a commission of enquiry which had forthrightly reported that their root cause was that the colony's constitution introduced as recently as 1946 had not met the legitimate aspirations of its people. So the Colonial Office set up a Committee on Constitutional Reform with an exclusively African membership chaired by Judge Henley Coussey, and including what were then regarded as the principal nationalist leaders. This committee's report was published in October 1949, the month in which Jean and I arrived on the Gold Coast, and in December its recommendations for a semi-responsible form of government were accepted. But younger, more radical politicians, led by Kwame Nkrumah, had by this time broken away from what had hitherto been the main nationalist grouping, the United Gold Coast Convention headed by J.B.Danquah, had formed the Convention People's Party, and launched a campaign for "Self-Government NOW". When the Coussey Report was accepted, they took advantage of post-war industrial unrest in Accra to enter upon a programme of "Positive Action". A very minor consequence of this was that I (together, I suppose, with other members of the academic staff of the University College) was enlisted as a Special Constable. But Nkrumah and most of his principal associates were soon arrested and given short prison sentences, and the unrest they had provoked quite quickly fizzled out.

The College's Department of Extra-Mural Studies, led by an active and ambitious Director, David Kimble, could not but take an active interest in such events – so active indeed that staid members of the colonial administration were apt to think of Kimble as a subversive firebrand. I had not been a month in the country before I was persuaded to join with two rather conservative African politicians and the first two Africans to be appointed district commissioners in the Gold Coast administration, A.L.Adu and Kofi Busia[1], to be a paper speaker in a discussion on the Coussey Report. Then, early in 1951, after elections to the new Legislative Assembly had been held (and won by the C.P.P.), along with other members of the College, I was one of those conscripted by Kimble to take part in a week-end conference for the newly elected legislators on "parliamentary institutions and procedure" and more than once I spoke at the Extra-Mural Department's summer schools. However my most alarming experience as a public speaker in the Gold Coast was when the Accra Dining Club – a select, fifty-strong inter-racial group, in no way to be confused with the Accra Club – had invited me to propose the toast of "The Commonwealth" at a dinner to celebrate the Queen's coronation at which the guests included not only the Governor, Sir Charles Arden-Clarke, but also Kwame Nkrumah, by then Prime Minister. Judging by my surviving notes, I seem to have given them something of a constitutional lecture! But most of my other sallies and speaking engagements outside our ivory towers on the hills of Achimota and Legon were in connection with my professional activities as a historian, and it is to these that I should now turn.

In the year prior to my arrival, all the work of the University College's Department of History had been done by Bernice Hamilton, but the teaching involved can have been no more than the two courses required by students taking history as a subject for the London Intermediate. With my arrival to support her, we had to embark also on teaching for the first year of the three-year course for the History Honours Degree, for which six of the previous year's intermediate students had been accepted. It was very hard work. I cannot now remember whether Bernice did any honours teaching that year, but since I did no intermediate teaching, she must certainly have continued to do all of that. She also had to represent us on the Academic Board, which in those days was the only committee overseeing the College's academic affairs, and seemed to be in almost continuous session. I was required to mount three lecture courses, each supported by tutorial supervision, for the Honours students. One of these was the new subject, "European activities in Africa", to which Professor Bellot had agreed; the other two were courses in the modern history of England and of Europe which I had mugged up from my reading and lecture notes for the Cambridge Tripos. Not long after I had begun on these three courses, it was realised that no one was available to teach a compulsory subject for students taking the B.Sc. Economics Degree which was called "The British Constitution", and I was persuaded to take this on also. I was by no means clear why economists needed to have such a subject in their degree syllabus, nor what was meant to be involved in it, and it proved to be a last straw which could easily break my back. I had to go to ask David Balme to relieve me of it. Looking back on this year 1949-50, I think Bernice may also have been hard pushed to survive, because at the end of the second term she went back to Britain on sick leave. This meant that it now fell to me to attend the interminable discussions in the Academic Board. But her departure had one advantage for me in that I was able to use her motor car at a time when Jean had taken ours with her to England when, in March, she had returned by sea for the birth of our son Michael. (At that time, on the ground that the Ridge Hospital in Accra might not be able to cope with a difficult delivery, it was not considered wise for European women to bear their first child in the Gold Coast. We were more than delighted when in 1953 our second child, Julia, was born at the Ridge Hospital in relative ease.)

I can remember calculating that something like five members were needed if a university department of history were to run a full programme of courses for an honours degree without strain, and providing some choice of second year optional subjects and third year special subjects. In my second year, 1950-51, we got close to this, since Bernice and I were joined by Edgar Metcalfe, who had been research assistant at Oxford to Sir Reginald Coupland, the Beit Professor of Colonial History, and Jack Lander, a medievalist from Cambridge working on the life of Edward IV. At the end of 1951-52, Bernice left us for a Simon Fellowship at Manchester, but the Department had continued to grow with the appointments of Douglas Coombs, from University College London, and Margaret Priestley, an Oxford graduate who had some experience of university teaching at Leeds. After Bernice left, I became acting head of department and a Senior Lecturer, while the College continued to search for someone to be its first Professor of History. So far as I am aware, the only person to be seriously interested in this was Caroline Ketelbey, number two in the history department at St Andrews, who came out to look at us in the second term of 1950-51, and who completed negotiations on our syllabus with Hale Bellot. She seemed to like both the country and the Department, but eventually turned the job down. I believe this was for reasons of health (she must have been in her later fifties), and also that she told Balme that I might be a suitable candidate for the chair. At that time I was more interested in finding a university post in Britain, and was making applications wherever and whenever I could see anything that might be suitable. At Cambridge, to which I dearly wanted to return, success went first to Gallagher and then to Robinson. I was not so disappointed by the failure of some of the other applications I made, and I experienced no difficulty in refusing suggestions that I might apply for posts in Canada and South Africa. Eventually, in the summer of 1955, the College's chair of history was again advertised. I went to ask Balme whether it was sensible for a youngster of thirty-three to think of applying for it, whereupon he pointed out to me that Gilbert Murray had been only twenty-three when he had been elected to his first chair, at Glasgow. The proper answer to that, of course, was that I was hardly in Gilbert Murray's class as a scholar – but I did not think of this at the time. So, taking Balme's remark for an encouragement, I sent in my application for the chair and, with only a handful of very modest publications to support me, I was elected to it.

I was responsible for three additions to the strength of the Department. The first was Robert Sprigge, who came to us in 1953-54 with a brilliant reputation from Caius College, Cambridge, and who as a specialist in the history of political ideas, was a replacement for Bernice. We then looked for someone with a developed interest in the early history of European expansion overseas, especially by the Portuguese and the Dutch, both of whom had been active in Africa. Our first choice was Ian Macgregor, who came to us from the University of Singapore in January 1956 and died suddenly and tragically of insulinitis only six months later. We were able to replace him with Graham Irwin, also from Singapore, who made a conversion to Africanist history and eventually succeeded me as head of department.

As I see it, the Department was in full working order by 1953-54. We then had an establishment of seven posts, one of which, that for a Professor, was vacant. This vacancy enabled us to secure Douglas Jones, Lecturer in West African History at the School of Oriental and African Studies in London, on a year's secondment. This was convenient for him as he wanted to do an extended period of fieldwork. It was also very opportune for us, as we had just secured London University's agreement to allow us to replace some of the English History courses that were standard fare for its Medieval and Modern History Honours Degree by introducing two courses in African History, and Douglas was an ideal man to help launch the teaching for the earlier of these, "The History of Africa to c. 1750". Hitherto we had had the knowledge and skill to approach the history of Africa only from the outside, in the courses which I taught on European activities in Africa and on Atlantic History – which, centering on the slave trade, dealt with the interaction between the histories of the Americas and of western Africa. But from 1953-54 onwards we had what we considered to be a mature and balanced Honours Degree syllabus for an African university institution. In their final examinations, after three years study, our students were required to sit nine historical papers. At least two of these had to relate to Africa, while if they wished they could choose up to as many as five Africa-related papers. We were able to provide choices of three second-year optional subjects and three third-year special subjects; in each case two of the options were Africa-related. Our main problem was that when Douglas Jones returned to S.O.A.S., we once again had a vacancy for a specialist teacher in African history. I was still the only member of the Department completely involved in the teaching of this history, Metcalfe's and Irwin's contributions being less of African history in a full sense, than of colonial history in an African context. This problem was not fully solved until after my departure in 1959, when the Department was able to recruit from among its own graduates. But for 1957-58 it was greatly eased when for two separate terms we were able to call on the services of two visitors, Roland Oliver, whom we had invited to share with us his great expertise in the history of the Bantu, and Thomas Hodgkin, who had just finished working on the second edition of his marvellous historical anthology, *Nigerian Perspectives*.

In one sense at least, we were very successful with what we were doing. The first Honours B.A. students from the University College graduated in 1952. By 1959, when I left the College, there had been 128 of them, and of these 60, or nearly half, had graduated in History. (Six other departments between them had produced only 68 Honours graduates - the next largest cohort, 23 strong, coming from the Department of English.)[2] But for some years I did have one nagging worry; we had not produced a graduate with First Class Honours. This was in fact an unnecessary worry, for in those days in the Modern and Medieval History course for London University's own internal students, the proportion of graduates attaining First Class honours was only about one in two hundred. Anyhow I was put out of my self-inflicted misery in 1956 when we internal examiners reckoned we had two candidates with a First. Although the London examiners were able to persuade us that one of our two was a very near miss (this was one of the very few occasions when we had anything like a difference of opinion with the London University examiners in history), I can say that the undergraduate class of two in which I had supervised Adu Boahen and Isaac Tufuoh was quite the most exciting and stimulating in my experience - at Cambridge as well as in Africa. Both Adu and Isaac were awarded scholarships to do postgraduate work in Britain, Adu going to S.O.A.S, (where he received excellent supervision from Roland Oliver) and Isaac to Oxford (where I think he was relatively neglected). When on 1 October 1959, the day after I had left the service of the University College, Adu and Isaac became the first African members of the staff of its History Department, I felt we had really achieved what we had left Britain to do.

Of course university lecturers and professors of history were expected to do rather more than simply provide tuition for students. But in the Gold Coast there was one job which faced our contemporaries in Nigeria at the University College at Ibadan – a job which involved the secondment of Kenneth Dike during 1952-54 to set up Nigeria's National Archives – which we did not have to do. A young Gold Coast graduate, J.M.Akita, had already been selected and trained as Government Archivist, and it was while Dike was visiting Accra to see how things were done in the Gold Coast that I first met him. But although there was a not inconsiderable interest in history outside our University College, in 1949 there was no national History Society to link this interest with what we were trying to do at Achimota. There were of course the secondary schools where teachers taught the largely English and European history which could secure for their students entry to our department. There were also the essentially non-literary histories still vital to the maintenance of the traditions of the courts and societies of the African states which had been brought under British rule, for the most part only in the later years of the nineteenth century. Then there was the history which lay behind the rhetoric of the nationalist politicians, a history based partly on a distillation of, or extrapolation from, their perception of the traditional history, and partly on what they had learnt from western-style education about the manner in which their peoples had been brought under British rule, and what aspects of the British tradition they could adapt to regain independence for them. So Bernice Hamilton and I decided to found a historical society to bring these interests together. Neither of us had experience of launching what might pass for a "learned society", so I got my F.R.S. father to send me a copy of the constitution of the Royal Society! With this before me, I constructed a draft set of rules for a "Gold Coast & Togoland Historical Society". This was then circulated to prospective members together with an invitation to them to come to an inaugural meeting at Achimota early in January 1952.

Perhaps the most obvious person to think of inviting to be the first President of the Society was Dr Danquah, who was fond of expressing his views on issues of Gold Coast history, including a belief in the mass migration of people from Ancient Ghana to the Gold Coast which was not to the taste of more academic historians, but he was too involved in politics. So we turned to a nationalist of an earlier generation, Dr J.W. de Graft Johnson, another lawyer, from Cape Coast in his case, who in the 1920s had written books and articles which had commanded academic respect. Others elected to our first Council were Akita, Michael Ribeiro, who had taught history at Achimota School, A.B.Attafua, also once a history teacher but in 1952 an officer of the Vernacular Literature Bureau, and Jack Lander; I became Secretary. De Graft Johnson was delighted to have been chosen as the Society's first President, and thereafter was one of its staunchest supporters, always willing to give time to its affairs, but for 1953 he insisted that he should give way to someone younger and more actively engaged in historical activities. So I was elected in his place and so continued until 1957, the year when the colony of the Gold Coast became the independent state of Ghana, when it seemed appropriate that the Society should turn again to its founding African father. A third or more of the Society's members could be counted on to turn up and enjoy themselves at its annual conferences each January. These were almost always residential affairs held at an educational institution and extending over two or three days at which papers by invited speakers – not always members of the Society – were read and discussed. I can remember meetings in Kumasi, Cape Coast (where no less than five of the best secondary schools in the country were situated), Accra, in halls of residence at Legon, and – most memorably – in the eighteenth-century coastal castle at Anomabu. Most of the papers presented were subsequently published, together with some other articles, in the Society's *Transactions*, for which I had secured a small subsidy from the University College, and of which I was editor so long as I remained in the country. In my day our Historical Society was always a modest little one, with a membership usually around 140. However the circulation of its *Transactions* was greater than this, and in it were printed one or two pieces which may still be worth at least a glance even in the 1990s. We also set an example for other parts of West Africa. When Dike became head of Ibadan's History Department, he consulted us about the running of a historical society, and in December 1955 I was invited to the inaugural meeting of the Historical Society of Nigeria, a country where a plurality both of people and of universities was to make possible the growth of a much more substantial society.

[1] Busia was soon to be Professor of Sociology at the University College, from which, of course, he went into politics as the leader of opposition to Nkrumah and the C.P.P.

[2] The Honours Degree provides a convenient level at which to measure the performance of the History Department as this was the only one which was entirely within its control – because, of course, General Degree students took three subjects, only one of which could be History. It may also be pointed out that more students chose to work for the B.A. Honours Degree than for the B.A. General Degree; thus in 1952-58 in the College as a whole 109 students secured B.A. Honours Degrees compared with 77 who secured B.A. General Degrees. In 1958-59, my final year, the department was teaching a total of 39 Honours students and 23 General Degree students (plus 2 Geography students taking History as a subsidiary subject). It may be added that, until in 1955-56 the University College raised its entry requirements to the level which universities in the U.K. had adopted in 1951, there were also always some Intermediate students to be taught.

CHAPTER 7

WIDER HORIZONS

A fair amount of my time at the University College was taken up with the reading and the writing of notes needed for new lecture courses. After I was no longer needed to teach the European and English history courses which I had to do in 1949-50, I was responsible at one time or another for four courses of lectures – on the European Expansion and on Atlantic History, and two courses in African History. Then, when the first two of these had been passed on to colleagues, I embarked on a new special subject exploring the value of the published fifteenth- and sixteenth-century European accounts of West Africa as sources for its history. But I also had to think what academic work I might do beyond this teaching.

The Gold Coast was hardly a relevant base from which to continue with the interest in the colonial history of southern and central Africa which had occasioned the thesis for my Ph.D. I might of course move to the chronologically comparable history of West Africa, for which I would be able to make use of the records preserved in the National Archives in Accra, which for the most part were the African end of the British colonial administration's correspondence with the Colonial Office from 1843 onwards, together with what had survived from that administration's own internal records beginning from much the same time. But living and working in West Africa had made me increasingly inquisitive about the nature and development of its society before it had come to be first influenced and ultimately dominated by Europeans. As far as our Department of History was concerned, the Gold Coast's nineteenth and twentieth centuries became Edgar Metcalfe's speciality, while outside the Department it was known that David Kimble was working on the development of Gold Coast nationalism from 1850 onwards. So while I followed up a suggestion which had been made to me by Jack Gallagher when he had learnt that I was going out to the Gold Coast, found a copy of the Minutes of the British Merchants' Council at Cape Coast during 1829-1844 (the original of which had been supposed lost) and used this to write an article on "The administration of George Maclean" for the *Transactions*, it was Metcalfe who wrote the standard biography of Maclean and published a great volume of documents to illustrate the relations between the Gold Coast and British government, and Kimble who produced a political history of the colonial Gold Coast after Maclean's time.

It took me some time to appreciate the extent to which external written sources – the accounts of European visitors coming by sea from the middle of the fifteenth century onwards and of writers in Arabic approaching from across the Sahara which began even earlier – might be used to illuminate society and its history in West Africa before the general spread of literacy there following the expansion of the world religions of Islam and Christianity. Initially I supposed that the two main ways into the exploration of pre-literate West African society and history must lie through archaeology and the study of oral traditions (in neither of which I had any experience or training). As befitted a classicist, David Balme was keen to establish archaeology in the University College. He once told me that one evening he was dining in Cambridge at Jesus College, and took advantage of sitting next to A.W.Lawrence, the Disney Professor of Archaeology, to ask him whether he knew of anyone who might like to go out to the Gold Coast as its first professor of his subject, whereupon Lawrence said he would. And so he did, arriving in 1951 and being almost immediately joined by a second archaeologist, Oliver Davies. But Davies's field was prehistory, while Lawrence's wide experience and great energies were directed to the setting up of a National Museum for the Gold Coast, and to the architectural history and the preservation of the forty or so forts and castles which Europeans had built on its shores from 1482 onwards. It was not until about the time that I left the country that significant excavations were begun on the material remains of the later iron age societies which interested me. However, discussing with Lawrence the extensive use he made in his work on the forts of the contemporary European written sources helped indicate to me how useful these sources could be for the history of the African peoples and polities that were the intimate neighbours of the Europeans in the forts. Furthermore it was Lawrence who suggested to me that if the early Arabic sources relating to West Africa were to be fully exploited as historical documents, they needed to be re-edited and re-translated by scholars who were not simply Arabists but who also had some familiarity with the history of Africa. He and I drew up a first list of texts to be worked on, the University College was persuaded to provide funds, and in 1956 I was able to recruit Dr Witwold Rajkowski from S.O.A.S. to undertake the work. But Rajkowski had completed a first draft dealing with no more than a third of the relevant texts when he met an untimely and tragic death on a Saharan expedition. By this time Lawrence had returned to Britain; I was shortly to follow him, but I was able to set on foot the complicated negotiations which led to the continuation of what Rajkowski had begun, and eventually, in 1981, to the publication of the invaluable *Corpus of early Arabic sources for West African history*, translated by J.F.P. Hopkins and edited and annotated by him and Nehemia Levtzion, as a volume sponsored by the University of Ghana in the Fontes Historiae Africanae series.

So far as the oral traditions of the Gold Coast peoples were concerned, by the time I arrived on the scene, quite a bit of work had already been done on them, not least by W.E.F. Ward, the pioneer history teacher at Achimota School. But much of the recording and use of these traditions had been the work of enthusiastic amateurs, who were either intent on glorifying the past of their ancestors or who, if outsiders, tended to take the traditions they had recorded at face value without seeking to interpret them in relation to the socio-political context of the societies from which they had emanated. The most sophisticated work on the societies whose history I was anxious to explore, in Africa generally as well as in the Gold Coast in particular, had for the most part been undertaken by social anthropologists. But most social anthropologists had not been particularly concerned with the history of the societies they were studying and – especially perhaps if they had been trained in the functionalist British school – tended to regard the traditions of these societies not as possible clues to a historical past but rather as oral charters manufactured as explanations of the societal present.

Nevertheless it seemed plain to me that if I were to get any historical sense out of the oral traditions of Gold Coast societies, I must try to understand something of the working of these societies, and that the way to do this would be by working through what the social anthropologists had achieved. The Gold Coast was inhabited by something like seventy separate ethnic groups, each with its own distinct socio-political structure and language. Each of these ethnic groups might be a unit of study for a social anthropologist, who would spend many months living among its people, learning its language and making a first acquaintance with it, and who might then return for further lengthy periods of fieldwork over many years to enrich and deepen his or her knowledge. But the existence of so many distinct ethnic units in an area of much the same size as Great Britain, but with only about a seventh of its population, meant that of necessity many of them were very small and had no need to maintain much in the way of historical tradition. Therefore it seemed to me that, unlike a social anthropologist, a historian – especially perhaps one who could not get substantial periods of leave from his teaching and administrative commitments – was unlikely to get an adequate return from learning any particular language and getting to know the society of its speakers in any depth. He would do better to engage in building up wider pictures from the interrelationship of the various historical traditions than in studying any one of them in great depth.

I think I was probably guided in this thinking by the fact that the University College was situated in the land of the Gã, one of the smaller ethnic groups, whose language was not closely related to those of most of the peoples of the Gold Coast. In different circumstances, I might well have thought differently. I think, for example, of two of my contemporaries, Ivor Wilks, who was for some years our Extramural Department's tutor in Asante, the greatest of the traditional kingdoms of the Gold Coast, and who was to spend the best part of a lifetime working towards his magnificent history of that kingdom, and Jan Vansina in the Bantu lands of the Congo basin, who had the good fortune to have been trained in anthropology as well as in history, and was initially employed as a full-time researcher with no commitment to teaching or administration, and who became the first great authority on the use of oral traditions as sources for African history.

I read widely in the anthropological literature dealing with West Africa, but such indoctrination as I had in the discipline of social anthropology came mainly from extensive discussions with two anthropologists, Jack Goody and David Tait, who were beginning their careers with fieldwork in the Northern Territories of the Gold Coast. Jack was just starting out as an assistant lecturer at Cambridge (where in due course he was to become the William Wyse Professor of Social Anthropology). David, who came to social anthropology as a second career after the war, securing his degree at

University College, London, took up a lectureship in the Sociology Department at Achimota a few months after my own appointment in history. Both were much more concerned with history than the senior anthropologists under whom they had studied, Meyer Fortes and Daryll Forde. Jack was endlessly stimulating on historical and other matters relating to the peoples of West Africa, which he would expound sitting on the floor in our Folly when he was passing through Achimota on his way to and from the field. David began in the Gold Coast with a solid block of twenty months or more working among the Dagomba and Konkomba peoples, but thereafter, having established this solid platform of fieldwork, his visits to the field tended to be restricted to university vacations. In term time we were in and out of each others' houses, and this was the milieu in which we came to conceive a scheme for the recording and study of historical traditions in the Northern Territories of the Gold Coast.

The Konkomba, who became David's main study, were a small group with little need for a corporate memory beyond a span of about three generations. But David had begun his researches among the Dagomba, whose Dagbon monarchy was a substantial member of the Mole-Dagbane family of kingdoms whose rulers all claimed descent from a group of horsemen who had conquered and made tributary almost all of the smaller ethnic groups (such as the Konkomba) who inhabited the basin of the Upper Volta. Three of the largest of these kingdoms became part of French West Africa, and the main lines of their historical traditions had been systematically recorded quite soon after the French conquest. David and I now aimed to record the official traditions of all the royal courts and their subordinate chieftaincies on the Gold Coast side of the colonial frontier. At Easter 1953 we travelled round the Northern Territories using David's extensive personal knowledge to select local informants who might be trusted to take down in writing the "drum histories" which were recited before a king or chief on major state occasions, and to make first translations of them. After studying the results, it was our intention to return to ask questions about the language and meaning of each individual recorded text and then, when each of these had been established to our satisfaction, to consider them and their interrelationship as a corpus, and to return again with wider questions. Following this we hoped to be able to integrate our knowledge with that of that of the Francophone authorities in an overall interpretation of the history of the Mole-Dagbane speaking peoples. But we had not got very far with our plan when, almost exactly three years after it had been launched, David Tait was killed in a tragic motor accident. Its only memorials are about a dozen collected texts, and a short essay of interpretation which I presented to an Ethnology Seminar of the International African Institute that was held at Dakar in 1961 (subsequently published, in 1964, in a volume entitled *The Historian in Tropical Africa*).

This seminar brought together some seventeen pioneer workers on African history, some of whom – Oliver, Goody, Wilks and Vansina – have already been mentioned in these memoirs, and a number of others with whom – especially perhaps workers from Francophone West Africa such as Gouverneur Hubert Deschamps, Raymond Mauny and Yves Person – I had already developed useful relations. Vansina was a central figure in the Dakar seminar, not simply because of his standing as an oral historian or because, virtually single-handed, he became the author of the published volume's "Introductory Summary", but also because he was by far the most readily bilingual of its members, and was often pressed into service to translate between English and French. This he did with some wit and with a perfect appreciation of the importance of what had been said in either language; thus on one occasion I remember he translated an impassioned tirade in French by no more than "He does not agree with the previous speaker" – a perfectly adequate rendering!

This was not the first time I had come across Vansina, because I had already become involved in international conference-going in connection with the study of African history. Together with about ten others with Gold Coast connections, I was present at what is generally accepted as the first ever international conference on African history and archaeology, that organised by Roland Oliver at S.O.A.S. in July 1953. This was a relatively modest affair designed to bring together teachers from the young university colleges in Africa, during their long vacation visits to Britain, to share news of what they were up to among themselves and with the handful of those in Europe who were concerned with the African past. Vansina was not one of those there; he had started on his fieldwork among the Kuba of the Congo only in the previous May. He was present at the substantially larger second S.O.A.S. Conference in 1957, when no less than seventy papers were circulated for discussion compared with the thirty-three of the first conference. But by then I had already seen Vansina more or less on his home ground. In 1955 I had gone to the first Inter-African Conference in the Social Sciences organised by the C.C.T.A., the Commission for Technical Cooperation in Africa South of the Sahara, which had been set up in 1950 by the four African colonial powers and the autonomous governments of the Union of South Africa and the Rhodesian Federation. Since this conference was held at Bukavu in the Belgian Congo, it was serviced by the Institut des Recherches Scientifiques de l'Afrique Centrale (I.R.S.A.C.) with which Vansina was a *Chercheur*, and he was the very lively and much admired *Rapporteur* of the section of the conference which dealt with matters pertaining to social anthropology, sociology and "ethno-history".

This C.C.T.A. conference was a very different affair from the friendly, informal gatherings organised by Roland Oliver, which have quite fairly been characterised as "enlarged seminars". Except for a few observers, all those at Bukavu were delegates of their governments. The British Delegation had fourteen members, some of whom, such as the geographer Robert Steel, the economist Ronald Tress, and the African linguists Malcolm Guthrie and Wilfred Whiteley, had come from universities in the U.K., while others were drawn from university or research institutions in the East and West African colonies. I am hazy about the mechanics of selection, except that I do know that the Gold Coast authorities had invited the University College of the Gold Coast to make nominations, and that this was how David Tait, John Williams – our Professor of Economics – and I were chosen to go to Bukavu. But when we got there we were surprised to find that we were the only delegates from British West Africa; I can only assume that its other governments or university colleges had failed to take any action.

As an official delegation, we were required to choose a chairman, who would represent us on the steering committee that managed the conference's business. Many of us thought that our chairman should be the eminent anthropologist, Audrey Richards, then Director of the East African Institute of Social Research at Makerere, but she proposed Henry Fosbrooke, a senior sociologist from Tanganyika – and by this means the Britons secured two seats on the steering committee, for at the conference's first plenary session, Audrey was elected as one of its Vice-Chairmen. The British delegation refused to take the conference as seriously as some of the others. These would seem to have had official policy guidelines to follow, whereas we tended to enjoy ourselves in friendly academic discussion. It might perhaps be thought that we acted in this way because we had no Colonial Office minder to keep us in order, but my later experience of inter-governmental conference meetings dealing with academic affairs, for example UNESCO conferences, has suggested to me that it was normal for U.K. delegations, even when they did contain "men from the ministry", to be more light-hearted and less politically intent than those of most other nations.

The official business of the conference was to make recommendations to the member governments of C.C.T.A., and plenty of these were made, some of them even thought up by the British. Whether much action was ever taken on them is quite another matter. Our little group from Achimota, who knew that the Gold Coast was very soon to become Ghana, were probably the only ones at the conference – at which there was not a single black delegate – likely to have appreciated that the whole colonial structure could quite soon vanish from Africa. In the event, of course, things were to move much faster than even we with our Gold Coast experience could have envisaged, so that independent African successor governments were to have little time or inclination to engage in any elaborate and expensive organisations of scientific cooperation. In retrospect one of the principal merits of the conference so far as I was concerned was the chance it provided for a brief look at parts of Africa which I had not seen before. I began by spending a few days at Makerere, "the Achimota of East Africa", and then motored to Bukavu with the East African delegates. By my Gold Coast standards, I found the parts of the Baganda and Ankole lands in Uganda through which we passed surprisingly empty of people and of any signs of markets or any other commercial activity. They were also scenically dull until at Kabale we began to enter a land of fantastic volcanoes, ten or more thousands of feet high, from which great flows of lava had spread, some of which were still barely colonised by vegetation. Then through Kisenyi and Goma we entered the Belgian Congo and journeyed along the shores of Lake Kivu through what must be the most perfectly beautiful scenery in Africa. In those days, Bukavu, with its European dwellings built spaciously and well on a series of peninsulas extending into the lake, must have been one of Africa's most attractive towns. The Belgians showed us the well-planned housing estates they were building for their black subjects and emphasised their insistence that populous hillsides must be cultivated in terraces running along the contours, and they took us into their trusteeship territory of Rwanda to show us the rural tranquillity in which the masses of Hutu cultivators lived alongside the tall and willowy cattle-owning aristocracy of the Tutsi. When the conference had ended, David Tait and I flew from one little landing ground to another all the way across the Congo to its sprawling and unlovely capital of Leopoldville with its vast proletariat, and it was perhaps only there that one began to sense that colonial paternalism might eventually end up in disaster and mayhem. Even so, it was impossible to think that less than forty years later Rwanda would have all but destroyed itself in Hutu-Tutsi strife, and that the lovely rural and urban countryside from Goma to Bukavu would have been devastated by the influx of refugees from Rwanda.

The other main merit of the conference from my point of view was that it provided plenty of informal occasions – in the buses which took us to see the sights, in the excellent restaurants overlooking Lake Kivu, or even in the showers at the luxurious Athenée School (built to European standards for a largely European clientele) in which the delegates were housed – to get to know such people as Desmond Clark and Roger Summers, the archaeologists from Rhodesia; Kenneth Ingham, my opposite number at Makerere; Avelino Teixeira da Mota, Portuguese naval officer and Africanist historian; Jean Rouch, the French anthropologist and film maker; and three of the observers, all anthropologists, Daryll Forde and Vinigi Grottanelli (both of whom I was later to see regularly at International African Institute meetings), and Melville Herskovits (as much the great panjandrum of American Africanists as Daryll Forde was for the British).

Except for the Bukavu conference, I did not travel widely in Africa during my time at Achimota and Legon. In the Gold Coast, there were the occasional trips to the Northern Territories, and I think I may say that I went to visit, and usually also to lecture, at virtually all of the country's main secondary schools and many of its teacher training colleges. We drove as a family more than once to Takoradi, usually to catch a boat, occasionally for a short break at its European Rest House. Further afield, in 1958, when Jean was staying in England to see our son into his new school, I broke my journey out to West Africa in Senegal to spend a profitable week exploring the resources of its long established Institut Francais d'Afrique Noire and talking with Raymond Mauny, its archaeologist and historian of what he called the "medieval" period of West African history. I made three short visits to Nigeria, twice by air, and only once driving there by road, and this was no great adventure since the road across Togo and Dahomey was remarkably good.

I can see a number of reasons why I was such a stay-at-home when I was based in Africa. For one thing, the academic staff of the University College were generously provided each long vacation with free passages to and from their countries of origin so that they would not lose touch with their academic life. Secondly, it did not seem practical to do much travelling in West Africa with young children, and I was not keen on leaving Jean with the sole responsibility of looking after them. Then, when in 1954 I was in a position to take a term of study leave, I used it to accept an invitation to spend it at Keith Hancock's Institute of Commonwealth Studies in London, where he thought I was a suitable person to work, together with Alison Smith, in putting together for publication a collection of documents on the history of the British tropical empire.

The main benefit of working at the Institute so far as I was concerned was that it was the first time that I experienced the stimulus of being able regularly to attend postgraduate seminars, notably those chaired by Roland Oliver in African history and by Gerald Graham in Imperial History. I also found myself a member of a small informal seminar which Hancock used to help brief himself before he was sent out to Uganda to investigate its Kabaka crisis. This may seem an odd assignment for one focussing on West African history, but it had occurred to Hancock's lively mind that the history of British relations with Ashanti in the Gold Coast colony might provide useful illumination of the impasse which had arisen in relations with the Baganda Kingdom within Uganda. However my contribution was to write a little paper which argued that the two sets of circumstances were more unalike than alike. So far as the collection of documents was concerned, quite a bit of groundwork was done with no immediate result, partly because Alison went down with a serious illness, and partly because within a few months Hancock was to leave the Institute.

But perhaps the main reason why I did not do more African travelling when I was based at Achimota and Legon was that the University College kept me pretty busy and, apart from the weekends when I would often enjoy myself on the cricket field or the whole family might go to the nearby beach at Labadi, most of my spare time came to be taken up by writing. During my ten years at the College, I was involved in writing four books, three of which were published.

Within a year or so after going to the Gold Coast, I embarked with Roland Oliver on the writing of a substantial one-volume history of Africa for which he had found a publisher. I think that we both found this a more difficult enterprise than we had supposed when we first sketched it out. (I was certainly not impressed when I recently discovered and re-read some of the draft chapters that I had written for it.) Looking back on it, I would say that this venture was premature, and that I certainly did not have sufficient understanding of large aspects of the very big slices of history that I was attempting to cover. But our struggles did ultimately bear some fruit. When ten or so years after Roland and I began work, Ronald Segal invited us to write *A Short History of Africa* for Penguin Books, we secured leave to do this from our original publisher, and found that what we had been struggling to express in 200,000 words slipped off the pen more readily in a third of the length.

By the time Roland and I started on the *Short History*, I had produced three books of my own, though – strangely – none of them was my own idea. The first came about because when we started teaching at Achimota there was very little available in the form of general textbooks for our students to read, especially perhaps if they were new to the study of African history. Furthermore, some books that might have been of some use to them in the early stages of their studies were out of print. One of these was Ifor Evans's *The British in Tropical Africa*, published by the Cambridge University Press in 1929. When, early in 1952, the Educational Secretary of the Press, Charles Carrington, came to see us at Achimota, I asked him whether Evans's book might be reprinted. To this he replied that much of it was too out of date for a straight reprint to be marketable, and he asked whether perhaps I might adapt it for 1950s readers. But when I looked again at Evans's work, I could see that neither its structure nor his preconceptions would stand the strain of this. So we ended up with the idea that I should write for the Cambridge Press a totally new book on the history of West Africa though, because of the limitations of my (or anybody else's) knowledge of the subject in 1952, I wanted it to be called *An Introduction to the History of West Africa*. I completed writing this in December 1953, and it was published in the summer of 1955.

Whereas in the early 1950s publishers could see little or no market for African history monographs (I found no one interested in any adaptation of my Rhodesian thesis), there certainly was one for simple textbooks of African history, and by the time my book was thought to have reached the end of its useful life in 1991, rather more than 300,000 copies of it had been sold. I was continually involved in revising and updating its text, so that when it reached its sixth edition in 1969, I was confident enough to change its title to *A History of West Africa: an introductory survey*! In fact it was not yet altogether dead because in 1992 it became a sort of historical document in the shape of a reprint published by Gregg Revivals. (Maybe a similar fate will ultimately overtake the Oliver & Fage Penguin, which by 1997 had also reached its sixth, revised and enlarged edition, with sales approaching 400,000.)

My second book also resulted from discussions with a visiting educational publisher, J.A.T. Morgan, of Edward Arnold Ltd, who came to see me in April 1954. He had fostered a series of simple historical atlases, and thought the time might have come to have one for African history. Since I have always been fond of maps, and have always enjoyed drawing them in a rough and ready way, I allowed myself to be persuaded that this was something I could have a shot at. Since I did not know of any existing historical atlas for Africa, it was quite a challenge to think out what aspects of African history ought to be illustrated by maps, and then which maps it was that could actually be drawn. I then made rough sketches which were passed on to a very talented artist, Mrs Maureen Verity, who had worked for the Royal Geographical Society, to turn into finished drawings. *An Atlas of African History* was published in 1958 in black and white, and was many times reprinted until in 1978 it entered a second, enlarged edition enlivened with a little colour and with Mrs Verity's name deservedly added to mine on the title page.

The third book that appeared during my time at Achimota and Legon was an incidental result of my second major extra-African excursion, which was to the University of Wisconsin. Towards the end of 1956 there came out of the blue an invitation to me to spend the spring semester of 1957 as a visiting professor of history at its main campus at Madison. At the time I was by no means au fait with the reputation of Wisconsin as one of the greatest of the universities that had developed out of the United States land grant colleges. But I did know something of the reputation of its department of History; here Frederick J. Turner had developed his seminal concept of the formative importance of the frontier in American history, and more recently it had been home to the distinguished imperial historian Paul Knaplund. When Knaplund retired, he was replaced by a young graduate of Swarthmore and Harvard, Philip Curtin, who, after working on West Indian history, was interested in the possibility of introducing the study of African history to Madison. He had available for this purpose a Commonwealth Visiting Professorship which had been established in commemoration of Knaplund's work. Curtin first tried to secure as the visiting professor for 1957 the most distinguished black African historian of Africa, Kenneth Dike, but when Dike proved unable to come, turned with some urgency to me. So in February 1957 the Fage family travelled by the magic carpet of air transport from the West African tropics to the deep winter of middle North America. A snow storm prevented our scheduled arrival at Chicago, so pending its clearance we were decanted in the middle of the night at Montreal, where the temperature quite literally took our breath away; I think it was something like 50°C less than that in which we had left Accra.

The people of Madison were very much more friendly than their climate, and we did not find their society and its lifestyle quite as exotic as did the Vansina family when it followed us to Madison three years later. Nor were the university, its faculty and students as strange as I had feared. Provided that I was willing to make some adjustments to my variety of our supposedly common language, they were really little different from those I knew on the other side of the Atlantic. Yet outside the university, we found the Mid-West of the United States strangely foreign. Although its people were endlessly and flatteringly curious about us and where we had come from, Canada was about the utmost limit of the ordinary citizens' conception of the outside world (and therefore the most common explanation of the odd way in which we spoke English), and I doubt very much whether many of them could understand much of what we told them about Africa, even when I was responding to the many requests I received to give formal talks to local clubs and associations. In their eyes Africa was still a land of nakedness and savagery to which missionaries should be sent. It seemed unbelievable to them that Accra had a department store with escalators just like they had in Madison. We for our part could not believe that the nearest place in which one might cash a sterling traveller's cheque was in Chicago, over a hundred miles distant, or that the only way that the authorities of the State of Wisconsin had of dealing with drivers with Gold Coast driving licences was to accept them as though they had come from another of their United States. I hate to think what would have happened if we had had an accident when driving with our Gold Coast licences in, say, Connecticut. This was of some importance because we used the secondhand car we had bought to make a substantial mid-semester return journey through the north-eastern United States to visit friends and relations and some universities, such as Columbia, where Joseph Greenberg was then based, or Boston, with its lively African Studies program. We will not easily forget when our leisurely traverse of a nearly empty Pennsylvania Turnpike brought us to the New Jersey Turnpike and ultimately, as the New York skyscrapers appeared on the north-eastern skyline, onto ten lanes of "pavement".

My main commitment as Visiting Professor at Madison was to give a substantial course of lectures to third and fourth year undergraduates, and also to conduct a graduate seminar, on the history of the British in Africa. But some weeks after my arrival, I was lunching informally with Phil Curtin when he said to me "When are you going to give your public lectures?" When I asked him what public lectures, he said that he meant the public lectures that all Paul Knaplund Visiting Professors were expected to give. I said that this was the first I had heard about this, and asked him how many public lectures were required. To this he replied that there should be at least two, but that there was no need for there to be more than four. So I said that I would give three, and then had to sit down and write them. This required a considerable reliance on my memory, because the University of Wisconsin's Memorial Library, now one of the best of the Africana libraries in the U.S.A., cannot at that time have held as many as fifty percent of the sources that I needed to refer to.

I was provided with an obvious subject for my lectures by the fact that, about a month after we had arrived in Madison, the colony of the Gold Coast had secured its independence and, adopting the new name of Ghana, had become a free and independent member of the British Commonwealth and of the United Nations. So I set out to try to explain to an American audience how a colonial polity had emerged from the interaction between African traditions of commerce and statehood and European – and increasingly British – expansion, and then how and why this polity had become an independent state. The lectures must have gone well enough because, after I had given the last of them, Curtin approached me once again saying "When can I have the text of your lectures for publication?" After replying that this was the first I had heard of *publication*, I then had in due course to set to and to go carefully through all the sources I thought I had relied upon to see whether they really did say what I had thought they said. The end result was a little book entitled *Ghana: a Historical Interpretation*, which appeared from the University of Wisconsin Press in 1959 and was subsequently three times reprinted. In some respects I like it the best of my books. It is very handsomely designed and printed, and I think it also has the merit that the circumstances of its conception have resulted in a fresh and clear text, with all its turgid building blocks being relegated to end-notes.

In June the Wisconsin semester had come to an end, I had awarded grades to my students which seemed to satisfy at once my own non-American standards and the expectations of the indigenous faculty, and we decided to spend a little time enjoying ourselves before returning across the Atlantic. We drove northwards the length of Wisconsin and into Michigan to enter Canada at Sault Ste Marie, then across the Laurentian shield to visit friends in Ottawa. There was a temporary hiccough when we crossed the St Lawrence River to re-enter the U.S.A. at Cornwall. The U.S. immigration officials were somewhat startled to receive from Canada British passport holders who were using Gold Coast licences to drive a car bearing Wisconsin licence plates. More to the point it was pointed out to us that whereas Jean and the children had come to the U.S.A. on a tourist visa which allowed more than one entry to the country, I had come with a visa specifying a single entry to take up a particular temporary job. Therefore, whereas my family could re-enter the U.S.A., I might not! Aware that U.S. and Canadian citizens could cross their mutual border without any let or hindrance, I explained that no one had taken any kind of notice of our documents when we had crossed into Canada, and that we had only spent a few days there; whereupon to my great relief the man dealing with us said that officialdom would take no notice of what I had done. (The moral of this, no doubt, is that if you want to transgress the very stringent U.S. immigration regulations, do it at a minor point of entry rather than at a major port or airport.) Following this we were able to enjoy both the scenery of the Adirondacks and the historical associations of the corridor cockpit of the French and Indian wars before traversing Massachusetts to Cape Cod, where we had a week's marvellous holiday in a cottage lent to us by cousins of Jean's. Finally we drove to Boston where, by previous arrangement, our old Dodge was sold to Arthur Porter, the future Professor of History and Vice- Chancellor at the University of Sierra Leone, who was then engaged in postgraduate studies at Boston University. Selling a car to a friend can be a doubtful business, but I am glad to say that in this case a friendship which dates back to 1949, when Arthur listened to my lectures in Cambridge, did not seem to have suffered.

We returned to Britain in time for Roland Oliver's second S.O.A.S. African History Conference. At this time, Philip Harris, who had taken Carrington's place for the African publications of the Cambridge University Press, was floating the idea that perhaps the time had come for a multi-volume *Cambridge History of Africa*. But Roland and I thought that the time was by no means yet ripe for such a venture, and that what should come first should be a *Journal of African History*, and the Conference set up a small committee to explore this possibility.

By the end of September we were back at Legon to find that things had much changed since we had left it in February. So far as we were concerned, the most important change was not that that the colony of the Gold Coast had turned into the independent state of Ghana, with the consequence that our institution had now automatically become the University College of Ghana. This had been anticipated for some time. I remember, for example, Arnold Lawrence asking me a year or so earlier whether our academic hostility to the thesis that the people of the Gold Coast descended from the people of ancient Ghana meant we should be critical of the renaming of the country – and so of its university college – when it ceased to be a British colony. We were of one mind that this would be absurd. "Gold Coast" after all was a colonial name expressed in a language that was foreign to the country; an independent African country deserved an African name. There was evidence of early trading and, possibly, cultural connections between the peoples of the Gold Coast and those of ancient Ghana and its successor states in the western Sudan, and so it was not inappropriate that the first modern West African colony to achieve its independence should take its name from that of the first West African state known to history.

In practical terms, Nkrumah's administration as Prime Minister of independent Ghana in its first years was not noticeably very different from his administration of the colonial Gold Coast during its last years; significant change did not really come until after 1960, when Nkrumah took on the office of President. The changes that we noticed when we came back to Ghana in 1957 were more changes in the University College than in the country at large. The first and foremost of these was that David Balme had left to take up a classics post in London University. He had been an excellent and far-seeing founding Principal, and a public tribute was paid to him by all the College's heads of department, many of whom had in the past not always been sympathetic to much of his collegiate policy. Among other things, he had thought that it would be sound politics that the College should cut its umbilical cord with London and become a university in its own right before the country achieved its independence. He thought that if at Ghana's birth it possessed a university which was already academically independent, there would be less temptation for the new rulers to establish their political control over it. With technical assistance from Harry Kidd, whom he had brought out as an adviser as early as 1949, Balme had engineered a constitution for the College which put nearly as much power in the hands of its academic staff as might be found in Oxford or Cambridge, and in 1954 he had persuaded the government-appointed College Council to enact this as a set of bye-laws under the Ordinance of the Gold Coast colony's Legislative Council which had instituted the College. But in 1956, when he tried to secure his academic staff's support to recommend to the Council that it should seek to secure the end of the College's special relationship with the University of London, he was outvoted. The majority of the staff, including almost all its African members, thought it better to go into the new Ghana with the link with London intact as a guarantee of the international standing of the degrees awarded to their students. It seemed they failed to appreciate the danger of a government of an independent Ghana taking the initiative in determining how it wanted its university institutions to operate.

Balme's successor as Principal, R.H.Stoughton, a Professor of Horticulture from the University of Reading who had worked on hydroponics in the deserts of Arabia, was a sad disappointment. It may not be too much to say that his only obvious qualification for the job was that he had been a founder member of the Inter-University Council. But the days when the I.U.C. guided, and often financed, the growth of nascent universities were long past in Ghana, and from the beginning both capital and recurrent funding for Legon had almost entirely come from local taxpayers. Stoughton had neither Balme's sense of principled purpose, nor any real understanding of the political realities in which the College had to operate. Nor was he good at accepting advice from friends of the College who had at least some experience of the country and the particular ways of its politicians and administrators. I was now one of these, for on my return to Legon in September 1957 I discovered that while I had been away in America, without anybody advising me of the fact, I had been chosen to be Stoughton's Deputy Principal.

Stoughton was not good at delegating, but I remember at least one fortnight in which he went away and left me in charge. So I went into his office each morning, looked at the post which had come in and decided what needed attention and what could or should be left for his return — which, in view of the shortness of his absence, was most of it. One morning I was sitting at his desk when the telephone rang and I heard a voice say: "Botsio here. Can the College accommodate a hundred Chinese acrobats?" Now Kojo Botsio was one of Nkrumah's two principal lieutenants in the foundation of the C.P.P., and was then Minister for External Affairs, so obviously this telephone call had to be taken seriously. But what Botsio had said seemed so outlandish that all I could immediately say was: "*What* did you say, sir?" It transpired that, during a recent official visit to China, Nkrumah had light-heartedly accepted an offer that one of the internationally famous Chinese acrobatic troupes should make a goodwill visit to Ghana. But apparently no one had thought to make any practical arrangements for this, and now Botsio had learnt that the hundred-strong party was actually in the air and shortly due to land at Accra airport. As it happened, I was able without difficulty to tell Botsio that the College could do what he wanted; a sizeable part of a large new hall of residence had just been completed, but was as yet not occupied by students. However some of its rooms were being used as temporary accommodation for newly arrived staff, and here hangs a small tailpiece to the story. One of the new arrivals was the archaeologist, Peter Shinnie, Lawrence's successor, and the following day he said to me: "You won't believe this, John, but last night I went out into the corridor to go to the loo, and there I saw a Chinaman standing on his head!"

I think that my main achievement during my time as Deputy Principal was to institute the process which eventually, in 1960, after I had left Ghana, led the College to set up its Institute of African Studies. A School of African Studies actually had been part of the original blueprint for the University College and, about the time of my arrival in the Gold Coast, Kofi Busia had been appointed as its head. But Busia argued that it was part of the duty of all departments of a university institution which was situated in

Africa to engage in African studies so far as was permitted by the nature of their academic disciplines. Since his own discipline was that of sociology, the department he headed should be a department of sociology, staffed by sociologists and members of allied disciplines such as social anthropology and social psychology. There was logic in this argument, so by 1950-51 the College had decreed that the School of African Studies should disappear and that a Department of Sociology should arise from its ashes. But there was a weakness in Busia's argument which I gradually came to appreciate. Part of the role of the original School of African Studies had been to provide teaching and research in the fields of West African languages and culture, but with the abolition of the School, the only part of this that survived was the excellent research in African music carried out by J.H.Nketia. In 1949-50 Jack Berry had been brought out from S.O.A.S. to advise on the nature and the number of the appointments that should be made on the language side, but his recommendations had been so extensive that the School of African Studies had been frightened off from making any language appointments at all, and after its demise it was difficult to see how any might be made.

I suppose that it was my work with David Tait on the oral traditions of the Mossi-Dagomba peoples that first demonstrated to me the need for the College to have on its staff linguists working on West African languages, and by February 1958 I had gone so far as to circulate a paper arguing that the College should have an Institute of West African Languages and Culture. This, I wrote, was urgently necessary not just because it was "a vital part of the College's duty to study the culture of the society within which it exists and which in fact supports it", and because language was both a central element in a culture and "an essential key to the study of almost all other aspects of it". It was also the case that the teaching and research of departments in the College like those of history, sociology, theology and geography was often dependent to a greater or lesser degree on "linguistic evidence or on evidence acquired through local languages", and that "the efficient use and understanding of such evidence presupposes a fundamental pool of scholarly and comparative knowledge of the languages of [Ghana] and adjacent territories which is not at present available except sometimes fortuitously".

This paper received support both within and without the College. The internal supporters included both Busia and Nketia (who at much the same time was urging the College to set up a Department of Music); the outsiders included the Director of S.O.A.S., African linguists in Britain and the U.S.A. and an officer of the Ford Foundation. It was also seen and approved by the General Board (the successor to the Academic Board), with the result that Stoughton asked for a formal proposal to be put to the College. Following this, a draft scheme and costings for an Institute of African Studies with a Director and five established fellows – three working on African languages, one in African musicology, and one qualified in Arabic and Islamic Studies – was produced by a working party which I chaired. But, for reasons which I cannot now remember, these were not completed until June 1959. It was therefore not until the 1959-60 academic year, after my departure from Ghana, that action could be taken on the working party's proposal. Peter Shinnie succeeded me as chairman of what was becoming an interim Committee for African Studies which, at a time when government was if anything trying to reduce the cost of university activities, spent much time trying to find where the £25,000 or so a year needed to fund the Institute might come from. It was not until June 1960 that Shinnie wrote to tell me that he was going to a meeting of Senate at which "the last touches will be put to the years of planning (mostly by yourself) for the Institute of African Studies". By the following October, the Institute was in being under Shinnie's acting directorship (pending the arrival of Thomas Hodgkin in 1962), and in due course the five research fellows that I had envisaged were appointed.

However the main memory of my time as Deputy Principal is of interminable meetings of the College Council and its Finance Committee. These were scheduled to take place on Saturday mornings two or three times a term, but almost invariably they would extend into the afternoons and often they would be adjourned into Sunday or some other later day, much to the aggravation of the College members and their wives who valued their weekend breaks. The Council, the supreme governing body of the College and its link with government, its paymaster, had both academic and lay members. The former, a minority, were the Principal and Deputy Principal, the Registrar, and three elected senior academic staff, usually Professors. The lay majority was partly elected by various representative bodies in the country, and partly directly nominated by government; the latter group always included the Ministers of Finance and Education. The Chairman was nominated by government from among the judges of the

High Court, and therefore was technically – and to at least some extent, in practice – a neutral figure.[1] With the academic representatives always in the minority, I cannot remember any issue being put to a vote; the idea was to achieve a consensus (which, of course helps to explain the way in which meetings dragged on). If a consensus were to be achieved, the academic members needed to convince the chairman that they were being reasonable, and to secure the support of the two government ministers, and of the more vocal of the elected laymen. The Chairman during my days on the Council was Sir Arku Korsah, then in his mid-sixties. He was an impressive man of vast relevant experience. As early as the 1920s and 1930s, he had been a member of the colonial legislature; he had then been one of the first Africans appointed to the colony's executive council, and a member of the Colonial Office's Commission on Higher Education in West Africa, chaired by Sir Walter Eliot, which had produced the blueprint for the University College; and he was now the Chief Justice of Ghana. In my time the Minister of Education was P.K.Quaidoo, a nice, quiet man who had been a schoolmaster before he had gone into politics. But the man who counted was the Minister of Finance, K.A.Gbedemah. This was partly because, like Botsio, he had been one of Nkrumah's principal lieutenants in the founding of the C.P.P. Gbedemah was a smoother, more tactful man than Botsio, and it appeared by no means impossible to convince him of the rightness of whatever policy it was that the academics wanted the Council to agree to, and most of the other lay members were happy enough to follow his lead. But where the Council and its Finance Committee ran into difficulty, and the greatest cause of their interminable meetings, was that one could never be sure that Gbedemah would successfully stand up for this policy in the offices and committees of the Ghana government. A fundamental reason for this was that, by the later 1950s, the recurrent cost of the University College had become very much greater than was ever envisaged when it was originally planned on the principle that "Nothing but the best is good enough for the Gold Coast", and there were now much greater demands on the country's public purse than there had ever been in the 1940s and the days of the great boom in the price not cocoa, by far and away the country's greatest and most remunerative export. So whereas in the first years of the College, government was perfectly ready to tell it how much it could expect in grants over the whole of a three-year period, by the end of the 1950s it was very reluctant to commit itself to the size of its grant even for the current year. Therefore the College Council and its Finance Committee had to be in almost continual session.

The difficult times in which the College had begun to live were one factor leading me to think that the time had come to leave Ghana. Another, in its own way as or more important, was that in 1958 our son Michael reached the age of eight, and it became desirable that he should return to Britain for his education. In 1958-59, Jean therefore spent half the year with Michael and Julia in England, and the other half with Julia and me in Ghana, and none of us thought this an ideal arrangement. Luckily there was no need for it to continue; two jobs became available to me in the U.K. Kenneth Robinson, a former senior Colonial Office man who had moved into academia and had succeeded Keith Hancock as Director of the Institute of Commonwealth Studies in London, asked me whether I would be willing to return to the Institute to complete the work I had begun under Hancock of preparing a book of documents for publication. I must have annoyed him considerably by saying that I thought this a very worthwhile enterprise, while at the same time failing to give him any positive answer. The explanation for this behaviour was that the job with Robinson could only be a temporary one without any sure prospects for the future, and that I had heard from Roland Oliver that it was possible that, by the end of the 1958-59 academic year, the School of Oriental and African Studies might have a vacancy for a lecturer in African history which he hoped would interest me. By October 1958, this vacancy was a certainty, and I told Roland that I would certainly be interested in it. He then set to work with the authorities of the School, and in January 1959 I received a formal offer of a lectureship which I was happy to accept.

---

[1] The council's membership also included two professors from U.K. universities who were nominated by the Inter-University Council. But at this late stage of the development of the University College in Ghana, these tended to appear at meetings only once a year, at the time of the annual degree ceremony.

CHAPTER 8
RETURN OF THE NATIVE

I did not find it easy to readjust to living and working in my native land. Together with the other members of the family, I dearly missed Ghana's sun and warmth. This was not entirely physical; it was also in some degree psychological, for compared to the Ghanaians, my fellow countrymen seemed very cold and remote. I could readily appreciate the difficulties of adjustment experienced by Africans arriving in Britain for further education. I can remember indeed a Sudanese student who was on the books at S.O.A.S.: he was seen on the first day of his first term at the beginning of October, but thereafter vanished from sight until the spring of the following year made it possible for him to come out of hibernation. (But the reactions of people of the Sudan to cooler climates may be somewhat extreme; I once met a Sudanese academic acquaintance at a conference at Dakar in Senegal one December who complained that its local example of a tropical African climate was so cold that he could not sleep at night!)

What was perhaps more surprising was that, although I had been born and brought up in a London suburb, I discovered that I did not like London all that much. It was still a place well worth penetrating for the enjoyment offered by magnificent buildings, and by its excellent shops, libraries, concerts, theatres and other facilities. But as a place in which to live and work, it was far from ideal. It was at once too big and too crowded. Too much time had to be spent travelling within it, fighting one's way through the crowds that thronged the pavements and the Underground, or through the traffic and the fumes it generated on the roads. Too often I felt besieged by unwanted noise, and at the end of the day the state of my shirt collars and cuffs showed how dirty a city London was.

However Jean and I saw no alternative but to seek to sell the lease of the house next door to her parents in rural Winchelsea which we had acquired for our annual leaves from Ghana, and to move to somewhere within reasonable distance of S.O.A.S. in Bloomsbury. We were quite soon disappointed by even the more respectable parts of the southern suburbs which I knew from my boyhood; either they were too shabbily depressing or the neighbourhoods and houses that we liked were too expensive. A Winchelsea friend suggested that we might try the Hampstead Garden Suburb on the other side of the city. Here we found a much more attractive and appealing environment. But we could not see how we could afford anything bigger than the tiniest two-bedroom house intended for "artisans" until we heard the mother of a local house agent (who looked after his office) say to him "I don't suppose they would be interested in 90 Falloden Way, would they?". This turned out to be a quite substantial four-bedroom house which, for years neglected by its previous occupant, a printer, who had eventually left it nearly knee deep in his professional detritus, was in a very sad state of repair and decoration. We looked at this house with rosy eyes and thought how nice it might be if we could do it up, told the agent that we were interested and gave him our deposit. A few days before Christmas, Jean and I moved in with campbeds to prepare for the arrival first of our furniture and then of our children; I think never before (or since) had we tried to sleep in such a cold building. Within a few days we realised that our house had another disadvantage: in the 1930s some short-sighted official had decided that Falloden Way, a residential road leading out of the Suburb's shopping centre, should become part of the Great North Road, Great Britain's A1 Trunk Road. But No.90 stood back quite a little way from the carriage-way; it was really only at rush hours that the noise of the traffic was at all obtrusive, and it still held out the promise of being a very pleasant house with a promising garden. When four years later we left it to move to Birmingham, I do not think that there was a paintable surface inside or out that Jean and I had not painted, a room that we had not wallpapered, or a floor or a roof that we had not put in order, and the garden bloomed with plants and young trees. When a buyer was found for it, he gave us nearly twice as much as we had paid for it.

One of the advantages of 90 Falloden Way was that, provided one could avoid the rush hours, it was little more than half an hour's journey away from my new place of work whether one went there by the Underground's Northern Line or by car. The School of Oriental and African Studies was quite the oddest university institution that I had come across. It was housed in a building, alongside London University's enormous Senate House, intended for an appreciably smaller institution which, because of the war, had never been completed, so that there were no satisfactory facilities for its students and little better for its staff, while the books of its substantial library were to be found all over the place, even in its corridors. It might not be too much to say that corridors were the most striking feature of the building, corridors lined with shut doors bearing the names of the academics to whom the rooms behind them had been allocated. In his autobiography, Professor C.H. (later Sir Cyril) Philips, the energetic Director of the School when I was there, characterised its academic staff when he joined it as an Assistant Lecturer in History in 1936 as a collection of "self-absorbed specialists whom it was difficult to get to know", and this was exactly my own impression when I arrived nearly a quarter of a century later. Although I gradually got to know most of the two dozen or so members of the Department of History, for the most part I found myself living in a completely different compartment from, let us say, the School's phoneticians or its teachers of Sanskrit or Japanese (or even of African languages!). Equally *their* academic lives were conducted in compartments which were almost entirely separate from mine. I wondered whether some of them really appreciated that the School had a large and, in its own style, eminent compartment labelled "History", and I suspect that some of them may not have known that within it there was a little sub-compartment for those who concerned themselves with the history Africa. (One might conceivably go further and wonder whether the substantial number of learned men and women of the School who were Orientalists, working in the long-established tradition of studying and teaching the languages of Asia, altogether appreciated that some twenty of their colleagues were involved in the relatively new game of exploring and expounding the mainly non-literate languages of Africa.) On the whole, at S.O.A.S. one talked academically only with one's own kind, so that although many of us were extremely learned, most of us were nothing like as well educated as we might have been.

The other main peculiarity of S.O.A.S. as a university institution was that it had remarkably few students. So far as I can remember, when I joined it, the number of its full time students working for first degrees of London University was about the same as the number of the academic staff, in each case around 180. History suggests that it was only the practical needs of the two world wars which had led government and university authorities to invest in a London University college specialising in teaching and research relating to Asia and Africa; it was clear that this had attracted the interest of only an insignificant proportion of those leaving British schools to go to universities. S.O.A.S. had more postgraduate students than it had undergraduates; at this level, indeed, it had a very high reputation, attracting students from all over the world - and not least from Asia and Africa. (There were those who thought that it should aim to be a purely postgraduate school.) Nevertheless, as things were, undergraduates and postgraduates together combined to give an overall staff:student ratio of only about 1:2, which contrasted oddly with the 1:8 or more which was then normal elsewhere in the U.K. universities.

S.O.A.S. must therefore have looked an unusually expensive part of the British university system, and Professor Philips, as well as seeking to complete, extend and improve the School's buildings, was also much concerned to increase the numbers of its students. My arrival on the scene was an incidental part of his expansion policy by helping to launch undergraduate teaching in African history. Hitherto Roland Oliver and Douglas Jones, the two Africanist historians in post when I arrived, had had effectively to confine their teaching activities to the supervision of postgraduate research; I think that their experience of undergraduate teaching had been limited to the occasions when they had been invited to Ghana. Not only had I had done more undergraduate teaching: I had also already actually had some experience in planning and administering undergraduate courses in African history for degrees of the University of London. This I believe was thought to outweigh the disadvantage that in the last few years my research interests obviously overlapped with Douglas's. (This meant that, when it came to teaching African history to S.O.A.S. undergraduates, to fit in with the established interests of my two colleagues, I had to revert to the central and southern African interests I had had before I went to West Africa.)

Anyhow, a not insignificant part of my early months at S.O.A.S. was concerned with helping in planning for a new branch of London University's B.A. History Honours Degree, one with particular reference to Africa. It was thought, not incorrectly, that this might be more attractive to British undergraduates than the corresponding branches which S.O.A.S. had promoted for the history of regions of Asia and the Near and Middle East. While the structure of the new branch was similar to that of S.O.A.S.'s other, more esoteric branches and, for that matter, not dissimilar to that of the history degree in Ghana, a fair amount had to be done to develop special subjects for it. One important new development, however, was that those studying for the new degree were not to be left to themselves for the substantial parts of British and European history which were involved. Roland initiated an agreement with Professor S.T. Bindoff, the excellent outward-looking head of the History Department at Queen Mary College, so that our undergraduates could do their work in non-African history in his department. At the same time some of his students might opt to take the African branch of the London degree, and spend some of their time with us at S.O.A.S. Through these means, entry into some non-European history was made to look a less risky option for ordinary British university entrants than it might otherwise have seemed.

In the event I did relatively little undergraduate teaching at S.O.A.S. The first year our B.A. History course with special reference to Africa was on offer was 1961-62. But, so far as I can remember, students taking it spent virtually all the first year of their course at Queen Mary College working on English and European history, and we at S.O.A.S. were not seriously involved until their second and third years. But as it happened I was in America during the first term of 1962-63 and then taught for only its second term before leaving S.O.A.S.

I was much more involved in work with postgraduates. My first Ph.D. student came to me through the connection with Bindoff. I still vividly remember how, in the summer of 1960, a good looking young man called Tony Hopkins knocked at my door and said something to the effect that he had just got his history degree from Q.M.C., and was now interested in exploring possible parallels between the nineteenth and twentieth century colonial development of European colonies overseas and the development of Tudor England, which he had just been studying with Bindoff. He asked whether I thought there might be something in this and, if so, whether he would do better to look at Latin America or at Africa? I told him that he might well find useful material if he chose to work on West Africa. A week or so later he came back, and it was decided that he should work on the nineteenth century economic and social history of Lagos. Three years later he got a very good Ph.D. and joined me in the new Centre of West African Studies at Birmingham. Since then he has never looked back, so that he is now the Smuts Professor of Commonwealth History at Cambridge. In the same year, Shula Marks arrived at S.O.A.S. after studying with Leonard Thompson at Cape Town, and for a short time I had the pleasure of being supervisor of her research on the Zulu rebellion in Natal in 1906-08. But she knew very well what she wanted to do before I ever met her, and thereafter it was a case of the blind claiming to guide the far-sighted. I had left S.O.A.S. some time before she had finished her thesis, but by then I think she was already preparing to take over the teaching of a special subject for our B.A. syllabus which I had designed together with Richard Gray, one of Roland's earliest Ph.D. students who in 1961 had joined the S.O.A.S. African history team after a spell of teaching at the University College at Khartoum and the completion of a substantial book on Southern Rhodesia. So far as Shula was concerned, I was not surprised when she was appointed to the lectureship I had vacated, or that she later went on to become not only Professor of Southern African History at S.O.A.S. but also, for some ten years, Director of the Institute of Commonwealth Studies.

Tony Hopkins and Shula Marks may have been outstanding among the half dozen or so Ph.D. students for whom I had some responsibility at S.O.A.S. during 1960-63. But these years were very good ones for exploring new avenues in African history, and I am sure that I learnt more from every one of the Ph.D. students than they could ever learn from me. I also very much enjoyed working with them, not least with those who came from Africa or the West Indies, who were educations in themselves. However on a broader front, the focal point for the education of all of us, those expected to teach about the African past as well as their research students, was the African History seminar which Roland Oliver had founded, and which met each term-time week in a very pleasant room in the Institute of Commonwealth Studies in Russell Square just round the corner from S.O.A.S. This was a theatre in which staff and students were expected to give papers on their current research, and to which we sought to invite the most relevant and interesting of the substantial number of Africanist academics visiting or passing through London. But we tried as far as possible to devise a major theme for each term's programme – memorable ones included "The Bantu expansion" and "The Indonesian influence on Africa" – which would often require us to seek contributions from other historians or from practitioners of other disciplines, most obviously those of archaeology, anthropology and language studies, but when necessary even such as agricultural botany and musicology.

However, graduate and undergraduate teaching and the African History seminar, and the work associated with them, were by no means enough to require attendance at the School for more than two or three days a week. Compared with Ghana, I now had very little in the way of university administrative or committee work except when Roland Oliver was away. His only significant absences were when he went to Brussels in the first half of 1961 and to the United States in the first half of 1962, but I then became involved in such matters as organising the African History seminar, liaising with Q.M.C., and keeping a tutorial eye on the affairs of our students. I can recall serving on only one S.O.A.S. Committee, and it was not until the beginning of 1962 that I became "a recognised teacher of the University", and so one of the members of the University's Board of Studies in History. In addition, however, now that I was working in London I was for the first time able to attend meetings of an academic committee to which I had belonged since 1954. This was a committee convened by the Institute of Historical Research to plan, and to secure publication for, a series of "Guides to Materials for West African History". The Chairman and guiding light of this committee, made up of heads of history departments and archivists in West Africa and interested historians in Britain (including Bindoff), was Professor Hale Bellot, and I like to think it germinated from the discussions I had had with Bellot in 1949, when we were first thinking what would be involved in Honours Degree History work in one of the new university colleges in West Africa. At any rate I know that Bellot, together with other members of London's Board of Studies in History, were anxious that the study of African History should be firmly based on acceptable original sources. It was not difficult to see that the national archives of the European countries which at one time or another had been active in African ventures might well provide valuable source material, so the idea was to commission suitable scholars to trawl through these archives and prepare guides to those of their contents which related to Africa. By 1960 I think that all but one of the Guides had already been commissioned, and in 1962 they began to appear in print (the one for Italy being largely the work of Richard Gray), so it will be appreciated that attendance at meetings of the West African Guides Committee was hardly a heavy burden.

However, if I had little to do in the way of committee work, there was quite a lot for me to do in other directions. For example, during my first year in London, there were still quite a few loose ends remaining from my time in Ghana. Much of my correspondence was with Graham Irwin, my successor as head of the Legon history department: I was, for example, still involved in some Legon examining, and in seeing an issue of the *Transactions of the Historical Society of Ghana* through the press. When such things tailed off, there was a good deal to be done assisting Roland with the organisation of the third S.O.A.S. Conference on History and Archaeology in Africa. I also discovered that a former professor of history from the University College of Ghana (which in 1962 became the University of Ghana) was someone of some use to the U.K. end of the operation which had launched the colonial university colleges. I was in demand by the division of the London University Senate House which oversaw the colleges' academic affairs to advise on syllabus changes or to serve as an external examiner, and by the Inter-University Council to serve on advisory appointments committees. (Indeed it was something like twenty years after my return from Ghana before I was relieved from activities of this kind). I did some reviewing of African books for *The Observer*, and I even did some broadcasting. Usually this was pretty humdrum stuff, but I remember one hilariously disastrous live programme in which speakers in New York, Washington, Pretoria and Brussels as well as London had been invited to discuss "The future of the white man in Africa": an American contributor completely escaped the control of the chairman, the redoubtable Robert Mackenzie. But one of my major activities immediately following my return from Ghana was extramural in the best sense of the word: in the two years 1960 and 1961, I know that there were two dozen or more occasions when I journeyed outside S.O.A.S to perform at seminars, conferences and day schools, or to lecture to some variety of invited audience. Part of this activity was occasioned by Philips's aim of increasing S.O.A.S.'s intake of undergraduates, particularly of ordinary British school-leavers. To this end, at about the same time as I had appeared on the scene, a full-time Education Officer, Dr Harold Blakemore, had been appointed to the staff of S.O.A.S., where he proved very assiduous in making arrangements for his academic colleagues to lecture at schools or to participate in sixth form conferences. (This is not to say that Blakemore was unacademic; but his expertise lay in the field of Latin American Studies.) However Blakemore was by no means responsible for all my extramural ventures. There was a staple fare of lecturing to branches of the Historical Association and of the Workers' Educational Association, and to an assortment of university departments and undergraduate societies concerned with Africa. Perhaps the most memorable occasions were lecturing to the Royal Naval Staff College in Wren's magnificent buildings at Greenwich (and being taken to and fro in a splendid Humber staff car), and – very soon indeed after my return from Ghana – presenting a seminar paper to Oxford's Institute of Commonwealth Studies with no less a person than the great Margery Perham sitting literally at my right hand assiduously writing down everything I said![1]

Perhaps the largest part of my professional outside activities at S.O.A.S. was spent collaborating with Roland Oliver on the writing of *A Short History of Africa* for Penguin Books, and on the editing of *The Journal of African History*. These activities were conducted from 90 Falloden Way rather than from the somewhat uncongenial and traffic-bound ambiance of the School of Oriental and African Studies. In retrospect, it is surprising how quick and relatively easy it was to write my share of the *Short History* and also, perhaps, how successful it has been (with translations into Catalan, Croat, Dutch, Finnish, German, Italian, Japanese, Portuguese, Spanish, and Swedish – plus a pirated edition in Arabic). So far as the writing of it was concerned, we divided the chapters between us, and then swapped what each of us had done for the other to read and, as necessary, to rewrite. So far as I can remember, there was no more than one serious difference of opinion between us, and quite a few readers have told me that they can detect no variation in style from one chapter to another.

As for *The Journal of African History*, it will be remembered that in 1957 Roland and I had told the Cambridge University Press that the time had not yet come for it to devote one of its great multi-volume histories to Africa: academic work on African history had been in progress for no more than a decade at most; there were far too few serious scholars in the field; and both the extent of knowledge and judgement of the significance of its aspects were changing from year to year. What should come first was a journal in which new researches into the African past might be published, and in which major issues of African history might be discerned and debated. The Press told us that it would not be willing to publish such a journal without some guarantee against financial losses during its first five or so years. Luckily at this time the Rockefeller Foundation was active in supporting academic activities relating to Africa and Asia. For a number of years, indeed, it provided generous support to S.O.A.S., and in Robert July it had an officer who was himself to make a not insubstantial contribution to African history by writing on the origins and the early development of nationalism in West Africa. Following talks with July, the Rockefeller Foundation agreed to provide a launching guarantee of up to £5000 to provide support against any losses incurred by an African history journal during its initial years. As a result of this, it became possible for the first number of *The Journal of African History*, edited by Roland and myself, to appear from the Cambridge Press in 1960. To start with, there were only two numbers a year, and we had commissioned most of what we printed. Since so much of the earlier past of Africa was not recoverable from strictly historical records, whether written or oral, we made a point from the outset of soliciting or encouraging contributions from workers in such disciplines as archaeology, anthropology and linguistics. Indeed we were soon happy to accept any meaningful contribution to the elucidation of the African past irrespective of its author's ostensible discipline, provided only that we thought it comprehensible for those outside that author's discipline. Very soon we found that more than enough unsolicited contributions were coming in. In 1964, the Cambridge University Press became agreeable to the *Journal* appearing three times a year, and by 1968 so much good material was coming in that we moved to publishing four times a year, and Richard Gray was co-opted as a third editor. In 1971 Shula Marks became a fourth member of the editorial team, and three years after this, Roland and I thought the time had come for us to bow out, and the editorship passed wholly to a younger generation, initially with a team consisting of Shula Marks, Tony Hopkins, Robin Law and Andrew Roberts. So far as I am aware, after the first five years there was never any call for the Cambridge University Press to draw on any part of the Rockefeller Foundation's financial guarantee.

I made three foreign excursions during my time at S.O.A.S. One of these, that to the Ethnohistory Seminar organised at Dakar by the International African Institute in December 1961, has already been mentioned. The School generously found the funds to send me to this, and it had earlier secured a grant from the Ariel Foundation so that I might go to the XXVth International Congress of Orientalists which was held at Moscow University in August 1960. On this occasion this enormous four-yearly jamboree had attracted some 1500 participants, about half of whom presented papers, but only one of the twenty working sections of the congress was devoted to Africa. This section had two parts, one concentrating on linguistic studies and the other – which I attended – on history and anthropology. Here over thirty papers were promised, but their presentation was a shambles because only the Russians, the Britons and – to some extent – the Americans managed to keep to the required timetable, distributing texts or summaries of their papers in advance, and speaking to these for no more than ten minutes. As a result, my memories of the Moscow Congress have little to do with its academic business, but are rather of the incidentals surrounding it. I stayed in a student hostel that was very well appointed, but which could provide very strange food – I can remember a breakfast with two courses: cottage cheese and yoghurt! There were illuminating conversations with the students who were around to help the foreign visitors. Together with Roland Oliver and others, I saw a fair amount of Moscow by trolley-bus, the marbled Metro and river boat, and on foot. We were impressed by the way the citizens would not permit litter to foul the main streets, and the way the police prevented country bumpkins from jay walking. We visited the opera at the Bolshoi Theatre, and we were conducted round the Kremlin by a neatly dressed lady guide who, in answer to a question, told us with some feeling that it was only since Stalin's death that ordinary people had been allowed inside. But in many ways the highlight of the visit to Russia was the weekend when we went on a trip to Leningrad in a luxurious sleeper train, and so were able to enjoy one of Europe's most magnificent architectural landscapes and the incredibly rich treasures of the Hermitage museum and art gallery.

The third excursion was altogether on a different scale, for in September 1962 the Fages crossed the Atlantic in a pleasant leisurely fashion on the M.V.*Maasdam* of the Holland-America Line so that I could spend the first semester of 1962-63 as Visiting Professor in the Non-Western Studies Program of the four Connecticut Valley Colleges in New England – Amherst, Mount Holyoke, Smith and the University of Massachusetts. The invitation to do this was not the first I had received since my return to England to spend time as a visiting professor in the U.S.A. In June 1960, I had been invited to the University of California at Los Angeles, which was already well on its way to having one of the best African Studies programs in the U.S.A. – at that time perhaps second only to Mel Herskovits's longer-established program at Northwestern. But I had to tell U.C.L.A. that I could hardly ask for leave from S.O.A.S. so soon after arriving there and when my colleagues and I were busy setting up our new undergraduate history degree. The result of this was that the following November Los Angeles sent me a second, even more pressing invitation, to which I saw no alternative but to give much the same answer. But by 1962, our under-graduate course was up and running, and our teaching programme was such that Roland Oliver could spend the second semester of 1961-62 with Herskovits's program at Northwestern. It was therefore not difficult for me to arrange to be away for the autumn term of 1962 provided only that I could be back in time for a full stint of teaching at S.O.A.S. in the follow-ing spring term.

The Connecticut Valley colleges had appreciably less strength in the African field than either U.C.L.A. or Northwestern, but the invitation had come from Gwen Carter at Smith College, and it was there, in the small Massachusetts town of Northampton, that I was to be based. I knew some-thing of Gwen's growing reputation as a political scientist who, despite the handicap of paraplegia, was extremely active, inspiring and productive in African studies. From all accounts, it seemed as though she would be a good person to know and work with, and from our earlier American expe-rience, we thought we would enjoy spending some months in New Eng-land (where two families of Jean's cousins lived). So in fact it proved. The New England countryside and campuses were delightful. This was espe-cially so of course in the fall, if not in the bleak midwinter: I can remember one afternoon when Michael and I had gone out to photograph snowy scenes and our car got stuck and we nearly froze to death *within the Northampton town limits*. But leaving out of account such a wholly exceptional experi-ence, we felt thoroughly at home in Northampton, especially with Gwen and her friends. Nevertheless there were some oddities in being employed, not by a particular college, but by a consortium of colleges. On three days of the week, I gave a lecture or took a class at Smith, but many of its aca-demics, even in its history department, and including its President, intelli-gent and charming though they all were, always seemed somewhat uncer-tain as to why I was there or what I was meant to be doing. Once a week I drove the twenty or thirty miles to the University of Massachusetts at Amherst, and there in the course of a long afternoon I repeated most of the week's teaching I had done at Smith. At U.Mass. my only academic contact was John Harris, another political science professor, though one interested in Asia rather than Africa, who was the well-organised Chair-man of the four-college Non-Western Studies Program. So far as concerns the other two colleges, I cannot recall Amherst taking any notice of me at all, but Mount Holyoke did at least invite me to dinner and to give a public lecture.

The ambivalence of my status as a resident at Smith but an employee of the Connecticut Valley consortium may help to explain why some time elapsed before – with one exception – I began to get much in the way of invitations to lecture elsewhere. The exception was U.C.L.A., which grabbed me soon after I had arrived at Northampton, with the result that in the space of thirty-six hours I was flown to the other side of the continent, gave two lectures and a seminar, talked with interesting people like Hilda Kuper, Leonard Thompson and Jim Coleman, and was flown back across the continent again to Massachusetts only too aware of what was meant by the term "jet lag". (On the return flight, a 150-seat Boeing 707 carried only three passengers so, but for the ministrations of twice that number of flight attendants, there should have been scope for sleeping.) I went to Washington for the annual conference of the African Studies Association, but its main role seemed to be to act as a hiring fair for new Ph.D.s, so that it became almost as chaotic an affair as the Moscow Orientalists' Congress. It so exhausted me that in the end I was driven to retreat to my hotel room and watch TV! Old acquaintances were renewed with the Africanists of Boston University, and I had interesting times at the Foreign Services Institute at Washington, at Princeton, and at the tiny little Goddard College in wildest Vermont – a college which I could only conclude was where rich parents sent unruly offspring who could not find places anywhere else. But news that I was in the U.S.A. was late in reaching the major African Programs at Indiana, Michigan State and Wisconsin Universities, so that the invitations they sent me were for dates in January. All these I had to refuse because early in that month we were booked to leave New York by S.S.*America* so that I could be back at S.O.A.S. by the beginning of the new term. In the event, as things turned out it might have been possible for me to visit more than one of the three mid-Western universities. The American longshoremen went on strike, so that the *America*'s sailing was cancelled. Eventually we got back to England a week late after journeying in a stuffy cabin on one of the lower decks of a tired and shopworn R.M.S.*Queen Mary*. When we disembarked at Southampton, the boat train was so cold that our breath froze on the windows; it was England's coldest winter since 1947. As our taxi climbed between four-foot-high snow-banks over Hampstead Heath, we could only congratulate ourselves that we had had the foresight to give the American tenants to whom 90 Falloden Way had been let the very English and un-American instructions that, before they left the house, the water should be turned off and the system drained.

---

[1] Margery Perham, Senior Fellow of Oxford's Nuffield College, was the greatest academic commentator and authority of the day in the U.K. on colonial affairs, and these were usually African colonial affairs. This may be an appropriate point to remark on the unusual prominence of women among those academics who were important to me at one time or another when my concerns were both African and colonial. Audrey Richards, quite as imposing as Margery Perham, has already been mentioned; she ended her career as the Smuts Reader at Cambridge. The most daunting was undoubtedly Dame Lilian Penson, a diplomatic and colonial historian who became the first woman to be Vice-Chancellor of the University of London, and who was a great power in the affairs of the colonial university colleges (and much else besides). To these one might add Lucy Mair and Monica Wilson, Professors of Anthropology respectively at the London School of Economics and Rhodes University; Eveline Martin, a retiring lady who ended her career as Reader at Westfield College, but who had contributed to the writing of West African history almost before any other university historian knew that there was such a thing, and Gwendolen Carter, who will be introduced later in this chapter. In this context, I cannot help quoting Ken Post who, after surveying his lecture class when he was at the Centre of West African Studies at the University of Birmingham about 1965, said: "I never realised before that Africa was such a female subject".

CHAPTER 9
TAKING AFRICA TO BIRMINGHAM

When we returned to Falloden Way in January 1963, we knew that our days there were numbered. The sequence of events which led to this had begun in September 1960 when Professor Roy Pascal called to see me at S.O.A.S. I knew a bit about Pascal, arising mainly from his recent book about the art of biography which quickly became a classic of comparative literature. In 1939 he had left a Cambridge fellowship to become Professor of German in the university of his home town, Birmingham. He had achieved a great reputation in German literary and social studies, had been elected a Fellow of the British Academy, and in 1946-49 had served as Dean of Birmingham's Faculty of Arts – but none of this served to explain why he should have chosen to come to talk with a young lecturer in African History in the University of London.

Pascal came to see me because he had seen the potential importance for Birmingham University of the work which was being done by a sub-committee set up in January 1960 by the University Grants Committee "to review developments in the Universities in the fields of Oriental, Slavonic, East European and African studies...; and to consider, and advise on, proposals for future developments." This sub-committee was chaired by Sir William Hayter, a former ambassador to Moscow who had become Warden of New College at Oxford, and it was not difficult to see from its terms of reference and from the visits it made to selected universities – in the United States as well as in Britain (where Birmingham was one of the universities that was visited) – that it was likely to recommend a considerable expansion in these fields of study, which had not been well supported since the years immediately after the 1939-45 war, when a committee chaired by Lord Scarbrough had concluded that the war had demonstrated the need for an expansion of teaching and research in such studies, and earmarked funds had been made available for them. But the Scarbrough pro-gramme had ground to a halt after 1952, and it had been criticised be-cause little had been done outside a handful of universities, principally Oxford, Cambridge and London (whose S.O.A.S. was by far the greatest beneficiary), and because it was thought that subjects like political and social sciences and geography and history had been unduly neglected com-pared with work on language and ancient literatures.

At the University of Birmingham, Pascal had come to believe that its students should have some opportunity for at least sampling what society and culture were like outside the western civilisation born of the Judaeo-Graeco-Roman tradition, and the advent of the Hayter sub-committee seemed to offer him a practical opportunity to achieve this. As early as June 1960 he had succeeded in persuading Birmingham's Faculty of Arts that it should seek "to extend its linguistic and historical studies to parts of the world other than Europe and the overseas extensions of European civilisation." A paper he put before the Faculty Board that month reported that a number of proposals had been considered for achieving this in the Faculty's development plan for the 1962-67 quinquennium. "Of these, West African studies appeared to be the most promising, both for their intrinsic interest and current importance, and as forming a limited field and one closely in line with other developments in the Faculty..." – and, it was thought, in the Faculty of Commerce and Social Science and in de-partments such as Geology, Botany and Law. I do not know exactly how and why it was that West Africa came to be singled out. But it had un-doubtedly been astutely realised that African Studies as a whole would be too big a field to be handled by any unit of the size that Birmingham might hope to achieve, while in the Faculty's departments of Geography and History there were already some three teachers with academic interests in West Africa, and in the city there were some sizeable companies – most obviously Cadbury Brothers Ltd – which had significant commercial con-nections with West Africa.

Pascal's paper of June 1960 represented virtually a complete embryo for the West African studies proposal as it was subsequently to be devel-oped in Birmingham. Towards the end of the long vacation, obviously think-ing it sensible to make some contact with universities in West Africa, he went to see Stoughton in the London Office of the University of Ghana. Stoughton undoubtedly told him something of what had been going on at

131

Legon to set up its Institute of African Studies, so early in September Pascal came to S.O.A.S to talk with me and with Peter Shinnie, my successor in the Legon Institute's affairs, who happened to be in London at the time. Among other things, I was able to provide Pascal with copies of the two principal planning papers I had written for the Institute at Legon. Hardly more than a month later, on 19 October, Pascal was writing to me to say "We have now got as far as a Senate Committee..., and I hope to speak to University Grants Committee members about it"; in fact, as I understand it, a version of the paper Pascal had written for the University of Birmingham Senate was sent to the U.G.C.

The Report of the Hayter Sub-Committee was published in June 1961. It recommended that the U.G.C. should embark on a programme of earmarked grants to support the development of Oriental, Slavonic, East European and African Studies for both the 1962-67 and 1967-72 quinquennia. On p.83 of the Report there was a paragraph specifically referring to Birmingham:

> Only one university, Birmingham, submitted proposals in any detail for a centre of African Studies... We were impressed with the scope and organisation of the Birmingham proposals. It is intended to create a School of West African Studies, with a Director, a small academic staff covering several disciplines, research fellows and research students, and funds for travel and a library. The aim is to develop research on West Africa, to train graduates in other fields to gain a qualification, by examination, in African studies, and to incorporate African studies into existing first-degree courses by means of "special subjects" in geography, history, law or social science degrees. This organisation...is very much in line with the kind of development which the Sub-Committee has in mind...

With such a reference to the University of Birmingham in the Hayter Report, it is hardly surprising that when the U.G.C. invited universities to make bids for earmarked grants to implement the Report, Birmingham was given more or less what it asked for.

The University made its formal proposal to the U.G.C. in March 1962, and in May I received a letter from Pascal telling me that the scheme which he and I had discussed in September 1960 "has prospered – so that now we are empowered actually to make appointments". He said that the West African Studies Committee which the University Senate had appointed, and of which he was Chairman, was due to meet on Saturday 26th, when it was hoped to make "some definite move" to find a Director. "I am writing to you to ask whether you'd be interested in this post, and if so, whether you could come here next Saturday morning to meet the committee?" So on Friday 25 May I took the train to Birmingham – the first time I had ever been there except for one wartime transit between its two great railway stations of New Street and Snow Hill. Pascal met me at Snow Hill, took me home to dinner, and then to spend the night in the University Staff Club, an enormous Victorian mansion called Westmere, built in a rather Italianate style in extensive grounds, which had once been the home of the Tangye family and which was now on the edge of the university's expanding Edgbaston campus. The following morning he introduced me to his committee.

I can remember very little about the meeting, except that it was a lovely sunny morning, that we talked together for what I think cannot have been much less than two hours, and that, even if Pascal was the chairman, most of the running seemed to be made by Sir Robert Aitken, the Vice-Chancellor. When that afternoon I returned home to Jean, I think I told her that I was impressed with the people I had met, but that there was nothing certain that I could report to her. But the upshot was that on 1 June I received a letter from Aitken which thanked me "very warmly for coming to Birmingham to talk to us... and also for the advice and help you gave to Pascal at an earlier stage", and continued, with an informality which I was later to know was typical of Aitken but which no Vice-Chancellor would indulge in today, with a sentence which included some remarkable words: "You captured the Committee on Saturday and, after you had left, *it turned itself into an Electoral Board* and decided unanimously that it would like to see you in charge of the Birmingham Centre. So it asked me to write to you and discuss that possibility." (As will also be seen with the appointment of Dr Alty a year later, one of Aitken's strengths was his ability to know what he wanted to do, and to go ahead and do it without bothering about the usual procedures. Some senior members of the University could be infuriated by what they considered this high-handedness; my own experience suggests that he believed he could see the best interest of the University more clearly and dispassionately than most other people, and that he was commonly right in his belief.)

When I asked Jean whether she would like us to move to Birmingham, she said "No" very firmly. She liked living in London, which had been her first home in England when her family returned from Persia after the war, and she had become very attached to the Hampstead area, where she had made many friends and was developing many interests, and where our children were happily at school. I had some doubts myself as to whether I should move to a university and a city which were both completely strange to me. I had indeed assumed that I was likely to spend the rest of my academic career at S.O.A.S. It was undoubtedly quite a new idea that I might leave it less than four years after my arrival, the more so perhaps because I had seen signs which suggested that I was gaining the confidence of its Director, Professor Philips; certainly he (as also the School's Secretary, Col. Moyse-Bartlett) had more than once gone out of their way to be friendly and helpful. However when I told Philips and Roland Oliver about Birmingham's offer to me, I was surprised to learn that they had both supposed that it might not be all that long before I would move on from S.O.A.S. (Philips, I discovered, already knew about Birmingham's interest in me since he was one of those who had been consulted about me; another, I believe, was Margery Perham).

I was obviously attracted by the opportunity of running my own show and of starting it from scratch, but there were some substantial issues to be considered before I could give Aitken a definite answer to the invitation he had sent me. One immediate question arose from my commitment to spend the second half of 1962 in the United States, and then to be available at S.O.A.S. for at least the first term of 1963 doing the teaching that was expected of me for the recently-launched undergraduate syllabus in African history. Would Birmingham be willing to wait until these commitments were out of the way before I took up its offer? I was quickly told that it would, and in due course 1 April 1963 became an agreed starting date. Although this meant that Birmingham's Centre of West African Studies could not start teaching until October 1964, the delay had the incidental advantage that it could do so with a full first-quinquennium establishment of six academic staff instead of the four which would have been all that could have been supported with the earmarked funds available in 1963. Beyond this issue, there were a whole series of explorations, or at least of reconnaissances, which had to be made. I needed to get some idea of what this strange new university, its people and its methods of operation were like; after all, I had never before had anything to do with any of the civic universities, let alone the archetypical "Redbrick" one at Birmingham. Then

Jean and I needed to begin to discover what the Birmingham area might be like as a place in which we might live, and where our children might be brought up and go to school.

To help with such problems, Aitken arranged for Jean and me to spend a few days at Westmere while Pascal and some of his colleagues (with some of their wives) arranged to introduce us to the university buildings and some of its people. When we had recovered from the contretemps that the little Fiat car we had brought back with us from Ghana objected to the idea of cruising at 60+ m.p.h. on the newly built Ml (it had never before seen anything like a motorway or such continuous speeding), we were treated almost as though we were visiting royalty. The weather was marvellous, the bluebells were out in the woods between Westmere and the Edgbaston golf course's lake behind it, and the university campus on the other side of the road from Westmere was a splendid contrast to anything that S.O.A.S. – or any metropolitan part of the University of London apart from Bedford College – could show. Birmingham University, in its first incarnation in 1880 as Mason College, had started life in a picturesque Victorian Gothic building in Edmund Street in the heart of the city. But by 1900 this had become inadequate for its needs, and building was begun – to the red brick Byzantine plans of Aston Webb – on what ultimately became a 125 acre campus 2½ miles from the city centre on the attractive tree-studded Calthorpe estate of Edgbaston where many of Birmingham's wealthier citizens had chosen to live. When we arrived on the scene, the Edmund Street building had just been abandoned, and the rather grandiloquent Aston Webb buildings had become the nucleus for a whole university of just under 5000 students working – and increasingly also living – in an attractive miscellany of more recent buildings laid out according to the plan of another notable architect, Hugh Casson, among the lawns and trees of well maintained grounds.

The people we met on our visit struck me as individually pleasant and also, and perhaps more importantly, conscious of themselves as members of a team who, virtually without exception, all knew and talked with each other irrespective of their own particular interests and disciplines. I could readily see that their university would be a good place in which to set an area studies centre which would necessarily involve cooperation between different and sometimes traditionally mutually suspicious academic disciplines. I was therefore tempted to believe that I should take up the challenge of moving to Birmingham even though, as an individual committed to the study of African history, I might well be better off staying at S.O.A.S., with its great tradition and its world-wide reputation for achievement in non-European studies, and with its well-established library – and with the Library of the British Museum and such institutions as the Institutes of Historical and of Commonwealth Studies just round the corner. But then, as Aitken had disarmingly remarked, "after all London is only two hours away"! I was also quite soon to realise that the Birmingham Department of History (of which I was to be a full member) was on its way to becoming one of the best in Britain. Furthermore I could hope that, at a time when most Africana could be quite cheaply obtained on the second-hand market, the special book-buying funds allocated to Birmingham by the U.G.C. in connection with the development of the Centre would be adequate to enable its University Library to build up a sufficient corpus of African books and periodicals to support most ordinary teaching and research on *West* Africa if not on the continent as a whole.

Jean never became wholly reconciled to the idea of moving from London to Birmingham. (Among other things, her ear, brought up no doubt to listen to the purer speech of English expatriate communities, was never wholly at home with the strange flat tones which issued from Brummie mouths.) Nevertheless in Edgbaston, and in parts of the adjacent suburbs, such as Harborne, where we first found a house to please us, it was quite possible to find environments to live in which were not too different from that of Hampstead Garden Suburb. They even had some advantages: they were within comfortable walking distance of the University, and not much further away from the city centre with its shops, theatres and other major facilities (including a cricket ground which was home to Test Matches). If these could not match those of central London in number, some of them, such as the Birmingham Repertory Theatre, the City of Birmingham Symphony Orchestra or the Welsh National Opera at the Hippodrome, were hardly inferior in quality. And if one still insisted on the National Theatre, the Albert Hall or Covent Garden, London was still no more than two hours away! Birmingham also had some good parks and, when one was fed up with them or with it, it was much easier and quicker to get out of than the vast wen of London. In no time at all, a car would take you into the pleasant countrysides of Warwickshire, Worcestershire and Shropshire – and then the whole of wild Wales would lie before one. All in all, for my taste Birmingham was much more usefully compact than London. To my surprise, it turned out to be cleaner too – no doubt because our arrival in it coincided with the application of Clean Air Acts.

So on April Fool's Day 1963 I became Director of the Centre of West African Studies and Professor of African History at the University of Birmingham. But at first there was very little for me to do at the University except to try to find my way around its departments and committees, to explain who I was and what I was going to do, and to seek to enlist the cooperation of those with whom I would have to work. The priorities were more for me to find a house for us to live in and a school for our daughter to go to (for our son we became resigned to boarding school, a possibility which had been with us since our time in Ghana). These two tasks were successfully accomplished in time for the new school and university terms in September and October, but before then I spent no more than two or three days a week in Birmingham, where at night I camped out in one of the attics at Westmere (which was no longer needed as a Staff Club, since Casson had designed a splendid new Staff House which had been built close by the Aston Webb buildings). At Westmere I was to find a fellow camper, Richard Hoggart, the author of *The Uses of Literacy*, who had recently been appointed to a second Chair of English, and who like me had left his family behind near his previous place of work, in his case the University of Leicester. He was keen to bring contemporary cultural studies to Birmingham and – although he had no prospect of earmarked funds from the U.G.C., and so would have to find funding elsewhere (which in due course he did with some success) – he was therefore interested in talking with me about the multi-disciplinary centre format which Hayter had favoured for area studies.

Some thought had in fact to be given as to how the "centre format" might operate in Birmingham, a university conditioned to operate with departments and faculties with firmly marked boundaries. As has been seen, though the initiative in the introduction of West African Studies had come from within the Faculty of Arts, Pascal had from the beginning seen that these studies would extend into the sphere of disciplines and departments which were the business of other Faculty Boards, most immediately that of the Faculty of Commerce and Social Science. In the long run there was little logical reason why disciplines and departments which were the affairs of the other Faculties of the University – Law, Science and Engineering, and Medicine and Dentistry – might not also be involved. Pascal and Aitken thought that if a multi-disciplinary West African Studies Centre were to operate successfully in this situation, three things were necessary. Anyone appointed to teach and research in the Centre should also have an appointment in the appropriate disciplinary department; the Centre's Director should be a member of any Faculty Board which administered any Degree for which students of the Centre might be working; and there should be a "Board of West African Studies" in which the Director of the Centre should sit with the heads of all the departments responsible for the disciplines within which the Centre operated.

There was some debate as to who should be chairman of such a Board. Pascal thought it should be the Director of the Centre, but Aitken suggested, and I agreed, that the Director would be in a better position if the Vice-Chancellor were to be chairman. As it happened, at this time Aitken was thinking that the times were such that Vice-Chancellors were becoming overloaded by too much detail, and that therefore, in addition to the Pro-Vice-Chancellor and Vice-Principal he already had, who was part-time and appointed for a limited term of years, he should have a full-time permanent deputy. In 1963 he told the Senate that he had created a new post of Deputy Principal, and that he had appointed to it Dr Thomas Alty, who had recently relinquished the Vice-Chancellorship of Rhodes University in South Africa. It was Alty who became the first Chairman of my Board, bringing to the role a personality, neutrality and authority that were admirably suited for securing the goodwill of the deans and heads of the traditional faculties and departments.

When formal legislation was enacted by the University's Senate and Council for the governance of the Centre, I think that the only changes from what had been informally agreed among Aitken, Pascal and myself in the summer of 1962 were that the Deans of all the Faculties (or their representatives), and one or two elected members of the Centre's staff, were added to the Board, and that it was renamed the "Committee for the Centre of West African Studies".

I think there was undoubtedly some suspicion and unease among the faculties and in some departments of the University at the apparently privileged new order of things that had been created for what was soon known simply as "C.W.A.S.", but I do not remember anything approaching serious open hostility. It obviously helped that a parallel constitution was also

138

enacted for what had hitherto been a smallish department within the Faculty of Commerce and Social Science concerning itself with the "Economics and Institutions of the U.S.S.R.", which had also received earmarked Hayter funding, and which then developed into a larger and very active Centre for Russian and East European Studies. With the institution of two centres of area studies, it became more apparent that the University had become host for a new kind of unit for teaching and research. Moreover, as Aitken once observed, the Centres did have "the great administrative lubricant" that during their initial years they were supported by money which did not come out of the general grant from the U.G.C. which was the main support of the rest of the University.

So far as relations with the rest of the University were concerned, it was significant that there was to be no *Board of Studies* for C.W.A.S. (or for C.R.E.E.S. for that matter). Area studies was not to be an academic activity separate from the rest of the University: with one minor (and transitory) exception, all the students taught by the Centre staff were registered for a Degree in one or other of the Faculties. A great deal of our undergraduate teaching in fact was for the degree syllabuses of the disciplinary departments to which the members of the Centre staff also belonged. Thus, for example, I provided students for the B.A.Honours Degree in History with an opportunity of studying some African history in both the second and third years of their courses. However, students in the Faculty of Arts were not all working for Single Honours Degrees; some of the best had chosen to work for Combined Honours Degrees for which, for example, a student might combine the study of history equally with the study of another subject such as French or geography (and there was an equivalent kind of combined degree in the Faculty of Commerce and Social Science). So for students who wished to specialise in African Studies, the undergraduate courses taught by the staff of the Centre could be put together to make half of their work for a Combined Honours Degree. In my time at the Centre we did not choose to offer a Single Honours Degree in African Studies. We thought it best that work studying Africa through a number of different disciplines, as varied as history, sociology and economics etc, should be accompanied by work in some depth in a particular one of these disciplines. I still believe this to have been educationally desirable. But after my retirement, shortage of funds to support postgraduate students meant that their numbers in the Centre fell off seriously (from fifty or more in the later 1970s, they had declined a decade later to ten or less), and this was at a time when the worth of university departments was being increasingly assessed by their ability to attract income, such as the fees paid by students. In this situation, a Single Honours Degree in African Studies was launched as an expedient – which proved successful – of increasing undergraduate numbers and fee income to offset the decline on the postgraduate front.

Virtually the only teaching which the Centre did which was not done in conjunction with a disciplinary department was in the postgraduate field, but even here the general practice was for a student to be registered in one of the Faculties for a Master's Degree or a Ph.D. This was an area in which Hayter had been very keen to encourage expansion, the principal agency for this being the provision of funds to make possible the award of specific postgraduate studentships in area studies. In due course C.W.A.S. was to attract probably more than its due proportion of British students holding such awards (as well as substantial numbers of Masters and Ph.D. students from abroad – about half of whom were attracted from Africa). But when C.W.A.S. was established, there was little tradition in U.K. university institutions outside S.O.A.S. of postgraduate work in African studies, so the Centre embarked on the experiment of offering a nine-month postgraduate African Studies Diploma course to potential students who might not have the normal minimum Faculty entry requirement of an Upper Second Class first degree, but who could show some good – often practical – reason why they would want to acquire or enlarge some knowledge of Africa. These were the only students of the Centre who were not enrolled in a Faculty. But by the mid 1970s the numbers of postgraduate degree students working at C.W.A.S. (about half of them for Ph.D.s and about half for Master's Degrees over a twelve-month taught course) were such that there was no longer any need to continue recruiting for this Diploma.

In Legon, the Institute of African Studies had been planned with work in African languages as its core activity. It was possible to believe that students in an African Studies centre outside Africa might have a greater need to study African languages than Africans in their homelands. But while I was keen that in the long run there should be a place at C.W.A.S. for African language studies, I could not see that this should be given a high priority. In the first place, our Hayter paymasters had declared that the main national need in Oriental and African studies was for more work in the "modern subjects" of history, geography and the social sciences; they said that there was already more than enough capacity available in the U.K. universities in the linguistic and literary fields. Secondly I thought that few if any British students would be attracted to an African Studies centre in Birmingham by the idea of gaining a first or second degree through work on African languages: it was at that time almost notorious that the internationally famous Department of Africa at S.O.A.S. which, with a strength of twenty or more scholars, possessed quite possibly the largest concentration of Africanist linguists anywhere in the world, had hardly more students than it had staff. I therefore concluded that, in the foreseeable future, C.W.A.S. could never expect to employ more than one or two language lecturers at most, and that their work would be essentially ancillary to what was done in other disciplines. Thus when an advertisement was issued inviting applications for lectureships in the Centre, it was specified that these should be in modern subjects.

I was confident that we would get a good response from scholars who had experience of practising their disciplines in Africa and who, as I had been five years before, were now thinking of returning to Britain. So in fact it proved, initially largely at the expense of the University of Ibadan, from which we were able to recruit "Brad" (Robert) Bradbury in social anthropology, Peter Lloyd in sociology, and Ken Post in political science, all of whom had established reputations by their work and publications – respectively on the Benin Kingdom, the Yoruba, and Nigerian politics. I was keen to find someone qualified to work in economic and social history to balance my own lack of expertise in this important aspect of African history. But this was a speciality as yet little developed in the African colleges and, as I had rather suspected, the ideal appointee turned out to be Tony Hopkins, who had already done the best part of a year's fieldwork in Lagos for his Ph.D., and who we immediately sent back into the field to broaden his experience. We failed to secure any good applications from economists to teach and research at C.W.A.S., possibly I think because economists were inclined to think of their subject as a pure one which ought not to become associated with a geographical area as eccentric as West Africa. But I then remembered that among the lecturers in Birmingham's Department of Economics there was Douglas Rimmer, who had begun a spell as an economist at Legon about the time when I was thinking of leaving it. I therefore approached Douglas and his head of department with a view

141

to securing his transfer to C.W.A.S. on secondment. In the event Douglas was with us on secondment for five years; these were so successful from both his and the Centre's point of view, that he then became an established member of the Centre's staff (eventually, indeed, becoming my successor as its Director).

I shall always be deeply grateful to these five pioneers for the mixture of experience and adventure with which they helped me launch the Centre. They were a perfect crew with which to embark on a kind of enterprise which was new to Birmingham and its ways, and none of them seemed to find it difficult to interest students in what interested them. I think that the worst thing that happened to C.W.A.S. during my time was Brad's premature and totally unexpected death from pneumonia just before Christmas in 1969; he was a man at once of great achievement and of infinite promise. By the time of Brad's death, the other two who had been attracted from Ibadan had also moved on, Peter Lloyd to a readership at Sussex (where a readership in psychology was available for his wife, Barbara, who could only find temporary employment in Birmingham), and Ken Post to an adventurous joint appointment between the Universities of Manchester and the West Indies. But their reputations helped us find worthy successors: in anthropology, Elizabeth Tonkin, with experience from Nigeria's Ahmadu Bello University; in sociology, Margaret Peil from Legon; and in political science, Arnold Hughes, who as a young researcher had worked alongside Tony Hopkins in western Nigeria. (In due course, the second and third of these were to become the third and fourth Directors of C.W.A.S.)

The Centre did not initially seek to recruit a lecturer in geography for the very good reason that, in the persons of Bill Morgan and Rowland Moss in its Department of Geography, the University already possessed two established geographers with substantial African interests. People like these (together with others, for example Ronald Wraith in the University's Department of Local Government, who had substantial experience, practical and academic, of government in Nigeria), were recognised as Associates of C.W.A.S., and were able to further their African interests by taking advantage of the earmarked U.G.C. funds for West African travel and research which had come to Birmingham with the establishment of the Centre. Thus in 1966 Morgan and Moss went off on a joint expedition to western Nigeria. But when, shortly afterwards, Morgan left Birmingham for a readership at King's College, London, the Centre thought it desirable to have a geographer of its own. This might have created something of a problem, for by this time all the earmarked U.G.C. funds available to the Centre for the 1962-67 quinquennium had been committed. However, the U.G.C. had just embarked on the great programme of general university expansion which had been recommended in the Robbins Report, and the Directors of C.W.A.S. and C.R.E.E.S. joined together and persuaded the University that the two area studies centres – spoilt babies though they might be – should not be denied their share of the extensive new funding that was coming to finance the growth of the University as a whole. In this way C.W.A.S. received funds for two further lectureships, one of which went to Peter Mitchell, a geographer from Fourah Bay College, and the other, to deal with the important Islamic side of West African history, to John Ralph Willis, an African-American Arabist who had been working for his Ph.D. on this theme at S.O.A.S.

We had hoped that for 1967-72 the promised second earmarked tranche of funds for the development of C.W.A.S. would be as big as the initial grant for 1962-67. This was not to be (had we supped too greedily at the Robbins table?). With the smaller funds that did come our way, we chose to establish only one new lectureship, in archaeology, for which we enticed Colin Flight from Legon. After this appointment, there would have been money enough for two further appointments at lecturer level, but in the event we decided to make neither. In the first place, as the Centre developed, I had come to see that it might be more effectively managed if it had an administrative assistant who would relieve its Director and his colleagues of much of the more intricate aspects of student and library affairs. Our student body was not large, and most administrative matters pertaining to the undergraduates we taught were handled according to well-established routines in the Faculty offices or in the other departments in which they worked. But the Centre was responsible for sieving through two hundred or more postgraduate applications a year, and then of having to care for those it had selected, who at any one time in the 1970s would add up to forty or fifty. For these there might be very little in the way of established routines. There was certainly no U.C.C.A. to smooth the process of selection. No more than half the postgraduates were likely to be British and relatively straightforward to deal with. The rest might come from anywhere in the world, but were most likely to come from African countries where it would be foolish to expect things to conform to a pattern immediately recognisable in Birmingham. Native and non-native together, the postgraduates presented a substantial variety of backgrounds and needs; many of them might have families to support and house, almost all were dependent on a variety of British or foreign grants (each of which would have its own particular regulations and customs) to finance themselves and the overseas travel that was essential for their work. It was therefore good for them, as well as convenient for the Director and his academic colleagues, that they should have a universal foster parent in the Centre. I also saw that it would be useful to have an administrative assistant to liaise with the University Library in the substantial work of building up the University's collection of Africana (just as the Library deputed a particular assistant librarian to deal with C.W.A.S.). An administrative assistant was particularly appropriate for this task, not only because he or she would be a neutral among our various and sometimes rival academic interests, but also to organise and control a swelling collection of ephemera and works of ready reference for which the proper place was on shelves in the Centre rather than in the main University Library. For this post we were lucky to secure Mrs Gillian Trevett, a graduate in geography from the University of Southampton, who in no time at all established the rationale for the post and set a tradition for all the Centre's staff, students and visitors which, beginning in forms such as "Ask Gill" or "See if Gill will do it", was in due time cheerfully taken up by equally willing successors.

Apart from the decision to have an administrative assistant, we also had to consider the further academic development of the Centre. The appointment of an archaeologist had served for the time being to round off what might be called the historical side of the Centre, which was the focus for about half of its postgraduate students; it now had four members, an ordinary historian (myself), an economic historian (Hopkins), an Islamic historian (Willis: later Paulo de Moraes Farias, ex Legon), and the newly recruited archaeologist (Flight). None of our other established disciplines (which in many respects were complementary) seemed to require urgent reinforcement. We therefore needed to consider what new direction the Centre might seek to take. So far as I can now remember, the favourite options were law and an environmental science, most probably botanical or agricultural. But if the Centre were to decide to advance in one of these directions, we could see problems. It would be entering the sphere of a new Faculty, with its own degrees and students, and it was questionable whether a single appointment, which was all that could immediately be afforded, would form an effective bridgehead. Furthermore, if it did perform well, it might well need reinforcement, and we had no idea whether any funds would be available in the new quinquennium beginning in 1972 to allow of this. It was wise to be cautious here, because in the event the U.G.C. ceased making earmarked grants for area studies in 1972 (by which time all the posts they had originally funded in this way had become charges on the general income of the University). We therefore concluded that the wisest course for C.W.A.S. was not to use the funds remaining from the earmarked grant for 1967-72 to add a new lecturer to the Centre's permanent establishment, but instead to use this money to create two research fellowships each tenable for up to three years. By this means we thought we could, without commitment, at once explore what new specialisms were worth having and might work well in our Centre and University, and gain some idea of what bright young men and women were coming forward in the field of African Studies and whom we might like to take on as colleagues.

However C.W.A.S. was not totally dependent on funds originating from the University Grants Committee. Much of the research done by its staff was, of course, funded by grants from research councils and foundations. In addition, quite early in its history it received two magnificent gifts.

One day in 1969 I was working at the Centre when I received a telephone call from Mr John Cadbury who asked whether he might come and see me. This senior member of the great Cadbury family was the director of Cadbury Bros Ltd who, since the 1930s, had been most concerned with its cocoa buying activities in West Africa. I had first met him very soon after I came to Birmingham, when he had been instrumental in getting the W.A.Cadbury Charitable Trust to provide £6000 over a period of six years to facilitate the buying of the rarest and most expensive items of Africana for the University Library. This time, however, he wanted to see me in a personal capacity, and within an hour or so he was striding into my room. No sooner had he had sat down than he told me that he was considering making a number of substantial gifts to educational institutions connected with West Africa. He then immediately went on to ask me what Birmingham's Centre of West African Studies might want to do with one of these gifts if the University were to receive one for its use. Luckily this was one of my brighter days and, after gently prising from him some indication of how large "substantial" might be, I came up with the answer that we would seek to use it to invite academics from the West African universities to come to C.W.A.S. for up to a year as Visiting Fellows or, possibly also, to award scholarships to graduates of West African universities to enable them to study at the Centre. He seemed happy with this, and quickly departed as unfussily as he had come. I heard no more until early in 1970 it was learnt that the University had received an anonymous gift of, I think, £70,000, the income from which was to be used for these purposes. It was not until the following year that the name of our benefactor could be made public. As a result of this generosity, from 1972-73 onwards it was usual each year to have a John Cadbury Fellow with us in the Centre, adding strength and variety to our teaching and research, and helping to keep us in touch with the academic life of West Africa. (A number of practical difficulties intervened to prevent the Centre making much use of the scheme to award postgraduate scholarships.)

The Centre's other great benefactor was John Danford, whom I had first met briefly in 1964, when I was touring the West African universities and when he was serving as the British Council's local representative in Ibadan. Danford's experience of Nigeria went back to war service there in the 1940s and, as a man who himself had some pretensions as a sculptor, he had become increasingly fascinated with the art he saw all around him. By the end of the 1950s he had made a considerable collection of African – mainly Nigerian – art, not only in its magnificent wooden sculpture, but also in such forms as cloth and musical instruments, and this had been placed on exhibition in Trenchard Hall at the University of Ibadan. But the time came when the British Council wanted to move Danford away from Ibadan, first to Manchester and then to Sierra Leone (where he was to make quite a few additions to his collection), and he had to decide what to do with what he had lent to the University of Ibadan. He expected that in due course he would retire to his family home in Ireland, and there he hoped he might be able to convert a barn into an exhibition gallery. But there were quite a few years to go before this could happen. So in the meantime Danford looked around the British Isles to see if he could find another suitable university to provide shelter for his collection. Birmingham's new Centre of West African Studies turned out to be what he was looking for, and for our part we were delighted that our students and visitors should be surrounded by so many excellent physical samples of the living culture of West Africa.

Danford's collection in the form that it had been exhibited at Ibadan arrived in Birmingham in 1964 when the Centre was still lodging in four rooms on the first floor of Westmere, which was now the home of the University's Shakespeare Institute, a much larger institution. I can still remember the excitement of opening a sizeable number of substantial packing cases, thinking as their contents were revealed that the Centre was beginning to acquire a cultural heritage which would help us hold up our heads when surrounded on every hand by so much prestigious Shakespearean scholarship. Once the collection had been installed, it began steadily to grow, not only because Danford added to it what he had collected when he was in Sierra Leone, but also because it inspired quite a few of those who came to see it to offer to give or to lend to it the good things from Africa that they themselves had collected. Unhappily in 1970, just after his retirement, but before he had been able to do anything to house his collection in his native Ireland, John Danford died. His heir was his mother, who generously agreed to maintain the loan of the Collection. But after her death a few years later, the Danford family decided that there was no alternative but to offer the Collection for sale. I was able to negotiate that the University should be given first refusal and, with generous help from John Cadbury and the Victoria and Albert Museum, the University was able to find the funds to purchase the Danford Collection.

It was lucky that by this time the Centre had moved to larger premises. The handful of rooms in Westmere had very quickly become inadequate to meet the needs of steadily growing numbers of staff and students (even though we were happy that something like half our staff should room with their disciplinary departments). In 1965, however, I heard that "Red Marley", a house on what had been the edge of the campus like Westmere – but smaller and more modern, though still very pleasant – was about to be vacated by the University's Department of Extramural Studies which, like ourselves, needed to move to larger premises. My enquiries revealed that no definite decision had been taken as to the future use of what was known to the Post Office as 32 Pritchatts Road, so I asked for it for the Centre and we were lucky enough to get it. It was a splendid place in which to display the Danford Collection and, with a few minor alterations, such as the transformation of a three-car (!) garage into a seminar room, it served the Centre's academic purposes very well. We all became very fond of it, especially perhaps because we did not seek to change the original domestic kitchen. As it happened, this was next door to what became the administrative assistant's office, and I often felt that, if perhaps some people might suppose that C.W.A.S.'s nerve centre lay in the Director's office upstairs, its heart certainly lay in or close by these two rooms on the ground floor.

Chapter 10
Some extramural activities

When I arrived at the University of Birmingham in 1963 I had three principal extramural activities. However – as has already been remarked – one of these disappeared in 1973 when Roland Oliver and I ceased to be editors of *The Journal of African History*. Invitations to give occasional lectures or seminars outside my own institution continued at first more or less as they had done at S.O.A.S., though perhaps somewhat less hectically. I can remember venturing as far afield as Durham to the north and Taunton to the southwest, but in the later 1970s this activity began to reduce. There was no longer as great a demand as there once had been for popular, general talks on the history of Africa, while it was only on occasion that I had something to say that could interest my fellow professionals.

I continued to be involved with the Inter-University Council. There was now less call for me to serve as an advisor on the selection committees, which it arranged for history appointments in the African colleges; these were now virtually all full universities with less need to recruit from overseas. However, sometimes the University of Birmingham would send me to represent it at the formal meetings of the Council, and I became a member of the Council's standing sub-committee which held a watching brief on university affairs in West Africa. In November 1970 this involved me in participating in a mission, which toured Nigeria to explore ways in which the I.U.C. and the universities of the United Kingdom might cooperate with the Nigerian universities to mitigate the consequences of the great civil war, which had ended the previous January. There were half a dozen of us, led by Elfyn Richards, hitherto known to me as one who had once been a colleague of my father's in the world of aeronautical research, but who was now Vice-Chancellor of Loughborough University, and Richard Griffiths, a former civil servant newly appointed as Director of the I.U.C By 1970, Nigeria's original, federal, university at Ibadan had been joined by regional or state universities at Lagos and Ife in the south-west and Zaria in the north, and by the two campuses of the University of Nigeria at Nsukka and Enugu in the south-east. There were also new university initiatives stirring at Jos in the north, at Port Harcourt in the southeast, and at Benin in the mid-western region of this vast and populous country. But there was time for our mission to see only what was happening at Benin, for it had not been easy for the I.U.C. to organise so wide a tour in the ten or twelve days which was the most that each of us had in common to take off from our normal responsibilities. Nigeria was not a land renowned for the efficiency of its communications. I can vividly remember that, when the authorities at Nsukka needed to be sure that some vital information would reach the I.U.C visitors at Ahmadu Bello University before they were due to leave it, they decided that the only thing to do was to entrust the relevant papers to an assistant registrar who was then driven in a university car all the way to Zaria, nearly 500 miles and some fifteen hours away. In the end the I.U.C. had come to the conclusion that it would be best if the mission's longer cross-country journeys were to be undertaken in a comfortable little twin-engined executive aircraft. This was something which I naturally found most enjoyable; more to the point it was something which certainly saved much time and aggravation and, I believe, cost little if any more than would have been spent buying tickets to fly on Nigeria's somewhat erratic local air services.

So far as the purpose of our travels was concerned, we found – as we expected – Ibadan to be a well established university, where I did little more than renew old acquaintances from previous visits and make some useful new contacts. The younger universities, of Lagos and Ife, and of Ahmadu Bello at Zaria, were all new to me. The politics of the establishment of the University of Lagos had not been exactly happy nor, I thought, was its situation in the suburbs of Nigeria's crowded and turbulent capital; the University of Ife, on its spacious, potentially grandiose, campus, seemed to be a happier place. Ahmadu Bello, a workmanlike institution devoid of any frills, seemed to be doing its best to grapple with the problems arising from the fact that the northern half of Nigeria that formed its catchment area was the poorest and least well developed and educated part of the country. Each of these universities had aspects in which it might benefit from continuing contacts with U.K. universities – such as the temporary secondment to them of teachers in some particular specialisms, or the provision of specialised training for some of their own staff – but such problems as they had were as nothing compared with those facing the new Institute of Technology at Benin or the campuses of the University of Nigeria. We all thought the Benin Institute somewhat bizarre, as much a creature of political ambition as of genuine academic purpose but, since it had been created only a few months before our visit, most of it was as yet no more than a phantom. The problem facing the University of Nigeria, on the other hand, was very far from phantasm; it was only too real. Its campuses at Nsukka and Enugu were no more than shells of what I had seen on my previous visit some six years before: war had passed through them, stripping their buildings bare of their contents. All their equipment – simple plumbing as well as scientific instruments and tools – their furniture and perhaps 90% of their library holdings, and sometimes even the buildings' roofing, had been looted. Before the war the weaknesses of the university had lain less in its materiel than with its academic staff; too many of its members were inadequately trained and motivated for the jobs they were meant to do. Perversely here war almost seemed to have done some good by removing the university's dullards. The staff that had returned, along with most of the students, had set to work with quite admirable spirit to recreate a working university as best they could. Thus when we found that the refectory had nothing for diners to sit on, it was because no meal was in progress, so that its benches had been carried across to a classroom; at the end of the day, they would be moved again, to a student hostel (but I am not sure that I ever saw a bed). It was obvious to us all that the University of Nigeria needed emergency aid on a considerable scale, and this the I.U.C. set about organising. Elfyn Richards's Loughborough took the lead in despatching technicians and spare parts to help put engineering and scientific equipment in working order, while I myself took a hand in urging U.K. universities and their members to donate duplicate books, redundant equipment, or money.

Although this may not have been apparent at the time, in the long run perhaps the most significant of my I.U.C. activities when I was at Birmingham was that in the 1970s I became one of three "academic advisers" chosen to support Ian Maxwell in the work of writing an "official" history of the I.U.C. This appeared in 1980 as *Universities in Partnership: the Inter-University Council and the growth of higher education in developing countries, 1946-70* – an invaluable work of reference. Maxwell was well suited to this job since, after four years as the man in the University of London

Registry who handled the "special relations" with the overseas university colleges, in 1959 he had moved to the I.U.C. as its Secretary (and, later, became Deputy to Richard Griffiths). I think he felt he needed "academic advice" because he had never actually served in one of the overseas colleges – though I have never understood why his advisers were all in the arts and social science fields of history, government (Professor D.G.Austin) and education (Professor L.J.Lewis), nor why their overseas experience was virtually all in the University College of the Gold Coast! Be this as it may, I cannot escape thinking that the writing and publication of its history presaged the ending of the perceived need for a really active Inter-University Council for Higher Education Overseas.

In 1963 I took a hand in inventing a new extramural activity for myself. Hitherto the Royal African Society had provided virtually the only common forum for British academics concerned with Africa. But for many of them the Society seemed to have largely departed from the ideals which had inspired its institution in 1900 as a memorial to Mary Kingsley and her researches into the peoples and governments of Africa, and to have become too much of an old boys' club for members and retired members of the Colonial Service. I suppose I was one of those who took this view, for it had never occurred to me to join the Society (and I did not do so until 1966). However Roland Oliver and some other academics, such as Tony Allott, S.O.A.S.'s Professor of African Law, who were members of the Society, came to the conclusion that they ought to try to reform it. But they got no further than to persuade it to call a meeting, at the Commonwealth Institute in London in July 1963, to consider whether "teachers and research workers from British universities...working on African subjects and problems" should not form an African Studies Association in the United Kingdom which would seek to advance academic studies of Africa in much the same way as the African Studies Association that had recently been very successfully launched in the U.S.A. There was a ready response to this initiative: 125 persons turned up at the meeting, while another 46 teachers and researchers from U.K. institutions of higher education wrote to express their support, and it was readily agreed that an African Studies Association of the United Kingdom should be founded. An Interim Council was elected to hold office until a constitution could be agreed at a first annual general meeting. Margery Perham was fittingly chosen to be the founding President, Roland Oliver and Audrey Richards became Vice-Presidents and Anthony Allott Honorary

Treasurer, while I was chosen to be the first Honorary Secretary – no doubt for the good reason that at the Centre of West African Studies at Birmingham I had an office and secretarial support which as yet were not overburdened with their own business.

I remember that one of my first actions was to write to Jim Coleman, the Africanist political scientist who was then Secretary of the American A.S.A., to secure details of its operations, and I think that I took some aspects of its constitution as models for our own that was adopted at our first Annual General Meeting and Conference, which was held at the University of Birmingham in September 1964. Our association was of necessity much smaller than that on the other side of the Atlantic whose conferences were perforce held in great characterless hotels. Our membership has been as high as 500 or so, but more generally it has fluctuated around 400, with perhaps no more than a third of it likely to attend a conference, which would then fit very comfortably in the more homely ambience of a university hall of residence. It was quickly appreciated that it would be too much to seek to hold each year a full, three- or four-day conference essaying to cover all aspects of African studies. So in alternate years the statutory annual general meeting has been accompanied by no more than a one-day symposium devoted to a single theme, which seemed of some significance at the time. In retrospect I find it interesting that in the formative years of the A.S.A.U.K. the themes chosen for these symposia touched as much on the natural sciences as they did on the human and social sciences which might be more commonly thought to be the sphere of "Africanist" activity. There is no doubt that the founders of the A.S.A.U.K. intended it to be a broad church – as had been the [Royal] African Society which, in its first years after its foundation in 1900 in memory of Mary Kingsley, had among its members more Fellows of the Royal Society than it did Fellows of the British Academy. However, although the early A.S.A.U.K. Councils had among their members geologists, foresters and physical geographers, and its Presidents have included the distinguished botanists Sir John Hutchinson, F.R.S., and R.W.J.Keay (soon to be appointed Executive Secretary of the Royal Society) and the soil scientist E.W.Russell, and a very active early Secretary and President was the physical geographer Rowland Moss, this was not to be. In the early years, no more than fifteen percent of the members of the Association were natural scientists, and since then the proportion has been no more than about half of that.

The bulk of the members have always been historians, human geographers, political scientists, anthropologists and sociologists, and economists.

I remained active in the affairs of the A.S.A.U.K. until 1968-69, the year in which I took my turn as President. Thereafter my active involvement in its affairs, together with that of others of its "founding fathers", gradually faded out. But its headquarters remained for many years in Birmingham at the Centre of West African Studies, where the day-to-day administrative work came to be a job for a part-time secretary, Mrs Priscilla Naish, and first Robert Bradbury and then Marion Johnson served as honorary editors of the A.S.A.U.K.'s *Bulletin*. In 1973 this merged with *Library Materials on Africa*, the bulletin of S.C.O.L.M.A., the Standing Conference – founded the year before the A.S.A.U.K. – of the university and other libraries which held significant holdings of African material, to become *African Research and Documentation*. Marion continued as editor of the new publication until 1981. Her retirement was a factor in leading the Association to take steps to bring about *de facto*, if not *de jure*, a considerable part of what Oliver and Allott and their friends had sought to achieve in 1963. The Royal African Society and the A.S.A.U.K. were not merged, but in 1982 it was agreed that they should have an interlocking membership with a single full-time secretary working from a common London office, and the Society's quarterly journal *African Affairs*, by now a thoroughly respectable academic publication, became additionally the medium through which the African Studies Association communicated with the world.

Since Marion Johnson has not been mentioned previously in this Memoir, this is perhaps an appropriate place to say something about one of C.W.A.S.'s more remarkable members. After some thirty years living as a wife and a mother in various parts of Africa, Marion eventually secured the liberty to turn her Oxford training as a historical geographer to good use in African research, especially at the Institute of African Studies in Ghana. As a result of this, Thomas Hodgkin recommended her to us when we were looking for a temporary replacement for Tony Hopkins when, in 1969-70, he had been granted a year's leave of absence. Following this, Marion stayed on in the Centre as a very active research fellow who had no difficulty securing financial support for a series of groundbreaking investigations into fundamental aspects of the economic life and material culture of pre-colonial West Africa. One of her greatest services to African studies, outside as well as inside C.W.A.S., was her readiness to put her experience and her data-handling skills at the service of others. In this way she won many friends among other researchers and students, and made a major contribution not only to the information work of the A.S.A.U.K., but also to the eight volumes of the *Cambridge History of Africa* for the extensive bibliographies of which she was the meticulous editor.

My lack of activity in the A.S.A.U.K. after 1969 did not mean any diminution in my extramural activities. One of these became some involvement in matters relating to southern Africa. This was largely involuntary; the manner in which *apartheid* was being pursued in South Africa, especially after the Sharpeville killings in 1960, and the unilateral declaration of independence by Ian Smith's regime in Southern Rhodesia in 1965 and its consequences, were not matters which responsible citizens of the United Kingdom could ignore. They were certainly matters of concern to a vocal section of Birmingham students, the more so as, under the special relationship scheme, our University had responsibility for the Faculty of Medicine at the University of Rhodesia. So, as Professor of African History, I was more than once called upon to speak or to preside at meetings called by students. In this context, I suppose I gained some kudos when in 1967 the two Birmingham newspapers, the *Post* and the *Evening Mail*, both reported that the Rhodesian Ministry of Education had seized copies of the Oliver & Fage *A Short History of Africa* that were being used as school textbooks. But if so, I daresay I might have lost it if our students had also appreciated that in 1969 the black students of Howard University in the U.S.A. had objected to the inclusion of our Penguin on a prescribed reading list, on the ground that it was white racist propaganda, and that in 1960 Kwame Nkrumah's Ministry of Education in Ghana had taken the same action as the Rhodesian Ministry in respect of my *Introduction to the History of West Africa*! (Can it be that the coloration of what one reads lies in the eye of the reader rather than in the pen of the writer?)

During this time when southern African affairs were commanding a great deal of attention in Britain, I received two invitations to make academic visits to the Republic of South Africa. The first was in 1969, when I was invited to lecture at the inaugural open meeting in Pretoria of the second Biennial Conference of the South African Historical Society. Then four years later I was asked to give the Tenth Raymond Dart Lecture for the Institute for the Study of Man in Africa at the University of the Witwatersrand in Johannesburg. Just as there were Birmingham students who felt that U.D.I. should automatically mean that their University must cease to be involved in the medical affairs of the Rhodesian university, so there were those who were concerned with African affairs in more senior positions in British universities who took the line that southern African universities should be boycotted, and that visits to them would be construed as approval of the political regimes under which they operated. However I could see that it would be useful to me I were to return briefly to southern Africa, none of which I had seen for some twenty-five years, and which had obviously much changed in the interval, and to have the opportunity of visiting some important parts of it – such as the Transvaal – which I had never seen at all. South African money would pay for my travel and I would be accepting South African hospitality, but enquiries gave me to understand that the relevant funds came from academic or charitable rather than from politicised sources. So on balance I concluded that there was something to be said for trying to help maintain intellectual dialogue between two societies which once had much in common, but which were now becoming ideologically dangerously divided, in part at least because they now conversed with each other much less than they once had done.

When I had to decide what I should say at my public lectures at Pretoria in 1969 and at Johannesburg in 1973, I could see little alternative to talking about the kind of African history to which my attention had been drawn as a result of the ten years in which I had lived and worked in West Africa. I would be a visitor in a society which had been so dominated by Europeans for so long that it was likely that the only African history my almost exclusively white audiences would know much about would in effect be colonial or imperial history. It would be essentially the history of what white people had done in Africa, with by far the greatest emphasis on the temperate southern lands, which they had begun to settle as recently as 1652. So I aimed to use what I had learnt about the past of West Africa to demonstrate that the history of the black indigenes of the continent could be reconstructed over many centuries, and by the use of much the same techniques as had been used to reconstruct the history of Europe and of other supposedly "more advanced" parts of the world. I would essay to show that this history was not – as no doubt many members of my audiences might think – no more than "the unrewarding gyrations of barbarous tribes" imagined by Professor Trevor-Roper when in 1963 he was addressing a B.B.C. audience in the United Kingdom. At Pretoria I spoke under the bland title "Some problems of African history". In Johannesburg four years later, under the title "States and subjects in sub-Saharan history", I tried something rather more sophisticated. Partly influenced by the work of the West Indian-born historian of Upper Guinea, Walter Rodney (see below, p.210-11), I concentrated on the part played by institutions of servitude in the economic and political development of black African societies. I concluded by suggesting that there might be some parallel here with the way cheap black labour provided the underpinning for white society in South Africa, and that the comparison was not necessarily favourable to the latter.

I did not spend much time in Pretoria in 1969. This was in some measure, I think, because the Historical Society's conference was not held at the University of Pretoria, but at the University of South Africa, generally referred to as "UNISA", which was not a residential university, and which indeed possessed no campus. Its ten thousand students were all external, some studying by correspondence, and some taking its examinations after studying at the university colleges and training colleges which had become virtually the only means by which Black or Asian inhabitants of South Africa might secure post-secondary education after *apartheid* had come to make it virtually impossible for them to enter any of the English language universities. Both in this respect and in its reaching out to isolated Afrikaner rural communities, UNISA had come to appear to be an arm of Afrikaner nationalism, and the majority of its staff were Afrikaners, even though much of their teaching and examining was in English, the preferred academic language of their non-European students.

But a more potent reason for my spending only a short time in Pretoria was that, hearing through the I.U.C. that I was visiting southern Africa, Ian Michael, the Vice-Chancellor of the University of Malawi, had asked me to visit his university to advise it on the development of African studies. So within a few days I found myself sitting in a Viscount aircraft on its way to Blantyre, and overhearing two very proper white ladies in the seats behind me discussing what it was about Harold Wilson's Labour administration that had made it quite impossible for people of "their class" to continue to live in Britain. At Blantyre I was met and very hospitably looked after by Bridglal Pachai, a South African Asian, and a very able historian who had secured his Ph.D. in history from UNISA, where he was fondly remembered by his teachers. I think indeed he may have been one of their earliest Ph.D.s in history; pioneering was certainly in his blood, for he had become the leading light in the University of Malawi's young Department of History. He was now to spend the best part of a week doing his best to display to me what Malawi had done to create a university of its own after the break-up of the Federation of Rhodesia and Nyasaland at the end of 1963 had made it impossible to continue with the idea of a single university for the three British territories in central Africa. I am not sure that Pachai was altogether successful in this. This was not his fault; he was very energetic in showing me round a substantial part of the very beautiful country in which he was working. As well as taking me all round Blantyre, the commercial capital in and around which most of Malawi's tertiary educational activities were situated, he took me to Zomba, the garden village which had been home to the colonial administration and which was now intended to be the seat of the university, and even as far north as the southern shores of Lake Malawi. The problem was that in 1969 not much had as yet been done to create a university other than to declare that four earlier institutions on four different sites – an embryo polytechnic, an agricultural college, a college of education, and an institute of public administration – *were* a university. Of a total of about a thousand students, only about a third were studying for degrees; the rest were engaged on a variety of vocational diploma courses. It seemed to me that Michael already had quite enough on his hands without needing to worry about instituting any scheme of African studies; so far as African history was concerned, Pachai and his colleagues were already doing as well as, or better than, anyone might expect.

I think in fact that Michael was being pressed into inaugurating an African Studies department by the country's President, Hastings Kamuzu Banda, who, after leaving Malawi to train as a doctor in Britain, had practised in Ghana, where no doubt he had learnt from Nkrumah and other nationalists that no university in Africa was a proper university until it had a full programme of African Studies. Banda was fond of inviting visitors of any standing to his university to come and see him, and before long I was bidden to his presence where, for nearly two hours, I was regaled with his ideas of what history in general, and African history in particular, were all about. It was a somewhat eerie experience, reminding me rather of the sort of fate likely to involve the protagonist of an Evelyn Waugh novel set in some outlandish tropical country.

My second South African visit, in 1973, based on Johannesburg, was in outline remarkably similar to the earlier visit to Pretoria and Malawi in that it involved giving a public lecture, attending a conference of the South African Historical Society, and giving advice on setting up a programme of African studies. It was unlike it in that it extended over three weeks rather than ten days, that I was able to see much more of South Africa and its people than had been possible before, and that it was possible for Jean to accompany me.

Very shortly after arriving at Johannesburg, we took to the air again to get to Grahamstown, in the eastern Cape Province, where the fourth biennial conference of the South African Historical Society was being held at Rhodes University. This venue was probably as complete a contrast as might be found in South Africa to that for the 1967 conference at UNISA in Pretoria. Despite its role as a national capital, Pretoria is very much an Afrikaner city, while Grahamstown is a small town which was the first centre for English settlement in South Africa and, in a rather rough and ready way, its origins are still proclaimed in its tree-lined streets, its cathedral and its residential English-speaking university. Jean and I quickly found ourselves at home in one of the latter's halls of residence with its refectory and common rooms. As in 1969, I gave a paper on the opening day of the conference (no doubt the native historians were saying to themselves "Why do they always get this Englishman to talk to us on the opening day of our conferences?"). However this time I had chosen to talk about a neutral topic, "The History of African History".

We then returned to Johannesburg where, in a large lecture room of the University of the Witwatersrand and with some formality, I delivered the tenth annual Raymond Dart Lecture for the Institute for the Study of Man in Africa. The Institute had been founded to commemorate Raymond Dart's pioneer research on the earliest ancestors of human kind in southern Africa, research which was now being very ably extended by people such as Philip Tobias. It was pleasing – if somewhat intimidating – to find both Dart and Tobias among my audience. (At times I was hard put to it to check my tongue's tendency to refer to "The Dart *Memorial* Lecture"!)

I am not sure of the exact relationship between the Institute and the University of the Witwatersrand (though Dart and Tobias were both professors in the University's Department of Anatomy). However I suspect that the Institute did not have the cash to spare to pay for my expenses in getting to and from Johannesburg, because I know that these were paid by the University. In return for this I had agreed to provide its Vice-Chancellor, Professor Guerino Bozzoli, a bright and energetic electrical engineer, with a report to help the University set up an African Studies Institute. Having given my lecture, I then had no more to do in Johannesburg than to work on this report. Since I had converted the first class air ticket provided for me by the University into two cheaper excursion tickets, one of which was for Jean, and these stipulated a three-week stay in South Africa, I had something like a fortnight in which to do this. It was not all that easy to timetable the necessary consultations and meetings; Bozzoli in particular was a very busy man. However it soon became apparent that there was not all that much that I could say to him and his colleagues that they did not already know or could easily find out for themselves. There were already, for example, organised and active African Studies activities at the Cape Town, Natal and Rhodes Universities, and there was a good deal of relevant talent already available in their own university, not least among its young research students (one a daughter of Bozzoli). I suspect, therefore, that my commission from the University was at least in some measure a device to help the Institute bring the lecturer it wanted out from Europe.

So it did not take me long to complete my report, and Jean and I had time to spare to see a bit more of South Africa. The Grahamstown visit had already allowed us to see something of the Eastern Province where, among other things, we had made a little pilgrimage to see Monica Wilson, the South African representative of the tribe of great women anthropologists, in her mountain retreat at Hogsback. So far as the Johannesburg area was concerned, once we had gazed at the mine dumps, at the endless ranks of little houses in the immense planned black township of Soweto and at the picturesque but much less salubrious slums that had grown into the alternative black township of Alexandra, at the plush and well protected northern suburbs of the white middle classes, and at the potentially Sohoesque district of Hillbrow, we could see little more than an endless, dusty, stiflingly hot, grid of ugly concrete buildings. So we hired a car and set out southwards across the blazingly hot and dry High Veldt towards Bloemfontein, where we had been invited to stay at the home of Professor J.J. Oberholster, whom I had got to know at the Historical Society conferences, and Lesotho, where David Kimble was now installed as Professor of Government at the Roma campus of the University of Botswana, Lesotho and Swaziland (and soon to succeed Ian Michael as Vice-Chancellor in Malawi).

John flying a Tiger Moth at University of Cambridge Air Squadron

John in 1948

Photographed on board RMS 'QUEEN MARY'.

Jean, John and Julia (where is Michael?) on their first visit to the United States

John at the Centre of West African Studies

Three incidents of this journey stand out in my memory. The first was when, on the road between Bloemfontein and Maseru – no doubt because of the heat: the temperature in the sun must have been approaching 130° F. – the tread came off one of the tyres of our car. We then discovered that our hire car's equipment did not include a jack to enable us to change a wheel, and we soon began to realise how empty much of South Africa is. There was nothing in sight besides grassland; there was not even any sound of any kind of human activity. We began to remember that some time had passed since we had last seen any motor vehicle on our by no means unimportant road, so there was nothing we could do but sit still and wait. Eventually in the far distance of the flat landscape we spied a lorry trundling along and, as it came up to us, and without the need for any action on our part, it slowed and stopped and a friendly black face asked what he could do to help us. Secondly, when we had entered Lesotho and were driving through the streets of Maseru, its capital and its only town of any significance, which is within a mile or two of the border, we suddenly realised that we had entered a different world. All the people in the streets were black and, unlike the Blacks of South Africa, they were walking about as though they owned the place – which indeed they did! Then we were to appreciate the reverse of this when, on our way back to Johannesburg, we passed through the coal-mining region near Vereeniging (a much more distressing sight than any coalfield I had known in Britain) and saw a warning sign for motorists saying "BEWARE *BANTU* CROSSING THE ROAD". In South Africa, men and women with black skins were not really people (and, presumably, proper people, those with pink skins, would not be walking on the road or crossing it on foot: if they were so unfortunate as to have to work in the Vereeniging coalfield, they would only be seen driving along the road in their motor cars).

Nevertheless in 1973 we came across some evidence that change was on its way in South Africa. One was that during our stay, *The Rand Daily Mail* and *The Sunday Times* were much concerned with the lessons to be learnt from a series of strikes that were being mounted by black workers. It was interesting to discover from their columns that, though strikes by black workers were technically illegal, no harsh measures seemed to be being taken against them, and that there was some support for them from whites, and not merely from committed radical whites. Industrialists like Harry Oppenheimer and Anton Rupert were reported as saying in public that the basic trouble was that too few Blacks could earn a decent living wage. (At the time an average weekly wage for a black worker was about £3, while it was estimated that the minimum living costs for an average family living in Soweto were about £42 a month.) Thus Oppenheimer was saying that, of the twenty-two million people in South Africa, eighteen million had no say in the conduct of the country's government, were deprived of the right of collective bargaining through legal trade unions, and that thirteen million of them were poverty stricken, while Rupert had coined the slogan "If the Blacks don't eat, the Whites won't sleep". The black strikers were even supported by some white workers; thus the President of the Railway Artisan Staff Association was saying that his members "strongly support the paying of liveable wages to African workers".

The most significant evidence that times were changing that Jean and I came across personally came when we were staying with the Oberholzers in Bloemfontein. They had invited fellow Afrikaners of some standing in the community to come to their house to meet us and, in the evening after supper, we found the wives of the party arriving at the theme that times were not what they had been. The point they all came to was "We do not understand our young people any more". By this they meant that the younger generation of South African whites, or at least of its educated elite, was no longer taking it as an article of faith — as they themselves and their ancestors had always done — that white people, the Afrikaners in particular, were born to be the masters of South Africa.

This, I think, throws some light on the question of why it was that South African academics, including some of their Afrikaner historians, twice chose to invite me, an English historian who in 1969 and 1973 had no especial connection with the southern part of the continent of Africa, to come to their country to talk with them. It seems to me that the reason was that they had begun to appreciate that white society in South Africa was in dire danger of losing touch with the mainstream of development of the western civilisation, which their ancestors had so proudly brought to it three hundred years before. It is possible, I think, that the people who were concerned with inviting me out to South Africa must have thought that I was an appropriate person to help prevent further deterioration in at least one aspect of academic dialogue between their country and mine.

One day in 1965, when I was talking with Kenneth Robinson, he remarked to me that he thought that, as director of an institute of Commonwealth Studies, he was not best suited to be one of the British members of the Executive Council of the International African Institute. He said that his period of office on the Executive Council was coming to an end, and that he was suggesting that I, director of a new British centre of African studies and an active member of the A.S.A.U.K., might be a suitable replacement for him. He was obviously listened to, for in July 1965 I received a letter appointing me to the Executive Council of the I.A.I for 1966-68. I thus became a member of a most distinguished and congenial body and, in the event, was able to continue to enjoy the company of its members for the next fifteen years.

The Institute had been founded, in 1926, as the "International Institute of African Languages and Cultures", largely following the initiative of the man who became its first Chairman, Lord Lugard, the celebrated founder of the British Colony of Nigeria, and then (1922-36) the British representative on the Permanent Mandates Commission of the League of Nations. The Institute was intended to be an information centre for those engaged in official, missionary or other work in Africa, and for this purpose it was to receive regular financial grants from colonial authorities active in the continent. However its governing body had nothing to do with governments; its members were nominated by thirty-nine universities and learned bodies spread throughout the world. The Institute began with two co-directors, each very distinguished for his contributions to African scholarship, Maurice Delafosse from France and Diedrich Westermann from Germany. By the mid-1930s under their guidance it had begun to embark on substantial programmes of research in African languages and cultures which were largely financed by the Rockefeller Foundation. However the

Institute's work was interrupted, if not wholly destroyed, by the 1939-45 war, and in 1944 a new beginning was made with the appointment of Professor Daryll Forde as Administrative Director.

At the age of 28, Daryll Forde had followed the great H.J.Fleure as Professor of Geography and Anthropology at Aberystwyth, and he was now about to take up the job of creating a Department of Anthropology at University College, London. I would say that, as a social anthropologist he was not in the class of Evans-Pritchard or Meyer Fortes, but as an organiser, planner and inspirer of research he was superb; I have never met his equal. He was helped in this by the possession of apparently inexhaustible energy coupled with a marvellous talent for making friends and for persuading others – not least U.S. Foundations – to do what he wanted. There could have been no better choice for rebuilding and, indeed, greatly enlarging, the activities and scope of the I.A.I. One of his University College colleagues, Mary Douglas, was to write of Daryll following his death in 1973, that "he was for nearly 30 years directly promoting or indirectly encouraging every piece of research conducted in Africa", and this was not hyperbole.

Such a man built an excellent team to support him. Thus, though Daryll Forde had a genius for seeing what social and anthropological research should be attracted for presentation in the Institute's quarterly journal, *Africa*, he was not the best man for the literary details of editorship, so he had secured as his assistant Barbara Pym who – unknown I think to many of those who entered the Institute's friendly offices in New Fetter Lane – was one of the most meticulous composers of novels of her generation. His Executive Council was full of people who were good to know. Some I had already come across: Bill Brown from Boston University, Kenneth Dike, Vinigi Grottanelli, Arthur Porter (now become Principal of the University College at Nairobi), and Hubert Deschamps (now transformed into the most puckish of Sorbonne history professors). But there were others whom I had hitherto admired only at a distance, but whom I was soon to count as friends, such as Archie Tucker, S.O.A.S.'s Professor of East African languages, always with his Peace Pledge Union badge in his button hole, and a whole galaxy of talented anthropologists, including Meyer Fortes and Max Gluckman, respectively professors at Cambridge and Manchester, and the French pair Claude Meillassoux and Germaine Dieterlen. These anthropologists were excellent company, though listening to them talk almost made one wonder whether they were all following the same discipline. Fortes and Gluckman, both originally from South Africa, demonstrated the width of British pragmatism, but with the one on the verge of social psychology and the other on that of law. Meillassoux professed Marxism but in practice seemed equally pragmatic, though I sometimes wondered whether he was not really a historian. Germaine was the only member of the Council of whom I went in awe (and I suspect I was not alone in this); I think this had nothing to do with her being its one woman, but because the mysticism of her kind of anthropology was totally beyond my understanding. Not all members of the Council were academics; there were also a sprinkling of former colonial administrators and of businessmen to keep our feet on the ground and to make sure that the Institute did not run out of money. I particularly remember Sir Arthur Smith, once high up in the United Africa Company, who became our Chairman, and Sir George Beresford-Stooke, once Governor of Sierra Leone but now so lame that he could reach and stay at our more far-flung meeting places only by caravanning with his wife.

Our duties were not onerous. A few of us were called "Consultative Directors" (a status which I eventually achieved), and so presumably were available for Daryll to consult whenever he wanted, but for the most part we were on duty only on the occasion of the Council's annual three-day meeting. Then Daryll would report orally and on paper what he had done in the past year and what he proposed to do next: what books had been published and which he was hoping to publish; how the Institute's great series of African ethnographic and language surveys were proceeding; what research schemes or seminars were in hand or projected; and how and where he proposed to get the money to pay for all these activities. I do not remember that any of us ever took serious exception to any of this; it was always admirable. If I remember aright, most meetings of the Executive Council were held either at the Institute's base in London, or in Paris, where Sir Arthur Smith's commercial connections provided an alternative *pied à terre*. But while English and French were the two languages of the Institute, Daryll was always very conscious that it was an *International* Institute, and always keen to demonstrate its value and its merits in other centres. Moving the Executive Council around was not perhaps the best way of doing this. It was also expensive, especially since the closing of the colonial period meant that less money was available to support the I.A.I. from

European colonial offices and administrations, and that more of what the I.A.I. did was becoming within the sphere of interest of African governments with their own universities and research institutions. It was for this reason that from the later 1950s onwards, Daryll Forde placed increasing emphasis on holding a series of week-long "International African Seminars", which the Ford Foundation was willing to fund. These were held in African academic institutions, the Dakar seminar, "The Historian in Tropical Africa", which I had attended in 1961, was one of these.

Nevertheless I think I can remember going to meetings of the I.A.I. Executive Council in locations as diverse as Brussels, Uppsala, Lusaka and Warsaw, but at this distance in time I cannot be wholly certain that it was the I.A.I. which took me to confer in these places because, soon after I had become involved with the I.A.I., I became engaged in two activities related to UNESCO (the United Nations Educational, Scientific and Cultural Organisation) which involved going regularly to meetings not only in Paris, its headquarters, but also in remoter and more exotic places such as Dahomey, Nairobi and Sofia.

In 1966 there arrived out of the blue a letter from Anthony Crosland, then the Secretary of State for Education and Science in Harold Wilson's Labour government, inviting me to become a member of the Culture Advisory Committee of the United Kingdom National Commission for UNESCO. I had quickly to find out what this meant. I was not unaware that UNESCO had been instituted as part of the post-war settlement in 1945-46, to some extent as a result of a British initiative and with Julian Huxley as its first Director-General. Its object was to promote peace and security through international collaboration in educational, scientific and cultural activities in general, and in particular to support and complement national activities to eliminate illiteracy, to extend free education and to encourage the free international exchange of ideas and knowledge. But I doubt whether I had been aware that the member states of UNESCO, besides subscribing to its financial support in proportion to the size of their Gross National Products (thus, for example, the U.S.A was meant to contribute 25% of UNESCO's regular income and the U.K. 4.6% percent), were required to maintain National Commissions to link their national activities in education, science and culture with what UNESCO did or tried to do in these fields. There was considerable variety in what was done in practice to meet this requirement. Small or poor countries might do no more than depute one or two officials in some relevant ministry to act as a National Commission. The U.K. had always taken the line that there was so much going on in its educational, scientific and cultural life that no one body could possibly keep an eye on it all, and had embarked on a variety of expedients to try and achieve what UNESCO required. By 1965, the National Commission took the form of a committee supported by a small secretariat attached to the Department of Education. This was underpinned by a number of larger advisory committees. It was one of the latter that I was being invited to join, and this Culture Advisory Committee continued in existence until the U.K.'s withdrawal from UNESCO twenty years later. However, by 1971 the superstructure of these arrangements had been altered. First it had been decided that, so far as the U.K. was concerned, the important part of UNESCO's work was what it might do help the development of Third World countries, so responsibility for the National Commission was transferred from the Department of Education to the Ministry of Overseas Development (which for most of my time had been demoted to being the Overseas Development Administration of the Foreign and Commonwealth Office). Secondly it was decided that the actual Commission, as a distinct and sizeable body of men and women, was really superfluous, and it was replaced by a "Coordinating Council" consisting of no more than the responsible Minister and the chairmen of five Advisory Committees.

It took me some time to get the hang of what the Culture Advisory Committee was meant to be doing. Since 1965 its chairman had been Lord Goodman, then approaching the peak of his public career. Among other things he was Chairman of the Arts Council, and it was to their splendid offices in Piccadilly that he liked to summon members of the Committee — thus involving its secretaries in a trek across Green Park from their offices in Victoria. Goodman seemed always to be short of time and tended to give the impression that, as he had already consulted with the secretariat, he already knew what the Committee should decide. So, whenever I tried to make a point or to ask a question, he almost invariably seemed to me to brush my intervention aside as something of little account. But in due course Goodman moved on, and Sir Misha Black, the distinguished architect and designer, once co-ordinating architect for the 1951 South Bank Exhibition, was appointed in his place. In 1976 I became Vice-Chairman to Black and, when in the following year he died, I was appointed Chairman myself. It was with Black and with the civil servants in the United Nations department of the O.D.A. (who had hitherto for me been no more than rather remote figures) that I began to get some idea of our role as an arm of the U.K. National Commission.

In general terms we were meant to keep an eye on what the U.K.'s writers, publishers, musicians, artists, actors, filmmakers, museum directors and so forth were doing and, more pertinently, what they might want UNESCO to do for them and their kind, and to try to help them to get it. This was not very onerous; all such people had national associations, usually affiliated to international organisations recognised by UNESCO, which could well look after their own interests. More importantly, it was our job to know what UNESCO was doing or planned to do in the cultural sphere, to judge whether it seemed sensible and might provide value for the money expended on it, and to express appropriate opinions to the United Nations department of the O.D.A. If these opinions were deemed by the O.D.A. or higher authority to fit in with the U.K. national interest, they might then be passed on to the headquarters of UNESCO in Paris, either directly to its officers or, perhaps more commonly, to the small U.K. Permanent Delegation at the UNESCO headquarters. In Paris it would be discussed with UNESCO officers and with other nations' delegations and friendly members of UNESCO's Executive Board, and ultimately perhaps become part of the briefing for the U.K. representatives at the next UNESCO General Conference. In the last resort, all UNESCO's policies were subject to decisions taken, usually by negotiated consensus rather than by a vote, by the 160 or so member nations of UNESCO at its General Conferences. These met for several weeks every other year, usually in Paris but occasionally in some national capital, and it was examination of the cultural section of the thick telephone directory size bi-annual books in which UNESCO's two-year programmes and budgets were set out that provided the main business for meetings of our Culture Advisory Committee in London in the months prior to a General Conference. Since what was in these books was an amalgam of what UNESCO officers and advisers wanted to do and what they thought a majority of the representatives of the member nations wanted to do, or at least were unwilling to object to, once it had been set down in print it became virtually impossible to alter. So if we in the Culture Advisory Committee took serious objection to something that UNESCO planned for the next biennium, or wished UNESCO to embark

on something new or different, and these things were accepted in the Overseas Development Administration, and, ultimately, by the British Government, and so appeared in what could be said by the U.K.'s representatives at a General Conference and in their discussions with UNESCO officials and with other nations' representatives, at least two years would elapse
before the first signs of any change would begin to be visible in UNESCO's
published programmes and budgets (and even longer, of course, before these
could begin to take effect on the ground).

What sort of people were the members of the U.K. National Commission who might seek to promote such Herculean labours? In my time as
Chairman of the Culture Advisory Committee, they were not as distinguished as they had been in the early days of the National Commission,
when its Chairman was a politician of Cabinet rank, and its rank and file
could include people like the Chairman of the British Council, scientists of
the stature of Lords Adrian and Blackett, a literary giant such as
J.B.Priestley, and a politician as distinguished as R.A.Butler. The nation
and the outside world could hardly fail to take notice of the views of such
people. I sense indeed a decline in my own time in the Culture Advisory
Committee: Misha Black was less of a public figure than Lord Goodman,
and when I followed Black my appointment must have been a reward for
long service and good attendance rather than because I had any standing
as a public figure. So far as the Culture Committee was concerned, the one
reminder of a more glorious past was that one of our members was Jacquetta
Hawkes, archaeologist and second wife to J.B.Priestley, who had in 1945-
49 actually been the first Secretary of the U.K. National Commission. I
cannot remember her contributing much to our discussions; no doubt she
was reflecting quietly to herself how dull and prosaic the Committee's work
had now become. Most of us were rather like me, career academics and
arts administrators. Among those who were fruitful contributors to our
discussions, I remember in particular Alan Bowness from the Tate Gallery,
John English from the Midland Arts Centre for Young People, Peter Lasko
from the Courtauld Institute, Malcolm Macleod from the Museum of Man-
kind, George Thompson from the Ulster Folk Museum, and James Noel
White, a leading light in the World Crafts Council. I found (and find) it
interesting and indicative that three much more public persons who had
been chosen for our Committee each came to no more than one or two of
its meetings and then vanished from sight: these were the novelist Margaret

Drabble, the philosopher Roger Scruton, and Roy Strong the polemical Director of the Victoria and Albert Museum. We also managed, less precipitately, to lose two M.P.s, the Conservative Patrick Cormack and the Labour Andrew Faulds, who had initially demonstrated genuine concern with what we were doing. I suspect that they may each have come to the conclusion that participation in the Committee was an activity of too little political moment. If so, they were doubtless right, as was illustrated by the fact that over the twelve years 1971-83, the chairmanship of the National Commission had changed hands six times. Only two of the politicians appointed to it, Judith Hart and Reg Prentice, ever achieved Cabinet rank, and only one, the last, Timothy Raison, to my knowledge demonstrated any deep understanding of the role of the Commission or of the United Kingdom in UNESCO.

Looking back on the meetings I attended, I think it would be fair to say that, prior to the early 1980s and the opening of the public debate as to whether the United Kingdom should withdraw from UNESCO (for which see pp.189-99), there was really only one issue which the Culture Advisory Committee had to deal with which was of some substantial public interest. This came up at the General Conference which I attended in Paris in 1978 when, following upon the report of a committee set up by the previous General Conference, it was formally proposed that there should be an international instrument under which a country which had lost some part of its "cultural property" to another country might claim its "return or restitution" by instituting action through a standing UNESCO inter-governmental committee.

In the event it was agreed at Paris in 1978 to go no further than to set up an advisory intergovernmental committee to help *promote* the return or restitution of cultural property to its country of origin. But the matter was (and still is) of importance to the United Kingdom because, of course, its wealthy and imperial past has meant that it and its citizens have acquired a great deal of cultural property – pictures, sculpture, manuscripts etc – created by people in other countries, and which these countries might think to be parts of their cultural heritage which they would like to have returned to them. The best known example in the United Kingdom, of course, and a matter of concern long before 1978, is the so-called Elgin marbles, which Greeks most certainly would like to see returned, if not to their original places on the frieze of the Parthenon, at least to a museum nearby.

170

In the circumstances of his time, Lord Elgin acquired the marbles "legally", since his action was covered by a licence he had received from the Ottoman Turkish authorities who then governed in Greece and, once the marbles had arrived in the British Museum, they became subject to British law which meant in effect that they could only be removed from the Museum by securing the passage of a specific Act of Parliament. If none of this legality means anything to modern Greeks whose ancestors fought to win their independence from the Turks and who still regard them as potential foes, it does perhaps place the Elgin marbles in a different category from, for example, the numerous brass or bronze cult objects and antiquities which were seized and removed from Benin by members of the British military expedition which captured and sacked that Nigerian city in 1897. Are the latter any different from the pictures and other objects which Nazi German military and political figures took from museums and private collections in occupied Europe during 1939-45? On the other hand, might there not be some cultural exports which should remain abroad to remind the outside world of the great cultural achievements of their creators?

The more the question of the return or restitution of cultural objects was discussed in the Cultural Advisory Committee, and the more we talked with those professionally concerned with it – such as the Director of the British Museum, David Wilson – the more complex and fraught with hazards it was seen to be. In the end we decided that we could not go beyond a few simple principles. In the first place, it would be morally wrong, and damaging to the international standing of our country, and particularly to its relations with its former colonies and with third world countries generally, if the U.K. maintained its original stance in the matter, which was little more than "what we have, we hold". On the other hand we could not see that setting up an international body with the aim of facilitating specific returns or restitutions would be a sensible course to follow. If it were much used, it could easily be submerged by problems of determining what was "legal" and what "illegal" and by masses of technical detail. Furthermore, it could not be expected that all countries would subscribe to the UNESCO instrument setting up the international body so that, if major "have" countries such as the United States and the United Kingdom (both of which in the event were shortly to withdraw from membership of UNESCO) stayed out, it would hardly be effective. Bilateral negotiations between dispossessed and possessing countries would be a much more sensible way of proceeding. Perhaps dispossessed countries might be given a right to embark publicly on such negotiations for the restitution of cultural objects removed as a result of military or other forcible action, especially perhaps if these objects were not adequately displayed and labelled for public exhibition in the possessing country, and if it could be demonstrated that they would be properly housed and displayed on return to their homeland.

The U.K. National Commission was not my only connection with UNESCO; I also became involved in the planning and production of the *General History of Africa* which UNESCO agreed to undertake following upon a Resolution of its 1964 General Conference. This Resolution was a consequence of the accession to UNESCO of the large number of new African states which secured their independence from colonial control from 1957 onwards. Their new rulers felt that Africa, more particularly perhaps Africa south of the Sahara, had too long been thought of by historians as the "dark continent", and that it was time that the history of its peoples and cultures received the same recognition as that of those of other continents. I think that I was first aware of what was afoot when in 1966 I received a telephone call from someone in the O.D.A. who asked me whether I could go to a first "meeting of experts" to consider what needed to be done to launch a UNESCO *General History of Africa*, and which was about to take place at Abidjan in the Côte d'Ivoire. But the notice was impossibly short for me, and in the end I think it was the Oxford colonial historian Colin Newbury who went from the U.K. to the Abidjan meeting. Following this and other preparatory meetings, UNESCO agreed to finance schemes for such things as the collection of oral traditions and the publication of an invaluable *Series of Guides to the Sources for the History of Africa* held in archives outside the continent, and then for the production and publication of an eight-volume *General History* in English, French and Arabic, with the possibility of continuing to other editions, sometimes abridged, in other languages, including major African languages such as KiSwahili and Hausa. Finally in 1971 an International Scientific Committee was set up to secure the writing and publication of this General History. I was one of those chosen for this Committee and appointed to it by UNESCO's Director-General.

The International Scientific Committee for the *General History of Africa* started life with thirty members, twenty of whom were Africans, five from northern Africa, eight from West Africa, four from East Africa and three from central and southern Africa. This uneven distribution reflected the uneven development of academic facilities across the continent and was a factor in the enlargement of the membership after 1975 to thirty-nine, with Africans again providing some two-thirds of the total. At our first meeting, we elected an Ethiopian, Dr Akilu Habte, as our President and, with two exceptions, we chose Africans to form our "Bureau", the inner cabinet of seven which kept a closer eye on the details of our business than was possible for a large committee which was not required to meet more than once in each UNESCO financial biennium. One of the exceptions was that, for the onerous duties of Rapporteur, it seemed sensible to choose Professor Jean Devisse who, as a Parisian, was in the best position to maintain close contact with our UNESCO Secretariat, amiably and efficiently led by Maurice Glele a native of the Republic of Benin. When we came to select editors for each of the eight volumes of the *General History*, once again we chose Africans, all but one from our own number. We chose four well-known professors of history from the relatively long-established university institutions of West Africa – Jacob Ajayi (from Nigeria), Adu Boahen (Ghana), Joseph Ki-Zerbo (Burkina Faso) and D.T.Niane (Senegal), and the equally well known Professor Bethwell Ogot (Kenya) from East Africa. From North Africa we chose Muhamad el Fasi, Rector of a Moroccan university, and Gabriel Mokhtar, Egypt's Director of Antiquities. The choice of a suitable editor for the volume dealing with the modern period since 1935 proved difficult, and was delayed until 1978, when it was agreed that we should go outside our own number, and we selected a Kenyan-born, but U.S.-based, political scientist, Ali Mazrui.

Having established the *General History*'s command structure, and it having been agreed that there would be funds sufficient for eight volumes each containing some thirty 8000-word chapters, the Committee then proceeded to set out the contents of each of the volumes and to debate who might be invited to contribute each of the chapters. But while the emphasis on Africans in the Committee's membership and in its upper echelons had abundantly demonstrated its intention to fulfil the mandate UNESCO had given it to view the history of Africa "from the inside... considering Africans as subjects and not merely objects of history", at this point things became more difficult. Whereas virtually all the non-African members of the Committee – including such illustrious names as Philip Curtin, Jan

Vansina and Ivan Hrbek (Czechoslovakia) – were professionals who had already made substantial contributions to the writing of African history, this was not the case, and could not be the case, with many of the Africans. Because so much of Africa had only recently been able to embark upon academic development, and was usually severely restricted in the funds it had available to spend on it, so many of its members of the Scientific Committee tended to have less the character of established historians than of national figureheads or of promising apprentice historians, the latter so burdened with teaching and administrative duties that they had relatively little time for research or writing. If this were the case in the Committee, so it followed that when it came to looking for candidates to write many of the chapters, it was often easier to see non-African than African possibilities. It was inevitable, therefore, that in the end rather less than sixty percent of the chapters of UNESCO's *General History of Africa* were written by African contributors.

So far as I was concerned, the most onerous part of the Committee's work was when, from about 1975 onwards, its members were involved in reviewing and assessing the draft chapters as they came in and were circulated for our comments. In theory each Committee member was meant to read and comment on the draft of each chapter, either in its English or its French version. In practice by this time only what I have called the "professional" members of the Committee were still taking a really active part in its deliberations, and by no means all of these were reading all that they were sent. Luckily, so far as I could see, we had very little that was unacceptable. I can remember one draft chapter, whose author was a Committee member, which many of his colleagues thought to be unacceptable on academic grounds. This occasioned much discussion, leading ultimately to a decision that it should be printed, but with a long following note of dissent. But this was unique; most criticisms that were made of draft chapters were relatively minor, and the volume editors were able to arrange to secure amendments without too much difficulty. What I found most worrying was the quality of the translations between the two languages English and French. These were made by professional translators employed, or hired, by UNESCO's translation bureau, and I do not doubt that they measured up to acceptable standards. But they seemed to know little about Africa and nothing of its history, with the result that they could easily misunderstand the English or French text they were required to translate, so that their version of it in the other language could well turn out to be in error or even incomprehensible. I eventually took to asking to see the drafts in both languages, and spent a good deal of time checking the translations. But I could foresee further, and worse, trouble when the time came to make translations into Arabic and other languages.

Many people have doubted whether any sensible work of history can ever result from planning by a committee, especially perhaps such a large UNESCO committee, with each member coming from a different country with its own particular cultural, academic and political heritage, and operating with the procedures and technical paraphernalia (such as simultaneous translation) of international conferences. In fact I think the Scientific Committee for the *General History of Africa* worked well. Its decisions were always the result of academic discussion, taken without flaunting nationalisms or dividing into ideological camps, and without ever really resorting to counting votes. In part this was because of the behind-the-scenes work done by its Bureau and of the hard work and diplomatic skills of the UNESCO secretariat. But it was also due to the fact that the members of the Committee, whatever their skills or their degree of professionalism, were all determined to make the best use of UNESCO's bounty to further the understanding of the history of Africa.

In my opinion the only significant weakness in the Committee's work was that it did not succeed in keeping up with the schedule, and so within the budget, that had been originally set for it. But I knew this was by no means to be unexpected of multi-volume, multi-author histories on this scale. I can say this with some authority because I was almost certainly the only member of UNESCO's Committee who had experience in the planning and execution of another eight- volume collaborative history. In 1966, the very year that UNESCO's "experts" first met at Abidjan, the Cambridge University Press had returned to Roland Oliver and me with the proposal, which we had earlier rejected (see p. 109, 124), that we should be the General Editors of a *Cambridge History of Africa*, and this time we accepted this charge. We thought that six years' experience with *The Journal of African History* had demonstrated that "the amount of work being undertaken to establish the past of Africa as an integrated whole rather than... as the story of a series of incursions into the continent by peoples coming from outside" now made it practicable to attempt a multi-volume collaborative Cambridge History in the tradition established at the beginning of the twentieth century by Lord Acton. Nevertheless Roland and I could see some problems ahead.

One was that it would not be easy to secure a balanced view of either the earliest or the latest period of Africa's past. In the first case, so much would depend on the results of on-going archaeological investigation, and in the latter we foresaw difficulty because of "the rapid changes in historical perspective that were occurring as a consequence of the ending of colonial rule". So in 1966-67 we decided initially not to plan the *Cambridge History* beyond c.1870, which we aimed to reach in five volumes, appearing at the rate of one a year, and we also decided that the archaeological Volume 1, "Africa to c.500 B.C." would be the last of the five to be published. We were also aware of the risk that dealing with a multiplicity of volume editors and contributors was a likely recipe for delay in the achievement of our task, and this we wanted to avoid so far as possible. (I was certainly mindful that the last volume of the eight volumes of the *Cambridge History of the British Empire* had not appeared until thirty years after the first, and only after all three of its original General Editors had died!) We therefore decided that the number of contributors to each volume should be kept to a minimum, each being asked "to essay a broad survey of a particular area or theme with which he was familiar for the whole of the period covered by the volume". Thus whereas a UNESCO volume would have as many as thirty chapters each of about 8000 words, a Cambridge volume of much the same size would have no more than nine to fifteen chapters, each usually of something like 20-25,000 words. This would make it easier to select contributors well known to the editors, and not least for their known reliability in producing acceptable work on time. Similar criteria guided our choice of volume editors. Richard Gray (Volume 4) and John Flint (Volume 5) were English near-contemporaries of ours with whom we had worked for many years; we chose ourselves to edit Volumes 2 (Fage) and 3 (Oliver); and we were lucky enough to secure Desmond Clark, whose African excavations and gift of clear exposition we had long admired, to take on the editorship of the archaeologically-based Volume 1. Then when our enterprise seemed to be going well enough, and we thought that sufficient sound work was being published on the post-1870 period, we followed much the same principles in selecting volume editors for three further volumes to cover the period from the European scramble for, and partition of, Africa to the continent's recovery of independence. Volume 7 was given to Andrew Roberts, a younger colleague of Roland's at S.O.A.S. (and eventually to succeed him in the Chair of African History there), while for Volume 8 we were able to secure Michael Crowder, author or editor of many admirable books of African history, particularly in the modern period. It was only with Volume 6, dealing with the vexed and tortuous subjects of the scramble and partition, that we ran into difficulty, with Roland having to come in to reinforce our original choice as editor of Neville Sanderson, another of our friends and contemporaries.

Despite all our precautions, however, it must be confessed that Roland and I did not keep to the publication schedule for which we had originally hoped. The first Cambridge volume to be published did not appear until 1975, which was later than we had expected and, though during 1975-78 we did keep up the planned rate of a volume a year, Desmond Clark required more time than we had allowed for to prepare Volume 1, which did not appear until 1982. There was then a gap of our own making before the last three volumes began to appear, but we did then succeed in getting these out at the rate of one a year during 1984-86. Nevertheless I think the Fage and Oliver team of two did have a better record than UNESCO's large Committee, which began work in 1971, and did not publish its first two volumes until ten years later, in 1981, and its final volume until as late as 1993.

I do not think that readers who choose to make use of one of these vast histories will get a picture of the African past very different from those who choose to work with the other. There is no great difference between their two plans except that half of UNESCO's Volume 1 is devoted to general discussions of methods and sources. As a result, its first five volumes each cover an earlier, and a longer, period than the Cambridge volume bearing the same number, and the UNESCO *History* gives less space to the nineteenth and twentieth centuries than does the Cambridge *History*. However I think that the much greater number of authors in the UNESCO *History* does mean that it is more uneven; its many excellent chapters seem to me to be counterweighted by as many which have some weakness. But if the Cambridge *History* maintains a more even standard, it is at the price of being open to the criticism that it is very much in an Anglo-American tradition: only about fifteen percent of its chapters are the work of African scholars or of men and women with white skins who did not graduate from British or North American universities, and only about ten percent of the contributions needed to be translated from a language other than English. (However I am glad to say that all the translations were made by Africanist historians rather than by narrowly professional translators!) But for those who want to follow up their reading in one of these multi-volume histories by looking at the specialist works consulted by their contributors, I think the Cambridge *History* is much to be preferred. Each of its chapters is supported and enhanced by a bibliographical essay contributed by its author, and the actual bibliographies (mostly edited by Marion Johnson) are meticulously done, while those in the UNESCO *History* are no more than long unchecked lists of titles. On the other hand, the UNESCO *History* is usefully illustrated by numerous plates, whereas its Cambridge counterpart has no illustrations other than maps and some line drawings to illustrate archaeological evidence. Because UNESCO has subsidised the publication of its *History*, its volumes are also much cheaper to buy; thus of volumes that appeared in 1981-82, one from UNESCO was marketed at £13.50 while one from Cambridge cost £48.00.

An unexpected bonus which I can only suppose to have been a by-product of the activities touched on in this and the preceding chapter was that my name must have got on a list of appropriate persons who might be invited to official lunches and dinners when African dignitaries were visiting the United Kingdom. Jean and I first went to dinner at 10 Downing Street in 1969 when Harold Wilson was entertaining Hamani Diori of Mali. Three years later we returned when Edward Heath was welcoming Léopold Senghor from Senegal, an occasion embroidered with music – madrigals commissioned by our host while we were eating, and after coffee a *kora* ensemble commissioned by the guest of honour. Then in 1979 there was an invitation from Margaret Thatcher to lunch when the visitor was President Tolbert of Liberia. I had met Mrs Thatcher before; she was our M.P. when Jean and I were living in Hampstead Garden Suburb, and a neighbour and I had been to tell her of objections to a road widening scheme; and I was later to see more of Mr Heath when I took the chair at a meeting at Birmingham University at which he lectured on the Brand Report on the plight of developing countries. On the basis of this slender evidence, I would say that Mrs Thatcher was much more on the ball than either Heath or Wilson, both of whom seemed to me to be unable to engage in polite chatter with their guests; I can remember Wilson wandering speechlessly around the reception he was giving as though he did not know what it was about. But maybe these two were unusual prime ministers, because when we came across Lord Home on one or other of these Downing Street occasions, we thought he was delightfully easy to chat with.

There were parallel occasions outside Downing Street, for example a grand lunch at the Mansion House during the visit of President Limann of Ghana in 1981, or more informal occasions when the visitor was not a head of state, as when the Lord Privy Seal, Sir Ian Gilmour, was lunching a Ghanaian visitor whose family had provided me with one of my students when I was at Legon. But the pinnacle of our politico-social high life was on 28 October 1970, when Jean and I found ourselves among the twenty guests invited by Her Majesty the Queen to luncheon at Buckingham Palace in honour of President Bongo of Gabon. The highlight of the occasion came when, relaxing after the departure of Bongo and his suite, the Queen entertained her British guests by showing us and chatting about the gifts which the President had given her. This was followed by a large anticlimax when Jean and I, having said goodbye to Her Majesty, and having been escorted by a Private Secretary down the great staircase to her front door, realised that – unlike the other guests, who had their cars to pick them up – we, who had arrived by taxi, were faced with making a public exit on foot across the wide expanse of the Palace forecourt before we could regain the life of ordinary mortals. We were greatly relieved when a fellow guest, Sir David Barran (then the Chairman of Shell), offered us a lift in his Rolls Royce, and delivered us in state to Jean's sister's doorstep in nearby Pimlico.

I think of the first eight years of the 1970s as a golden period in the history of the Centre of West African Studies at Birmingham. We were not then giving much attention to work with undergraduates, but we had about as many postgraduate students as we could comfortably handle. We regularly had a class of twenty or so taking the twelve-month courses for Master's Degrees, and there would be as many or more postgraduates working for their higher degrees, usually Ph.D.s, by research. By and large about half our postgraduate students were British and somewhat less than half were Africans; there were usually also two or three from North America and there was the occasional student from Asia or mainland Europe. I would say that their standard was never less than competent; certainly I do not recall any one who did not secure the degree at which he or she was aiming. Their quality may be somewhat more objectively measured if I say that two thirds of the British postgraduates had competed successfully for awards from the Social Science Research Council or the Department of Education and Science, while about three quarters of the Africans were supported by awards from their home governments or universities, or from the British Council.

Not a few of our graduate students went on to successful academic careers. I can remember the historians more easily than the economists, geographers, political scientists, and the sociologists and anthropologists (but then half of our postgraduate students were historians and economic historians). I find it interesting that some of the most successful and productive of the European students, Robin Law (who was to become Professor of History at the University of Stirling), Robin Cohen (Professor of Sociology at Warwick), Finn Fuglestad (Professor of History at Oslo), and Adam Jones (Professor of History at Leipzig), had spent one or two years teaching or researching in Africa before settling to work for their Birmingham Ph.D.s, the two Robins in Nigeria, the Norwegian Finn in French Niger, and Adam with V.S.O. in Sierra Leone. I have particular reasons for remembering some of those who had chosen to come from further afield in search of higher degrees at C.W.A.S. Among these were four West Africans who were somewhat unusual among their kind in that they arrived knowing exactly what research they wanted to do. Two of these were Nigerians, E.A.Oroge, a comparatively elderly man who had conceived a passionate desire to study slavery in nineteenth century Yorubaland, and Mahdi Adamu, a younger man very determined to assess the important transnational role of his own Hausa people in West African history. Arthur Abraham, from Sierra Leone, worked on the politics of his own Mende people in the early colonial period, while Abdoulaye Bathily, our first student from Francophone West Africa, ventured to explore the many-sided competition for trade and power in the upper Senegal valley in the nineteenth century. All these went on to successful careers in West African universities – Adamu going as far as to become a Vice-Chancellor. But in many respects the most remarkable non-Briton to be so obsessed by African history as to conceive the idea of going to Birmingham to work for a Ph.D. in it was an Indian, Jyoti Pal Chaudhuri. His first African venture was to go to teach in a school in Ethiopia, and it was from there that he applied to do postgraduate work at C.W.A.S. I could not see how this would be possible, since no one would offer funds in aid of a student with such an eccentric pedigree who also had a wife and child to support. But he told us that he and his wife would finance themselves by securing teaching posts in Birmingham schools. *Mirabile dictu*, this is exactly what they did while he worked part-time for some years on a thesis on British policy towards Liberia during 1912-39. He followed this up by a spell as a professor in Liberia, and then returned to his homeland, where he must have become the only internationally-known authority on Liberian history employed by an Indian university.

During 1970-1976, the Centre's strength in postgraduate research was matched by its ability to use its own funds to support two three-year research fellowships. Here too we secured some excellent recruits (Cohen and Law were the first two). Their quality was such that only one of them lasted for the whole of their possible three years; all the others were enticed away after one or two years to tenured lectureships at other universities or in other departments in the University of Birmingham.

However while C.W.A.S. was flourishing, the university scene in the United Kingdom was beginning seriously to change. So far as the University of Birmingham is concerned, I am inclined, instinctively if unfairly, to date the beginning of this change from the retirement in 1965 of Sir Robert Aitken as our Vice-Chancellor and the arrival in his place of Robert Brockie Hunter, for twenty years Professor of Materia Medica at the Universities of St Andrews and Dundee. To my mind, the change resembled the replacement of Balme by Stoughton as Principal of the University College of the Gold Coast. I think of Aitken as a great Vice-Chancellor, whose wealth of imaginative ideas for the development of his university more than compensated for the authoritarian ways in which they were sometimes implemented. (His summary announcement to Senate in 1963 that the work required of a Vice-Chancellor had now become so great that he had appointed a full-time Deputy Principal is an example of this.) Hunter struck me as a less lively man who, although anxious to do well for his university and to be on good terms with his staff and students, often – although always well-intentioned – had rather little idea of how to set about achieving these ends. So far as I could see, just as I supposed that Stoughton's main qualification for university management had been seen to be his experience on the Inter-University Council, Hunter's must have been his four-year term as a member of the University Grants Committee. But this could not provide him with experience in dealing with university staff and students beyond that which he had already acquired in the rather specific circumstances of faculties of medicine in Scottish universities. It should however be said that, whereas Aitken had worked in an environment in which he could be sure that a university's income would steadily increase from one year to the next, so that if he did make a mistake, it could soon be buried, Hunter reigned as vice-chancellor in much more difficult times in which the money available for universities began in real terms steadily to decline. I should also say that in his dealings with me he was always, in his somewhat pawky way, kind and understanding, and it may be that other people may well have thought better of his abilities than I did. Thus in the year immediately following the award to him of the knighthood which Birmingham Vice-Chancellors could ordinarily expect, he was quite exceptionally the recipient of a life peerage. To this it must be added that, within a few weeks of his arrival, Hunter had the enormous misfortune to be faced with something which hitherto had been quite outside the experience of British vice-chancellors: a student occupation of his university's Great Hall and central administrative offices.

The Birmingham University student "sit-in" was nothing like as bad as it seemed to us at the time. It had little or nothing of the violence that was apparent more or less contemporaneously in Paris or in some United States universities or, to a lesser extent, in some other universities elsewhere in Europe or the United Kingdom. There is indeed some evidence that at least some of the rougher edges of what happened in Birmingham came in from elsewhere, perhaps in particular from the London School of Economics. However the sit-in's origins were essentially internal; they lay with the adoption by the Guild of Students at the beginning of 1968 of a well-argued report asking for the institution of staff/student liaison committees in all teaching departments, and recommending a degree of student representation in most of the University's decision-making bodies. By the beginning of the autumn term, virtually all the Guild of Students' report had been accepted in principle by the University's Council and Senate and their committees. The institution of departmental staff/student committees involved no more than the fiat of the University Registrar, and this was issued in June. But implementation of the other recommendations was not as simple because they raised wider issues. The governmental structure of the university was far from democratic. In academic affairs, under the Vice-Chancellor, power rested with the professors, who occupied all the seats in Senate except the three allocated to elected representatives of the non-professorial academic staff. In non-academic matters, the governing authority was the University Council, in which even professors were not present: the majority of its members were laymen, the only academics there beside the Vice-Chancellor and his deputy, the Vice-Principal, were the Deans of the five faculties and a single representative of the non-professorial staff. So, if it were right that students were to have some voice in the conduct of university business, it was probably even more right that the non-professorial staff should have a greater voice. The whole constitution of the University – which derived from days when the total number of students was measured in hundreds rather than in thousands, and when a department might consist of no more than a professor, his assistant and a dozen or so students – needed a thorough overhaul, so that ultimately an approach would have to be made to the Queen's Privy Council for the amendment of the University's Royal Charter and Statutes.

These things would take time, very likely more time than the three years that the average student spent at the university. So all of a sudden the university authorities found themselves facing a situation reminiscent of that facing the colonial government when Jean and I had arrived in the Gold Coast twenty years earlier. At the end of October the Council of the Guild of Students decided that if the University had not agreed by the end of the following month to implement its proposals *in toto*, it would embark on "direct action", and on 28 November there began the occupation of the University's Great Hall and administrative offices. Following this and a succession of mass meetings, the Guild Council began to lose control to a radical *ad hoc* "Committee of Ten". This led to a reaction among more conservative students, so that on 4 December officers of the Guild embarked on informal talks with senior members and officers of the University. These led on the following day to a mass meeting of some 4000 students at which it was agreed that the sit-in should be ended in return for a promise that no disciplinary action would be taken against students simply for opinions expressed during the sit-in, and to a meeting of Senate to which the Guild President and two of his colleagues were invited to discuss the way forward. I remember this meeting mainly because Hunter, in the chair, appeared to find it difficult to understand much of what the President said, so that his Deputy Principal and the Dean of Arts began to act more or less as interpreters. A kind of counterpoint developed, with Hunter saying things to the student President like "Are you really supposing such and such...?", and the Dean or Deputy Principal coming in to say things like "No, Vice-Chancellor, what the President actually said (*or perhaps*, What the President meant) was so and so..." In the end each side seemed prepared to believe that it did understand the other, and it was agreed that the University should return to conventional behaviour.

After Christmas, student representatives and increased numbers of non-professorial staff were brought in to attend – if not as yet with the right to vote at – meetings of Council and Senate and most of their committees, and there began numerous discussions in all committees and at all levels about the future structure of the University. In January 1971 these culminated in the appointment by Council of an eleven-member "Review Body" charged with looking at the whole constitution and functioning of the University and making recommendations for its future. The membership of the Review Body was cunningly devised to provide balances between academic and lay, Birmingham and external, arts and science, young and old. It was chaired by the distinguished Liberal politician Joe Grimond, and its other members included Dorothy Hodgkin, Nobel Prize winner and holder of the Order of Merit (and wife to Thomas Hodgkin), and Sir Peter Venables, the recently retired founding Vice-Chancellor of Birmingham's new second university at Aston; its secretary was an eminent retired civil servant, Sir Maurice Dean. They laboured for twenty months, considering seventy-three submissions of evidence from individuals and from corporate bodies within and without the University, and publishing a consultative document which occasioned an even larger number of comments. Finally in September 1972 they produced a *Report* which in the following year became the basis for a petition to the Privy Council seeking changes in the University's Charter and Statutes. It was not until the academic year 1975-76 that the new University constitution was in full operation. Increased representation for students and non-professorial staff in the governing bodies of the University was by no means the only important change, but so far as this was concerned the general principle adopted can be seen from the new distribution of places in the Senate. Here only such officers as the Vice-Chancellor, the Registrar and the Deans remained as members by right; all the others were elective, the professors choosing seventy of their number to represent them, the non-professorial staff electing fifty representatives and students electing twenty representatives. Much the same proportions were employed for most other representative bodies. The irony of this was that, seven years after the "sit-in", many – perhaps most – students did not appear all that interested in the fruits of their victory; sometimes indeed not enough of them would come forward for election to all the representative places allotted to them.

I was not particularly active in these goings on. I did submit a paper to the Review Body, in which I suggested that the University of Birmingham might move to a completely different kind of constitution from the somewhat authoritarian model which it and other "Redbrick" universities had received at birth. I sketched out something more like the constitution of the collegiate Oxbridge universities, which I thought had the advantage of giving more power to ordinary dons (if not to students), and less to Vice-Chancellors and their acolytes. But when I was orally examined on my submission, I did not feel that I was making a very good case, and I began to think that perhaps I had been doing no more than longing for a romantic past which may never have actually existed. Doubtless this is what my inquisitors thought: certainly the subsequent development of British universities has made it clear enough that I was trying to swim against a strengthening current running in the opposite direction. But if I had little effect on what was going on, in one particular it certainly had an effect on me.

This came about because in 1966, Jack Plumb, then on the point of becoming Professor of Modern English History at Cambridge, had invited me to contribute a 120,000 word volume on Africa to the "History of Human Society" series which he had recently begun to edit and which was being published in some style by Hutchinson in London and Knopf in New York. I did not think this would be an easy task. I would have to enter in some depth into parts of African history for which, in *A Short History of Africa*, my co-author Roland Oliver had taken prime responsibility with his especial knowledge, or which, in a book of only 70,000 words, the pair of us had been able to pass over relatively lightly and which in a longer work would require considerable exploration of slender and difficult data. For these reasons I thought I was likely to have a more difficult assignment than that which had faced, or which might face, some of the other authors in Plumb's series. Quite a few of these were personally known to me: John Parry had been invited to write on the Spanish seaborne empire, Charles Boxer on both the Dutch and the Portuguese seaborne empires, Jacquetta Hawkes on "the first great civilisations", and Donald Dudley (Professor of Latin at Birmingham) on the Romans. They seemed a goodly company to join and, since I now had behind me the experience and knowledge I had gained through editing volumes of *The Cambridge History of Africa*, and since Plumb did not expect to see a typescript before 1970, I thought it might be feasible to attempt what I came to call "a discursive account" of the whole of the African past from the appearance of *homo sapiens* onwards.

Since my arrival in Birmingham I had been regularly providing an outline course of lectures on the history of Africa for first year students, and I hoped to use this as some sort of guide to what I would have to write. But I soon discovered that my lecture notes were far from providing a sure foundation on which a polished literary work could be constructed. When the end of 1970 was upon me, the best I could tell Plumb was that I was "learning all the time", that while I had a complete outline I had no more than about 70,000 words of draft text, and that with any luck he might hope to receive what he had commissioned no later than about the end of 1971. In fact by the middle of that year, out of seventeen planned chapters, no more than seven or eight existed in drafts, which had been shown to colleagues for their comments as well as to Plumb. At the end of November 1972, I could see no alternative but to write to Plumb in these terms:

> My delay must be infuriating to you, and I can only apologise for it. But 1971-72 was a pretty disastrous year as far as my writing was concerned. This University is conducting a wholesale review of its government and organisation. This is disturbing enough generally. But one of the ideas that has come up in the course of this involved changes in the organisation and mode of operation of this Centre of West African Studies, which I and my colleagues regarded as quite impossible. A great deal of time and energy has had to go in combating these, with very unfortunate results as far as any writing of mine is concerned. We are not out of the wood yet by any means, but there are now signs that things may be satisfactorily settled by the end of this term. My intention is then to complete my book for you by about June or July [1973].

It was doubtless inevitable that those responsible for a new look at, and a general tidying-up of, the way the University operated would question whether it was sensible and right that C.W.A.S. and its sister Centre of Russian and East European Studies should operate outside, and be financed separately from, the established Faculty groupings of departments. The individuals involved in the exercise had not been involved in the discussions which had occasioned the two Centres' extra-faculty status when they had been conceived, and the two Directors and their colleagues found it very wearing to have to rehearse the arguments for this status over and over again at various stages of the constitutional reform process. However in the end the University proved willing to accept that it had not been foolish ten years before, in 1962-63, when it had decided that the best way to handle multi-disciplinary area studies centres was to place them outside the discipline-based faculties. It was not until after my retirement, and in part as a consequence of a reform which I had helped initiate, to give departments or groups of departments greater financial independence, that the two area studies centres were each placed within a Faculty.

In the end a complete text of my *A History of Africa* did not reach Plumb until early in 1975. It is, I think, a substantially different kind of history from those other volumes in "The History of Human Society" series that are known to me, and Plumb criticised what I had given him as having too much narrative detail, and not enough of the real social meat of Africa's human history. I was not surprised by this, and indeed made changes at specific points to meet some of his criticisms. Nevertheless I also maintained that, with the enormous mass and variety of humanity contained within Africa, and with so much of the history of the continent having been so little studied, I was obliged to establish much "rather tiresome narrative" before I could "begin to see what the 'history of human society' in Africa really was". With so large and varied a canvas, if I did not set the details out as correctly as I could, it would be too easy to perceive, and to try and interpret, social patterns which might not accord with reality.[1] Luckily Plumb seemed willing to be convinced by this line of reasoning.

However, the narrative and the detail that I thought necessary for a subject as big and diffuse as mine also meant that my book turned out to be appreciably longer than other books in the series, nearer 500 pages than their 300 or 400 pages. I think this length helps to explain why, after all the pressure on me to finish the book as soon as possible, it was not until 1977 that Hutchinson and Knopf began to prepare it for publication. The "History of Human Society" had been intended for the general reader rather than the student, and its books had been beautifully printed on good quality paper, nicely bound and provided with good illustrations. As a result, by the mid 1970s, the series was becoming rather uneconomic, and the advent of my bumper length book seems to have stimulated a rethinking that led eventually to a decision to transfer the series to the educational side of the publishers' business, and to produce its books in a somewhat less expensive format. This must have paid off, because I think mine is the only volume in the series which is still in print (and, indeed, now exists in a third, revised and enlarged edition).[2]

But by 1978, the year in which my *A History of Africa* finally appeared, it was already something of a luxury to have been allowed ten years in which to write it; the real world was becoming increasingly reluctant to fund any kind of academic venture which was not quickly remunerative. This may perhaps be illustrated by what happened in the 1970s and early 1980s to my two major extramural interests, the International African Institute and the U.K. National Commission for UNESCO.

The creator of the postwar International African Institute, Daryll Forde, died in 1973. This was some years after his retirement from his chair at

University College, and he had stayed on as Director of the I.A.I., a tired and increasingly disillusioned man, essentially because no one could see how to replace him. It was becoming less and less easy to secure funds to maintain the kind of activities he had so brilliantly promoted; European governments no longer had colonial offices which might subsidise the I.A.I., and the American foundations had become less interested in African research than they had been. The rents that were now being required for offices in central London were becoming prohibitive; it was no longer feasible to maintain the Institute's excellent library – it was sold for a pittance to the University of Manchester. But with Daryll gone, something had to be done, and in a young man from the School of Oriental and African Studies we thought we might have discovered someone possessing initiative and enterprise in devising new programmes in African research and publication comparable to those which were characteristic of Daryll in his younger days. We offered him, and he accepted, a five-year contract as Director. But, perhaps not surprisingly, he did not have Daryll's remarkable talent for understanding and dealing with people, and this was a serious handicap in times when adequate funding was not easily come by. So in 1980 it had to be accepted that the I.A.I. could no longer continue in the style and at the levels established by Daryll Forde, and those who like myself had grown up in his shadow quietly faded from the scene.

The U.K. National Commission for UNESCO, and my role in it, continued very much in the manner described in the previous chapter until the end of 1983, when the United States gave twelve months' notice of its intention to withdraw from UNESCO. The formal letter which gave this notice was not very precise in explaining why the U.S. wanted to withdraw, though it did indicate that the reasons were largely political. In this context, much attention was necessarily given to the highly critical report on "the management, budgeting and personnel practices" of UNESCO, which was published at much the same time by the U.S. Government's General Accounting Office. This body was by no means alone in criticising UNESCO; it would, for example, be a rare member of the U.K. National Commission who, from experience, had not been at some time or other critical of some aspects of UNESCO's activities and policies, and especially perhaps of the cumbersome and far from straightforward way in which this large international bureaucracy commonly found it necessary to conduct these. Those closely concerned with UNESCO in the U.K. could

189

therefore agree that the institution spent too much of its money in over-centralised and not very efficient bureaucratic administration at the expense of practical actions in the field which would be of benefit to the poorer peoples of the world. Therefore at the very time that the G.A.O. Report was published and the United States was giving its notice of withdrawal, the Chairman of the U.K. National Commission, Timothy Raison, Minister for Overseas Development, was taking the unusual step of bringing all the members of the Commission's Advisory Committees together to discuss the worth of UNESCO, not only to the United Kingdom, but also to the third world and, indeed, to humanity in general. The effect of the criticisms and proposed action from across the Atlantic was both to widen, and to raise the temperature of the discussion in the U.K.

This was done mainly, I think, by drawing attention to political criticisms that could be made of UNESCO. These arose especially because, whereas UNESCO had started life as a club for the wealthy victor nations of the Second World War, it had grown into a worldwide body, most of whose members were third and second world countries prone to be jealous and suspicious of the great material power of the developed nations and their near monopoly of the world's modern communications. This majority had therefore secured the establishment of a number of UNESCO programmes which sought to redress the balance by means which many Americans might deem "communist" or "communist inspired", thus turning UNESCO into a "threat to the free world". I would be surprised, however, if even as many as half a dozen of the hundred or so members of the U.K. National Commission who attended Mr Raison's meeting in December 1983 thought in anything like such terms. Britons concerned with UNESCO were aware that the politically questionable parts of UNESCO's programme were a very small part of the whole; thus for the two years 1984 and 1985, they were costed at something less than $26 million out of a total regular budget of over $400 million. Nor was it easy to see why the departure of the U.K. from UNESCO would help cure its ills. The withdrawal of the United States, which was responsible for 25 per cent of UNESCO's regular budget, was bound to have some effect (even if the U.S. was usually behindhand with its contributions), but the U.K.'s 4.6 percent contribution was not all that significant.

Led by short speeches from the chairmen of the Commission's Advisory Comittees, Raison's meeting in December 1983 had no difficulty in arriving at the general conclusions that, despite its faults, UNESCO had a beneficial role to play in the world in general and the third world in particular; that – not least perhaps because English was a world language – it was of value to the U.K. in helping disseminate British ideas and interests; and that the proper course for the U.K. was to stay in UNESCO and seek to reform it from within. I think that Raison's own opinions were much the same, and he undertook to write to UNESCO's Director-General setting out proposals for the reform of his institution based on the experience of the U.K. and its National Commission. At the time, Raison's colleagues in Mrs Thatcher's Conservative government do not seem to have raised objections to what he and the National Commission were up to, for towards the end of March 1984 the Chairmen of the Advisory Committees were shown the draft of a letter to the Director-General which was sent off, with only minor amendments, on 2 April. It was a very good letter, which began by emphasising that the U.K. remained "firmly committed to the ideals and principles" of UNESCO, but which continued "with particular regret" to say that "the government and people of the U.K. felt unease about the political aspects of certain programmes" and, "above all" questioned "whether many of UNESCO's programmes represent good value for money" especially in the task of "assisting the developing countries to find solutions to their problems in education, science and culture..." Raison went on to say that he "and his Ministerial colleagues" had decided that "the United Kingdom should remain a member of UNESCO for the time being, but that we should intensify our efforts to achieve the radical improvements in UNESCO's programmes and procedures we believe to be needed..." Raison hoped to see "significant indications of change" by the end of 1984 when, he said, he had told Parliament the U.K. would again review its position. Raison attached to his letter "a paper setting out in broad terms those areas in which we believe that ... changes are necessary".

Raison's letter was shown in advance to the permanent representatives of other western nations at the UNESCO headquarters in Paris, and was favourably received by them, and by the time of the next meeting of the UNESCO Executive Board in May the Director-General had already set up a number of "working groups to strengthen and improve" the functioning of the institution. The Executive Board itself responded directly to Raison's letter by setting up an ad hoc committee to make recommendations on the matters it had raised directly to the next General Conference, due at Sofia at the end of 1985. For the October 1984 Executive Board, the U.K. National Commission took the unusual step of sending each of its Advisory Committee chairman for a few days to Paris to reinforce its regular team. I returned from my brief visit with the definite impression that most national representatives were impressed by the U.K.'s initiative, and that many were saying that it was high time that action was taken of the kind Raison had suggested. On the other hand, I had seen that when the representative of the United States had got up to speak, no one seemed the slight bit interested in whatever it was she wanted to say. It seemed clear enough to me that if reform were to come to UNESCO, it was not going to come in response to criticism from without.

At the beginning of November 1984 there was a second general meeting of the whole National Commission chaired by the Minister to listen to what the Advisory Committee chairmen might want to say after their Paris visits, and to see what general advice the Commission might want to give to the Minister. Here I remember saying that it seemed to me that there was evidence that changes were taking place in UNESCO and its mode of operation in directions for which the U.K. had been arguing for some time even before Raison's letter of 2 April; that it would probably take at least two years before the effects of these changes could begin to be apparent; that an increasing number of member states were listening to and supporting the U.K.; and therefore that it would be wrong for the U.K. to follow the American example and to give notice of withdrawal from UNESCO. We should stay to keep up the pressure for reform, and remain a member of UNESCO at least as long as was necessary to see whether the changes which were being made largely at our instigation were going to be effective in practice. Few members of the Commission (and I think none of the other Advisory Committee chairmen) spoke in a contrary sense, and at the end of the meeting it was agreed, first, that a substantial majority thought that the U.K. should continue pressure to achieve the necessary reform of UNESCO *from within the organisation* and, secondly, I think on Raison's proposal, that there would be a further assessment by the National Commission of the desirability of the U.K.'s continued membership of UNESCO in the light of the results of the 1985 General Conference at Sofia.

However, by the time Raison was writing his letter to the Director-General, it became apparent that there was a growing hostility in British Conservative circles to the U.K.'s continued membership of UNESCO. As early as February, this led me to join a small group to combat this which was being organised by Peter Williams, Professor of Education in Developing Countries at London University's Institute of Education. Among the other members of the group was Richard Hoggart who, between his professorship at Birmingham and being the Warden of Goldsmiths' College, had spent five years as an Assistant Director-General at UNESCO, which meant that he was as well equipped as anyone to know about the faults of UNESCO as well as of its importance and value in international affairs.

I think the anti-UNESCO movement in the U.K. arose from the conjunction of influences from two directions. One was the inherent Conservative desire to keep a check on public spending, and here overseas aid – which had come to be thought a principal justification for U.K. membership of UNESCO – was especially vulnerable, because it seemed such a never-ending drain on U.K. resources. In addition to this, there were also influences from the United States. There was certainly active public anti-UNESCO propaganda from bodies like the Heritage Foundation. But I suspect too that, behind the scenes, Mrs Thatcher and her senior colleagues, remembering how supportive of the U.K. the United States had been at the time of the Falklands war, thought it politic to rescue President Reagan's administration from the self-imposed isolation of their country's withdrawal from UNESCO. The anti-UNESCO party went public on 5 November when, on the morning before the meeting of the National Commission and on the eve of a House of Commons debate on overseas aid on which it was likely that the future of the U.K.'s membership of UNESCO would be debated, *The Times* had a substantial leader entitled "Withdraw and Reflect". In this Britain's withdrawal from UNESCO was urged on the specious argument that if the U.K. joined with the United States, UNESCO would be seen to be an unrepresentative international institution, while if the U.K. stayed in UNESCO, even when urging radical reform, it would be thought to be condoning inefficiency and corruption. This leader was the signal for a considerable campaign of letters to the press and of lobbying of politicians and other persons of standing. My own contributions included two letters published in *The Times* and one in *The Guardian*, and letters to the President of the British Academy, Owen Chadwick, O.M., and Francis Pym, M.P., who until 1983 had been a senior member of Mrs Thatcher's cabinet (these two were known to me from my days at Tonbridge and Magdalene respectively). I also wrote to the Foreign Secretary, Sir Geoffrey Howe. All this was of no avail. In his speech in the Overseas Aid debate in the House of Commons on 22 November, Howe said that the end-of-year review of what had been done towards reforming UNESCO, following upon Raison's April letter to the Director-General, had recently taken place, and that, while "some progress has been made,... much remains to be done...", so that "we cannot be confident at this stage that adequate reforms will necessarily have been achieved by the end of 1985". Therefore "it would be wrong not to safeguard our position". He was therefore writing to the Director-General giving notice of the U.K.'s withdrawal from UNESCO on 31 December 1985 unless a reconsideration of what had been achieved in the way of reform by the time of that year's General Conference at Sofia was to persuade the British government to rescind its notice. Howe concluded the UNESCO section of his speech with an interesting little note:

> It is only right to point out that [this] decision will not have any effect on [U.K.] expenditure for 1985-86. But, by giving notice now, we retain the option for 1986, *which we should otherwise forfeit*, of being able to devote to better purposes in that year the amount which we would be due to pay to UNESCO in 1986.

In other words, Mrs Thatcher's government had apparently decided that it might be more important to ensure the good use of one year's government expenditure of some £6 million in a year's subscription to UNESCO than to continue fighting to secure the better management of one of the major agencies of the United Nations system.

Sir Geoffrey Howe's announcement that the United Kingdom was giving twelve months' notice that she might quit UNESCO had an effect on those concerned with the future of their country's relations with that international organisation not unlike that on Dr Johnson's man's mind when he was told that in a fortnight's time he was to be hanged. Those who thought that the U.K. should stay in UNESCO became even more active in holding meetings, publishing leaflets, writing to the press and lobbying politicians and other persons supposedly possessed of power and influence. Those who held the opposite opinion perforce had to riposte, though, secure in the knowledge that Howe would have virtually the whole of the large Conservative majority in the House of Commons[3] behind him if in due course he should come to implement the notice he had given, they did not think it necessary to do much more than produce letters and articles for publication in newspapers and magazines at what they thought were appropriate moments. The antis, on the other hand, led by members of bodies like the United Nations Association and the Council for Education in World Citizenship, decided in April to set up a specific "Keep Britain in Unesco" Campaign. While wholly in sympathy with the Campaign, I thought it inadvisable that a chairman of one of the advisory committees of the U.K. National Commission should take an active part in a movement which was already committed to keeping Britain in UNESCO. As I saw it, members of the National Commission were now charged with the responsibility of keeping a close watch on the extent to which UNESCO was moving to achieve the reforms mentioned in Raison's 2 April 1984 letter to UNESCO, so that in due course the Commission could advise Raison and Howe whether the government of which they were a part would or would not be justified in acting on the notice of withdrawal it had given. This responsibility was quasi-judicial and would be compromised if I became an active member of an organisation which was already committed to keeping the U.K. in UNESCO. In retrospect, I wonder whether I was right to think in this way. Since the earliest days of the National Commission, it had never been clear whether its members had been appointed by the Minister only to give advice to him. It could well be argued that they had some responsibility to keep the British public informed about UNESCO issues, and not least when it came to one as important as whether or not the British nation should remain a member of the organisation. Since from their presumably expert knowledge of UNESCO, almost every member of the National Commission had already decided that the right course for the U.K. was to fight for the reform of UNESCO while remaining a member of the organisation, it might have been better if those members of the Commission who held this view had publicly declared support for the Keep Britain in UNESCO Campaign.

As it was, for most of the time public expression of my views tended to be defensive responses to public statements by those hostile to UNESCO and the U.K.'s membership of it. These statements often seemed to me to based less on objective assessments of the merits and demerits of what UNESCO was actually doing than declarations of an almost religious belief that UNESCO was a creature of Satan. Thus when *The Times* of 9 May

1985 printed a leader headed "Death Wish at Unesco", I said in a letter (printed 18 May) that the author of this leader seemed not to have read UNESCO's recently-published draft programme and budget for 1986-7, which was appreciably more transparent than previous documents of this kind. Another leader, "Seeing through the Dream" (15 August) drew from me a riposte (printed 2 September) that it was the critics of UNESCO who had not done their homework who were the real dreamers; most British supporters of UNESCO had no illusions as to the faults of the organisation, but thought that if these were to be remedied Britain should stay in it as the principal leader of the movement for its reform.[4] The one occasion that I can remember on which a full public expression of my views was given was when, along with the other chairmen of the National Commission's advisory committees, I was asked to give written evidence on U.K. membership of UNESCO to the Foreign Affairs Committee of the House of Commons. As may seen from the Committee's *Report* (No.461, July 1985), all five of us were of the opinion that, provided that by the time of the General Conference of UNESCO at Sofia in October and November reasonable movement was perceptible towards meeting the criticisms expressed in Raison's 2 April 1984 letter to the Director-General, the U.K. should not implement its current notice of withdrawal from UNESCO. This in fact turned out to be a principal recommendation of the Select Committee, and when its Report was eventually debated in the Commons – as late as 22 November 1985, after the Sofia General Conference – there was support for it from all but two of the private members who spoke. It was a Friday debate, so there was no motion to be voted on and a small attendance in the House (in any case few M.P.s were much concerned whether or not their country should remain a member of UNESCO), but fourteen members, half of them Conservatives, spoke in support of UNESCO.

Throughout much of 1985 the National Commission was perforce uncommonly active. Each of its advisory committees was occupied scrutinising, in a rather more closely focussed way than usual, the programme and budget documents put out by UNESCO in its particular spheres of interest, expressly to see what changes there were from previous years and whether these had been influenced by the criticisms attached to Raison's letter. I suggested that the chairmen of the five advisory committees should come together from time to time to review progress and to see to what extent they might arrive at a common front for future meetings with the Minister. Professor Ray Beverton (chairman of the Science Committee) and Gerald Mansell (Communications) thought this was a good idea, and Ray Rickett (later Sir Raymond; Education) and Gavin Kennedy (Social Sciences) were prepared to go along with it. Since this had been my idea, I found myself in the chair at these meetings and involved in a fair amount of correspondence and telephoning with my colleagues and the National Commission's secretariat within the Overseas Development Administration. By July we were looking at working papers prepared for us by the secretariat, one setting out criteria for assessing responses to Raison's proposed reforms, and the other outlining a whole range of implications should the U.K. leave UNESCO, and we had begun to plan the sequence of meetings which would be needed to consider the results of the Sofia General Conference. In October and early November each of us spent a few days at Sofia while the conference was debating those parts of the 1986-7 programme which related to our committees. Except that we each had the opportunity to address the Conference on the U.K. reactions to these parts of the programme, I thought that this was something of an anticlimax. This may to some extent have resulted from the business being despatched somewhat more expeditiously than I remember to have been the case at previous General Conferences. It must have been too early for this to have had much to do with changes brought about by the reform movement; perhaps it was more likely that it was because at least some delegates were awaiting a storm of change which they thought might lie over the horizon. Nevertheless it seemed to me that the U.K. was still being held in high esteem by a substantial number of delegations, and I thought too that the number of these that were paying at least lip service to the cause of reform seemed to have increased – even the Soviet Union was now one of them.

At the end of November, in the light of what had been heard and seen at Sofia, each of the Advisory Committees met to formulate its opinion as to whether the U.K. should implement its notice of withdrawal from UNESCO. The views of members proved much the same throughout the committees. We learnt of two dissentients in the Communications Advisory Committee (one of whom may well have been the author of at least some of the anti-UNESCO leaders printed by *The Times*) but, this apart, at one of their informal gatherings the five Chairmen had no difficulty in summing them up in a single form of words which they agreed to put forward to a meeting of the whole National Committee on 29 November:

> The United Kingdom National Commission for UNESCO has examined the outcome of the 23rd General Conference at Sofia.
> It considers that, while not all the reforms proposed by Britain have as yet been achieved, sufficient progress has been made to recommend to the Government that it should rescind its notice of withdrawal from UNESCO. This would be in the national interest and would enable Britain to play its part in maintaining the momentum of reform.
> The National Commission also recommends that the Government should undertake a further comprehensive review of the progress of reform in about three years' time.

I remember only a small handful of speakers at the National Committee meeting on 29 November who voiced any opposition to these words, which thus became the verdict of the National Commission on the immediate future of the United Kingdom's relations with the United Nations Economic, Social and Cultural Organisation. I believe it to be a realistic verdict. The Organisation was a valuable part of the United Nations system, but it needed a substantial overhaul if it were properly to fulfil its functions. However it was important to realise that so large and so multifarious an international body could not be changed at all quickly, and that the most reasonable way to bring change about was not by standing aside from it, but by continuing pressure from within it alongside our friends in the Commonwealth and western Europe, none of whom had the slightest desire to withdraw and who were urging us not to. I believe the Chairman of the National Commission may well have been in sympathy with what the great majority of the men and women that he and his predecessors had appointed to the Commission had decided. I cannot remember Raison saying anything positive to this effect at the National Commission meeting on 29 November, but it does appear to be the sense of what *The Guardian* reported him as saying on the previous evening to members of the Keep Britain in UNESCO Campaign. But the National Commission's chairman was also Minister of Overseas Development, and his masters in the Thatcher government would have none of it. The world outside Britain and the United States was a dangerous place; small but irritating deviations from its rulers' norms were cancerous growths which should be quickly cut out.

On 5 December Timothy Raison's job was to tell the House of Commons that the United Kingdom would be acting on its notice of withdrawal, and that after 31 December 1985, it would no longer be a member of the United Nations Economic, Social and Cultural Organisation.

The Observer of 22 December went so far as to call this "Mrs Thatcher's Christmas present to Ronald Reagan"; the O.D.A. secretariat of the U.K. National Commission invited its members to a wake to mark its demise; twelve years were to elapse and a change of government was necessary before a United Kingdom government could think of returning to this branch of the community of nations.

---

1 Although I did not tell Plumb this, together with other historians, I had long been of the opinion that two very well-known general surveys of African humanity, by the anthropologists Charles Seligman (*Races of Africa* 1930, 1966) and George Peter Murdock (*Africa: its peoples and their culture history*, 1959) had been vitiated because they had not got their history straight.

2 It is an interesting comment on what has been happening to publishing in recent years that, in 1988, Hutchinson Education transferred my book, with others of its academic list, to the firm of Unwin Hyman (which became responsible for its second edition), and that in 1993 this was absorbed into the venerable firm of Routledge (which produced its third edition). But in some ways wheels had come full circle; at Routledge I was reunited with Ms Claire l'Enfant, my very efficient editor in 1977-78, and for the third edition I found her and her colleagues inhabiting 11 Fetter Lane, once home to the International African Institute.

3 It is impossible to be at all precise about the size of "virtually the whole of the large Conservative majority". At the end of the debate in the House of Commons on 22 November, 311 M.P.s voted with the government and 184 against. But the UNESCO issue was merely a part of a debate on the government's general policy on overseas aid. Of the twenty-four M.P.s who spoke in the debate as well as Howe and Raison, eleven mentioned the UNESCO issue. It is interesting that only one of these, Colin Moynihan (Conservative), expressed agreement with what Howe had said, while of

the ten who thought Howe was wrong or unwise, as many as four were
Conservatives – Sir Edward Heath, Francis Pym, Bowen Wells and Edward
du Cann. I suspect that there were some other Conservative M.P.s who did
not favour or were doubtful about giving notice to leave UNESCO, but
who either abstained from voting or who did not attend the debate. Most
M.P.s were little interested in the question of whether or not their country
should remain a member of UNESCO.

4 I was not alone in thinking that the anti-UNESCO party might rely
more on faith than facts in their polemics. See for example the criticism of
The Times leader of 8 September 1985 by no less a person than the Minister of Overseas Development in the letter which *The Times* printed two
days later.

Chapter 13
A Changing Situation: 2

In the Annual Report of the Centre of West African Studies for 1973-74 I wrote:

> The year under review will undoubtedly be remembered as that when, after many years of consistent expansion, the universities of the United Kingdom entered upon a period of considerable financial uncertainty and difficulty. The modest plan approved by the University for the development of the Centre during 1972-77 has been halted... For the first time since the Centre's foundation eleven years ago, 1973-74 saw a decrease in its resources when compared with the previous year...

So far as the Centre was concerned, inflation had seriously cut into the fund available for travel and research in West Africa. The University as a whole, like all other universities, learnt that it could no longer expect to see annual grants from the University Grants Committee steadily increasing through each five year period. Grants were now to be made on a simple year-to-year basis, and one year's grant might well be smaller than that for the previous year. In these circumstances the University of Birmingham thought it only prudent to declare that, when for any reason an academic or academic support post became vacant it could not, as hitherto, be more or less taken for granted that it should be refilled; it had first to be successfully argued that if the post were not refilled, essential work of the relevant department would be seriously impaired.

This doctrine – which was hardly ever varied throughout the rest of my time in Birmingham – had the immediate effect of causing the Centre to lose a lectureship in history which had only come into existence in January 1973, and to which we had appointed a talented American scholar, David Henige. Unfortunately Henige's young family did not take as well to life in Birmingham as he himself did, and at the end of the 1973-74 academic year he availed himself of an opening which presented itself to return to his previous post as Africana librarian in the Memorial Library on the Madison campus of the University of Wisconsin. Since the Birmingham post which he left had been created on the ground that it was needed to enable the Centre to fulfil a growing commitment to mount African history courses for undergraduates working for degrees *in the School of History*, it was hardly feasible to argue that its continuance was essential for the purposes of the *Centre of West African Studies*. But the new financial climate for universities, and problems facing an American family in Britain, had between them meant that it was the University of Wisconsin at Madison and not Birmingham's Centre of West African Studies that became the academic base for the editor of the very successful "journal of method" entitled *History in Africa* that began publication in 1974 and of the remarkable supporting series of monographs which this spawned.

Further misfortunes were to follow. As has been seen (p.145), the Centre had chosen to invest a substantial proportion of the funds for the second phase of its development, not in established lectureships devoted to teaching in specific disciplines, but rather in research fellowships, each tenable for a maximum of three years, which might be used, as seemed appropriate at the time, to provide support for exciting young scholars and to gain experience of lines of teaching and research not hitherto practised in the Centre. By their very nature, it was virtually impossible to argue that the occupation of any one of these research fellowships was essential for the continuation of the Centre's work. So after those who had been appointed in 1973-74 had come to the end of their appointments, it had to be accepted that the two Centre fellowships financed from the U.G.C. grant to the University could not be continued. So by 1976-77 the established academic strength of the Centre had been reduced from twelve to nine, and it was only through its good fortune in possessing John Cadbury's gift of the Visiting Fellowship named after him, filled each year by a different academic from an African university, that the Centre could be certain of gaining any novelty or variety in its programmes of teaching and research.

However there were occasional brief moments when a little light peeped round the edge of the clouds blown over the University from the U.G.C. By the end of 1977-78, the caution which the University had exercised in refilling vacant academic posts had produced a little reserve fund from which new appointments might be financed. Although it was unlikely that the money for any one new appointment would last for more than two years, departments were asked to make bids to compete for what was available in the form of "new initiatives", i.e. teaching and research activities of a kind that they had not had before. The Centre put in a bid which was successful, and so for the next two years had a temporary additional lecturer working in the borderland encompassing twentieth century history and political science. Then in the 1980s the U.G.C. responded to the argument that, with so few new appointments in the universities, teachers and researchers were becoming increasingly old and stale, and a little money was allowed to filter down to the universities to permit the recruitment of younger and more lively "new blood". Once again the departments of Birmingham University were asked to bid in a competition for new posts, which this time were intended to be permanent, and again C.W.A.S. was successful. In 1984 an advance was made into the field of African Drama and Performance Arts in which, with the appointment of Dr Karin Barber, the Centre soon acquired an international reputation. Finally, in 1985 a first fruit of a U.G.C. enquiry, conducted by Sir Peter Parker, into how African and Asian Studies had fared since Hayter and were faring in the years of ever increasing financial stringency, was an instruction to the University of Birmingham that it should not reduce its support to C.W.A.S.

The University Grants Committee was not the only government agency which was cutting back on its financial support for universities. So far as C.W.A.S. was concerned, just as serious was the decline in the supply of graduate studentships financed by the Social Science Research Council which, consequent upon the Hayter Report, had been entrusted with the prime responsibility of awarding studentships for postgraduate study and research in area studies. The S.S.R.C. had set up an Area Studies Panel – on which during 1970-74 I was the member representing African Studies interests – which placed quotas of studentships in the gift of approved area studies centres and departments, and which also itself awarded a few studentships to students registered in universities which did not possess such centres or departments. The result of this for C.W.A.S. was that by the 1970s, on average it could expect each year to see eleven or twelve of its postgraduate students holding one- or three-year S.S.R.C. studentships. This was just about half of those of its graduate students who were U.K. residents. By 1979-80, however, the government money supporting the S.S.R.C. was being trimmed, and in this situation the Council had clearly decided that postgraduate work in area studies was no more than "applied" social science, and so merited a lower priority than work in "pure" social sciences like economics or sociology. In the C.W.A.S. Report for 1979-80, I commented that the number of studentships the S.S.R.C. was now offering in area studies was "barely greater than the number of university centres it had recognised for such awards. As earlier award-holders finish their courses, the number will presumably dwindle to unity..." At C.W.A.S. unity was in fact achieved for 1981-82, and the number of the Centre's graduate students holding S.S.R.C. awards remained at one for the rest of my time in Birmingham.

Another threat to the health of postgraduate studies at C.W.A.S. was the government decision that, beginning in 1980-81, overseas students studying in U.K. universities should not, as hitherto, pay the same – essentially nominal – fees hitherto charged by U.K. universities on all their students, but should pay "full-cost" fees related to the actual cost of the courses they were taking. This had been on the cards for some time. In 1976, for example, *The Times* had summarised the report of a joint working party of the University Grants Committee and the Committee of Vice-Chancellors and Principals in the words "Overseas students at British universities are costing the country about £50m a year". This did not take into account that – as I pointed out in a letter to the newspaper – the foreign students were in all probability bringing into the country for their maintenance at least £46m a year. Nevertheless, when the cost-conscious Conservative Party came into power, it seized the opportunity presented by the working party report to cut back on government spending by reducing the funding of the U.G.C. by an amount equivalent to what teaching foreign university students was deemed to cost.

As has been seen, about half C.W.A.S.'s graduate students had come from outside the U.K., and it was reasonable to expect that an increase in their fees from £1500 to £3000 a year in round terms would bring about a noticeable reduction in their numbers. In the event, this did not happen at C.W.A.S. until after my retirement in 1984. In a long letter which I received from Mrs Thatcher in February 1980 in reply to one I had written to her protesting at what was happening, or would happen, to the Area Studies programme in the U.K. universities as a result of the cut-back in S.S.R.C. support and the increase in the fees required from overseas students, she seemed to suggest that the effect of the fee increases would be at least mitigated by various aid funds administered through bodies like the U.G.C. and the O.D.A. In fact, so far as C.W.A.S. was concerned, the initial relative buoyancy of overseas student numbers was largely due to the considerable contribution to them from Nigeria and the current sloshing around in that country of oil revenues. It was not until oil prices declined and circumstances in Nigeria changed that C.W.A.S. began to feel the pinch.

While accepting that the U.K. had "a responsibility to non-Western countries", Mrs Thatcher's general argument in defence of what was happening to Area Studies was no more than that the funds supporting them "could not be protected from taking a share of the reduction which the Government [had] decided to make in public expenditure in the current year", and that "cuts in public expenditure cannot be made painlessly". In these circumstances, those working in, or interested in the Area Studies Centres throughout the U.K. universities were naturally anxious that sight should not be completely lost of the initiative launched in 1961 by the Hayter Report (and extended a little later by the Parry Report on Latin American Studies). Michael Kaser, an economist based at St Antony's College at Oxford, who was very active in the Soviet field, and I were certainly not alone in thinking that the number and variety of the geographical areas embraced by workers in Area Studies might make it difficult for at least some of them to realise that they could share many common interests in the political and financial affairs of the British universities. However in 1980 it fell largely to the two of us to plan and launch a Co-ordinating Council of Area Studies Associations. We were able to persuade Robert Steel, the 1930s pioneer of geographical research in West Africa who in 1974-82 was Principal of University College, Swansea, to become the Council's first Chairman, while I became Vice-Chairman and Michael Kaser our first Secretary. The Council's first task was to seek to ensure that, in a period of universal retrenchment, the University Grants Committee and the Social Science Research Council remained aware that universities were not entirely organised on a pattern of subject disciplines, and that they should not forget the existence and the needs of area studies centres. The U.G.C., I believe, had not forgotten that it had appointed the Hayter and Parry Committees and had produced the initial money to implement their reports, and in no time at all it had appointed an Advisory Committee on Area Studies (and I found myself one of its members). On the other hand, I doubt whether the Social Scientists understood what we were talking about. In the midst of a reorganisation of the whole structure of their Council (which ended up with it being renamed the Economic and Social Research Council), they could suggest no better place for Area Studies than within a Human Geography and Town Planning Committee. I cannot now remember the upshot of our approach to the S.S.R.C./E.S.R.C. I left the Coordinating Council in 1986, after two years as its Chairman, and I am not sure that anything sensible had been agreed by that time.

If Birmingham's Centre of West African Studies were to survive, there was really no alternative but to expand and develop undergraduate teaching, and this was done very successfully. By 1985-86 there were already more undergraduates working for their degrees in the Centre than there were postgraduates. The figures were then 20 undergraduates to 14 postgraduates, and by the following year they had become 26 to 9. By the 1990s, while there was still very good research being done at C.W.A.S., it had become one of the most successful undergraduate schools in the University. When in 1996-97, the Higher Education Funding Council for England – a successor to the University Grants Committee – undertook formal assessments of the teaching and research being done in the universities, C.W.A.S. was given a score for teaching of 23/24, and in the whole university only one department did better, being credited with the maximum 24/24. So far as research was concerned, C.W.A.S. was one of four departments in the University to receive the highest possible rating of 5*.[1]

I can claim little or no credit for the successful way undergraduate teaching was developed at C.W.A.S. because in 1982 I ceased to be Director of the Centre. To explain how this came about, it is necessary to go back to something that happened in the Faculty of Arts in 1973. Although during the whole of my time in the University of Birmingham its two area studies centres were extra-faculty organisations, as has been explained, members of their academic staff taught in degree courses which were administered by the faculties, and they were "attached members" of the appropriate disciplinary departments in the faculties. Because of this interlinking, the Directors of the Centres became members of the appropriate Faculty Boards, which in the case of C.W.A.S. were the Arts Faculty Board and the Board of the Faculty of Commerce and Social Science. However within a year or two of my appointment, I decided that much of the material and the manner of the Commerce Faculty Board's business was of little interest to me, and I started to attend this Board's meetings only when there were items of business which specifically concerned my Centre. On the other hand, I became an assiduous attender at meetings of the Arts Faculty Board because I became increasingly absorbed by almost everything that found its way onto their agenda papers. No doubt the fact that by training and outlook I was a historian rather than a social scientist contributed to my choice between the two faculty boards, but I had also been greatly influenced by the impressive authority displayed by the first two Deans of the Faculty of Arts known to me. These were the two professors who between them directed what went on in the very prestigious cultural facility known as the Barber Institute. Anthony Lewis, Dean from 1961 to 1964, was a very distinguished musician, who had come to Birmingham as Professor in 1947 after working for the B.B.C. and planning music for its Third Programme (and was to go on to the Principalship of the Royal Academy of Music and a knighthood). He was in every way a great man. All the music he performed, but especially the Handel operas he directed each summer in what might be described as the atmosphere of a miniature Glyndebourne (and which introduced us and many others to the glorious singing of a young Janet Baker), greatly enhanced my musical education. As Dean, since he had always done all his homework, knew exactly how to treat each individual member of the Board, and was marvellously even-tempered, I have never known his equal. His successor (1964-67), Ellis Waterhouse, Professor of Fine Arts from 1952 to 1970 and previously Director of the National Gallery of Scotland, was not so smooth an operator – indeed he could go wrong and make something of a fool of himself – but he was a man of stature, equally established as a scholar, and also achieving a knighthood. The successors to these two, if relatively lesser men, were all hardworking and more than competent in the job of Dean. Gordon Davies (1967-70) was a Professor of Theology who had very little career outside Birmingham University. The next two, Robert North (1970-73, then going on to be Vice-Principal), Professor of French, and Bryn Rees (1973-75), Professor of Greek, shared the peculiarity that they had both recently come to Birmingham from chairs in other universities in which they had held deanships or other senior administrative appointments (which almost suggests that members of the Faculty Board thought that there were no established members of their Faculty who might be thought suitable for election to the office of Dean).

This brings us to what happened to me in 1973. In the autumn of that year, before what may well have been his first Faculty Board as Dean, Bryn Rees asked whether, after the meeting, he might have a word with me. I remember it was pouring with rain that afternoon, so that I had come to the Arts building from C.W.A.S. in my car, and it was in my car that Bryn and I sat in secret conclave after the meeting. He told me that, as had happened to Vice-Chancellors, the work which the Deans were now called upon to do had become so large and varied that it had been agreed that they could have deputies, and he asked me whether he might nominate me for election as his Deputy Dean. I was quite taken aback by this because I had supposed that, as someone who belonged to an extra-faculty organisation, I was exempt from any of the responsibilities of faculty administration. Bryn must have convinced me that this was not the case, and since his invitation rather took my fancy by offering the chance of some relief from what had now become the somewhat static job of directing C.W.A.S., in due course I found myself Deputy Dean of the Faculty of Arts. I found this was not an onerous job, but in the course of attending the regular meetings with the Dean, the Sub-Dean, and the Faculty's Assistant Registrar before each monthly meeting of the Faculty Board, I began to learn quite a bit about the Faculty and its departments and their problems, and also about the personalities involved in these. Then in the summer of 1975 we learnt that Bryn was going to leave Birmingham to be Principal of the University College at Lampeter, whereupon the Arts Faculty Board chose to elect me as Dean of its Faculty for 1975-78.

I was now on the threshold of the busiest part of my university career. While it was not unlike the busy-ness that had afflicted my last two years at Legon, it was on a larger scale and built up in a greater crescendo. Only part of it arose directly from the affairs of the Faculty of Arts. These must have been small beer compared with what faced the Deans of much larger and much more costly Faculties like those of Science and Engineering or Medicine and Dentistry, and in my case I had the benefit of having at my elbow one of the most senior and experienced of the University's Assistant Registrars, Cliff Brackwell. Much of the work, possibly the larger part of it, came from the role that Deans had in the larger government of the University as a whole. A Dean was ex officio a member of the University Court, the supreme governing body of the University, though of such remote grandeur that it needed to meet only once a year; of the University Council and its Finance and General Purposes and Planning and Priorities

Committees; and of the Senate and its Academic Executive, which between them did the work of governing for the Court. But above all deans were members of the Committee of Principals and Deans, of what in effect was the Vice-Chancellor's Cabinet. Attending, and preparing for, the meetings of all these bodies, over and above those of the Faculty Board and whatever committees it might spawn, necessarily ate deeply into time which otherwise would have been given to teaching and research. This could be damaging to the work of the department from which a Dean was drawn, especially if it were a small one like C.W.A.S. – which in the days of my Deanship never had more than ten full-time teachers, of whom, besides myself, only two were involved with the Centre's large commitment in the field of history. Luckily the University had appreciated this, so that a department which had provided a Dean was entitled during his tenure of office to an additional post of "Dean's relief". This was how C.W.A.S. was able to recruit to its strength Tom McCaskie, whose work as a historian of pre-colonial West Africa, Asante in particular, I had found increasingly impressive ever since I had first come across him when I was the external examiner of his Cambridge Ph.D. thesis. (In the event, as will be seen, C.W.A.S. was able to hang on to him in a series of temporary appointments until eventually, on my retirement, it was possible to add him to its establishment.)

From the time that I became Dean onwards, the work of people like myself who had become involved in the higher echelons of university administration was made appreciably more onerous because of the stop-go policy (if "policy" is the appropriate word) followed in the management of the nation's finances, and so of what the University Grants Committee could do to help finance universities by annual grants. Thus the first planning document I presented to the Arts Faculty Board after being elected Dean in 1975, one of which I must admit to being rather proud, and which I called "Arts in a Cold Climate", was one trying to assess the work of each of the Faculty's departments and deciding how "profitable" each of them was. There were first of all those departments which excelled in teaching and research and could attract as many students as they could efficiently teach, and which therefore should as far as possible be protected from cuts in their staffing. At the other end of the scale, there were those which had been less successful and which might therefore be expected to shrink as, for whatever reason, staff were to leave them. In between these two extremes there was a more difficult group of departments to assess, departments which, for particular reasons, were unlikely ever to recruit large numbers of students, but which it might be important to maintain at an adequate level. Then three years later I had to write another planning paper entitled "Possible new developments in the Faculty of Arts". This began with the words "It would seem that the financial climate affecting universities is somewhat less bleak than it has been during the last two or three years". I therefore suggested to the Faculty that it might like to reinforce its support staff, which had always been thin on the ground and which had recently suffered because of its relatively rapid turnover, and I asked the Faculty to suggest areas in which it would like to make bids for academic "new initiatives" (cf. p.202-03).

I remember in one of my annual addresses to the Faculty that I likened a university dean of the 1970s to the captain of an airliner who did not know how many passengers he was expected to carry, who was not quite sure how many members he had in his crew, or where his aeroplane was going and whether there would be enough fuel to get there, and who was continually receiving a series of different instructions from the air traffic controllers. I began to think that the life of a historian was much to be preferred. So as I approached the end of my Deanship, I thought I should do something to try to rehabilitate myself as a working historian. I therefore applied to the Social Science Research Council for a twelve-month research fellowship. This I was successful in getting, which meant in practice that for the academic year 1978-79, the University granted me leave of absence, while the S.S.R.C. provided the money to support Tom McCaskie in his temporary lectureship for a fourth year while he took over my teaching duties.

The idea for the research topic that I had proposed to the S.S.R.C. had been growing in my mind for some time. It derived from a Ph.D. thesis, which I had examined in 1966 at S.O.A.S., by a very bright West Indian student called Walter Rodney. As Richard Gray observed in an obituary notice, Rodney, who had gone into politics in his native Guyana and in 1980 was assassinated there, was a pioneer in focussing African historical research "on the agricultural basis of African communities, on the productive forces within them, and on the processes of social differentiation", rather than on "the inter-relations of African trade and politics" which had hitherto been the dominant interests. As may be seen from the title of the book in which his thesis appeared in print in 1970, it was the history of the

Upper Guinea Coast between 1545 and 1800 which provided Rodney with his first laboratory, and here he concluded from the evidence available to him that all economic and political activity outside the family was dependent on slave labour, but that a slave class did not come into being until Europeans had come to West Africa to trade in slaves. I remember being greatly impressed by this work of Rodney's – as indeed were other people – but as time passed I began to wonder how appropriate his conclusions might be for other parts of West Africa and for other periods. After all, Europeans had begun trading to West Africa in the fifteenth century, and their slave trade extended all along the west coast and was not brought to an end until well on in the nineteenth century. So what I proposed to the S.S.R.C. was that I should see what was said in contemporary written sources about the role of slavery and the trade in slaves in the societies of the whole of western Africa, from the Senegal in the north to Angola in the south, and from the mid-fifteenth to the mid-nineteenth centuries.

To make this a practical enterprise, I thought that, if I limited myself to sources that had been printed, whether at the time they had been written or subsequently, I would be working through a sample which would be readily accessible and yet adequate. Ultimately I found myself dealing with something like seven hundred separate or ostensibly separate published sources. I originally supposed that I would need to write a book to cover my conclusions, but in fact I found these remarkably uniform throughout the whole vast area I was surveying, so that substantive answers to the questions I had set myself could be presented in no more space than was required for an article published in 1980 in *The Journal of African History*. In the first place, various types or degrees of lack of personal freedom seemed indeed to be central to the fabric of pre-colonial society throughout western Africa. But, secondly, it seemed to me that Rodney had been wrong to suppose that classes of unfree persons had only come into existence as a consequence of the European demand at the coasts for African slaves. In the period when he had chosen to study them, it happened that the Upper Guinea coastlands were economically and politically less developed than was the case with many other parts of western Africa. Elsewhere there need be no occasion for economic and political change to run chronologically parallel with the growth of European trade at the coast.

However my research did ultimately lead to a book, the nature of which has already been suggested in the phrase "seven hundred separate or *osten-*

sibly separate sources". In the course of my work I had probably come to learn almost as much about the writing and publishing of books before the latter part of the nineteenth century as I had learnt about the nature of pre-colonial African societies. Authors and publishers could, without acknowledgement, produce works which were copies, or in part copies, or compilations, or translations, or part translations, or indifferent translations of other people's work. An extreme example of the dangers and difficulties of using early publications as historical sources became apparent in the 1960s when growing numbers of young scholars were turning their attention to the writing of African history. Two invaluable sources for those embarking on work on the later seventeenth and earlier eighteenth century history of West Africa were the two great descriptions of Guinea that were published in England at that time, those written by William (Willem) Bosman published in 1705 and by John (Jean) Barbot published in 1732. Since Barbot's work appeared nearly thirty years after Bosman's book, in the 1960s it was possible to suppose that it must be a later and more authoritative source. But whereas it was clear from the way in which Bosman had presented his work that its basis was his personal experience of fourteen years of living and working in Guinea between 1688 and 1702, it was by no means apparent that Barbot's book had a very different genesis. Most of it is in fact a compilation; his personal experience of Guinea was limited to two trading voyages in which he may well have spent altogether no more than six weeks ashore; these voyages took place as early as 1678-79 and 1681-82; the first draft of his book (in French) was composed shortly afterwards and was finished by 1688; and none of the final (English) version published in 1732 was written later than 1713. A complete understanding and evaluation of Barbot's book was not possible before the publication in 1992 in the Hakluyt Series of an edition based on twenty or more years of painstaking research by a team led by Professor Paul Hair. I had a small part in initiating this enterprise, and I am proud that Hair's two principal lieutenants, Adam Jones and Robin Law, had both worked for their PhDs under my supervision.

Of course, not every early printed work which might be used as a source for the writing of African history needs as much attention as Hair and his colleagues gave to Barbot (with the result that today we can be sure that we know the provenance and the acceptability of virtually every statement made in the 500,000 words of Barbot's printed text). There are perhaps no more than half a dozen or so significant printed sources for the precolonial history of western Africa that require such treatment before they can be fully usable (and perhaps there are not many people as competent as Hair and his colleagues to do this kind of work, and with the time to do it, and not many publishers willing to publish the fruits of their labours). But it occurred to me that in the process of my research into the history of precolonial western Africa I had begun to acquire quite a lot of information about the reliability, the coverage, and the peculiarities of the printed sources available for it. If I were to make this information as complete as possible, I would be in a position to compile a guide which might be of value to other researchers. The accomplishment of this task became the obsession of my working hours for some three years until I was able to produce *A Guide to Original Sources for Precolonial Western Africa published in European Languages*. By the time of its second edition, in 1994, this Guide contained information and critiques on nearly nine hundred printed works which purported to provide first hand or original information on precolonial western Africa. But the first edition of the Guide did not appear until 1987, after my retirement indeed, because towards the end of my research fellowship, Birmingham's Vice-Chancellor, Lord Hunter, had asked me to be one of his team of Pro-Vice-Chancellors, and I was to spend the last five years of my time at the University of Birmingham even more enmeshed in administration than before.

When I first went to Birmingham, the Vice-Chancellor and Principal of the University, Sir Robert Aitken, had just the one part-time deputy, in the form of one of the more senior of the professors, who was styled "Pro-Vice-Chancellor and Vice-Principal". However in 1963, just after my arrival, as I have already mentioned (p.138), Aitken decided that his job had become so big that he also needed a full time deputy, who was styled "Deputy Principal". When the first holder of this post, Thomas Alty, retired, Aitken persuaded a quite outstanding Professor of Metallurgy in the University, Geoffrey Raynor, to be the second full time Deputy Principal. Then when in 1973 Raynor also came to retire, Hunter decided that the time had come for the full time Deputy Principal to be replaced by three part-time Pro-Vice-Chancellors drawn from among the University's professors, the senior of whom would be appointed for five years and would also be "Vice-Principal", while the other two would each be appointed for only three years. It was usual for one of these three Pro-Vice-Chancellors to be a scientist or engineer and one a medical man, while the third would come from arts, social science, law or education. Hunter was obviously thinking of me as a replacement for Robert North, who was retiring from the University after five years as Vice-Principal. It was to North that I went to ask advice as to whether I should take on the job of Pro-Vice-Chancellor; it had occurred to me that I might find difficulties working as one of Hunter's deputies since he and I had such different personalities and backgrounds. I found it a slightly odd interview since previously I had often been to talk to North as a suppliant, because one of the jobs of the Vice-Principal had been to be chairman of C.W.A.S.'s governing committee. However he seemed to think that, as a recent Dean of Arts, I was the right person to follow him as a Pro-Vice-Chancellor, and so I agreed to do the job for 1979-82. My two colleagues were Ted Marsland, a remarkable man who had lived in a wheelchair since as a young man he had been crippled by polio, and yet had carved out a career as Professor of Oral Pathology and Director of the Birmingham Dental School, who now followed North as Vice-Principal, and Harry Prime, a cheerful and resourceful Professor of Electrical Engineering, both of whom became my good friends.

I was indeed to find that the little group of rooms allocated to us, and even more the secretaries who supported us there, provided an extremely friendly environment to serve as a base for the business of being a Pro-Vice-Chancellor. But much of this business was perforce carried on away from it, especially in committee rooms elsewhere in the university. If I had thought I had been committee-ridden when I was Dean of Arts, I was now infinitely more so. Memory of course can play tricks, but I think I must be more likely to forget committees than to invent them, and memory suggests that in my time as Pro-Vice-Chancellor I was expected in all to attend the meetings of something like twenty-three committees. This is to exclude ad hoc committees, but includes committees as various as those in which the affairs were discussed of things like the Safety Executive, appointments to the Academic and the Administrative Staff, Works and Maintenance, the University Library, and the "Joint Board of Studies for the Degree of Bachelor of Education". It was only occasionally that I was the chairman of a committee, and so in a position to try to ensure that its meetings were conducted expeditiously. More often I was present as the representative of the Vice-Chancellor, his eyes and ears, and if necessary his spokesman, in some part of the university which he had no time to attend to personally if no dire emergency had arisen.

There are a few of these committees whose affairs were sufficiently absorbing or eccentric for me not wholly to forget them. They tend to be rather on the fringe of the main activities of the University, and were ones which had been entrusted to me as chairman. I remember the Television and Film Committee, partly because I have always been interested in films, but also because our TV and Film Unit had a very talented producer and director who was generally at loggerheads with its administrative head. Then there was the COBUILD Committee, COBUILD being the acronym for the "Collins Birmingham University International Language Database", a database of some twenty million words of current English language together with their contexts, which was electronically culled from books, conversations, newspapers, broadcasts and other media. This was a joint enterprise between the University of Birmingham and its department of English Language, led by Professor John Sinclair, and Collins Publishers. It was being used in the first instance for the production of an entirely new kind of dictionary, one dealing with language as it was actually in current use. Rather like the Anglo-French Concorde supersonic airliner, this enterprise proved to be, by a large factor, very much more long term and costly than either of the two partners, the university and the publishing company, had envisaged when they agreed to embark on it. But in due course I convinced myself that it would eventually produce financial profit as well as substantial academic credit, and I had a hand in persuading the University and Collins not to cut the losses that were mounting along the very difficult road they were travelling.

A more orthodox academic committee which I chaired was the Board of Extramural Studies, which remains memorable to me partly because the whole nature of university extramural studies was beginning to undergo radical change. But my association with Extramural Studies is chiefly memorable to me for something which was exceptionally extramural. J.B.Butterworth, the Vice-Chancellor of the University of Warwick, which had been founded down the road at Coventry as recently as 1965, was determined that his university should have a share of the extramural work in the West Midlands which had hitherto been conducted solely from Birmingham, while the members of our very experienced Extramural Department were by no means convinced that people at Warwick properly understood what extramural work was about, and were prepared to concede no more than some kind of partnership with them. I vividly remember a series of lunch meetings at the two universities at which Hunter and Butterworth – who had not yet gained the peerage to stand on terms of equality with Hunter – could never see eye to eye. In the end it was left to the Department of Education and Science in London to decide that Warwick must have its, not very large, share of the cake.

But – as with other universities – more and more of the time of Birmingham's Vice-Chancellor and his deputies, Deans, Registrar, and Secretary was taken up by preparing "academic plans" to present to Senate and Council which might enable the University to meet the ever-changing financial scene. This became virtually an annual exercise and was exceedingly tiresome. However the monotony of our existence was broken when Lord Hunter gave notice of his intention to retire at the end of September 1981. A committee made up of the Pro-Chancellor – the chairman of the University's Council – and two of his senior lay officers, together with the Vice-Principal and two senior members of the Senate, of whom I was one, was set up to find someone who might be thought suitable to succeed him as Vice-Chancellor. We did not find this easy. The young hopefuls who were recommended to us either did not, for one reason or another, meet with our approval, or proved uninterested in coming to Birmingham. The alternative ploy, of finding an established vice-chancellor, perhaps of a smaller university, who might like to move to Birmingham – an idea which I myself favoured, and which was to be successful in 1987 and again nine years later – did not succeed. Perhaps we had not been energetic enough. In no time at all, September was upon us and it was necessary to appoint Ted Marsland Vice-Chancellor ad interim. It was becoming urgent to do something, and by 9 December we had come to two decisions which it fell to me to announce to Senate.

First of all, I said, the Committee had come firmly to the view "that present and foreseeable circumstances are such that it would be sensible if Vice-Chancellors were to be appointed for a fixed term", such as five years. Secondly, after considering "a very large number of names", the Committee had decided that, "especially in the very difficult circumstances that had developed since it began its work, none of the individuals who might have responded positively to an invitation to come to Birmingham, at least in the immediately foreseeable future, offered clear positive advantages over possible internal candidates who were already well acquainted with the University and its problems".

I said that when the Committee had got as far as this, Marsland had withdrawn from it, and that it was now being suggested to Senate that it should recommend to Council that he should be appointed Vice-Chancellor for five years from 1 October 1981. I went on to add that it should be remembered that

> Professor Marsland has already had to shoulder the onerous responsibility of beginning to plot the University's course through the present financial shallows. Had the Committee chosen otherwise, and preferred someone from outside, by the time that person could have arrived to take over..., he would have found the groundwork of University policy for at least the next two or three years already laid, and he would also be heavily dependent on his predecessor for information and advice.

The consequence of this was that Ted Marsland became Vice-Chancellor and that he asked me to serve as his Vice-Principal. I thought this was something I could hardly refuse, though I thought it wise that I should cut back on other commitments. One of these was the Scientific Committee for the UNESCO History of Africa, so I wrote a letter of resignation to the Secretary-General of UNESCO and received in return a letter of thanks for my services.

A much more serious step was that I asked that I might be relieved from the directorship of C.W.A.S. As I said in a letter to Ted Marsland early in 1982, the prime reason for this request was that "in present circumstances, the Vice-Principalship, with its heavy responsibilities for staff matters, has become something akin to a full-time job". I then went on to say that I had been brought to Birmingham eighteen years earlier to build up an African Studies Centre "based on a flourishing postgraduate school. Now, however, the situation governing universities is so radically different from what it was in the 1960s that I think it might be better for the Centre if it could be given the opportunity to have a new Director with a new set of ideas more attuned to the 1980s". I intimated that Douglas Rimmer had been an excellent deputy to the Director of the Centre for a number of years, and that perhaps the time had come for him to become Director and for my functions in the Centre to be limited to those of Professor of African History. And this is what happened.

I had of course arrived in Birmingham in 1963 at the time of the Robbins Report and the nation's acceptance of the principle that there should be a university place for every qualified student who wanted one. So far as Birmingham was concerned, the consequence was that in the next eighteen years its university grew from one of 4800 students and 680 academic staff, to one of 8600 students and 1100 staff. In money terms, the annual cost of the university rose tenfold to £40m, of which three-quarters was public money channelled through the University Grants Committee. But in 1981 the tap was firmly turned off; the government had decided that the nation could not afford to spend so much on universities. In the University of Birmingham, we were told that by 1983-84 our annual grant from the U.G.C. would have been reduced by at least fifteen per cent.

Since something like seventy percent of the cost of running a university was the cost of paying wages and salaries to its people, a reduction in income of this size within so short a period of time could only be achieved if staff could be made redundant. By early 1982, therefore, the U.G.C. had secured money for a scheme of funding early retirement which was thought to be attractive enough to secure the necessary reduction in university staffs. I decided to take advantage of this scheme, and in the summer of 1982 I asked the University to agree to my retiring at the end of September 1984, when I would be 63, two years younger than the normal age of retirement for university staff (and coincidentally the same age as that at which my father had chosen to retire from the National Physical Laboratory). My reasons for this decision were partly selfish. University life was obviously no longer as attractive as it once had been; in particular, perhaps, it was becoming ever more hectic. It therefore seemed sensible to take advantage of the chance of getting out of it while it was still on offer. I also felt as a one time Ghana colleague said in a letter to me early in 1983, "I think it is better to go while I am still respected rather than to wait to hear mutterings in corridors... to the effect 'Why doesn't the senile old sod get up and go!'" But I was also thinking about the future of the Centre of West African Studies. Its staff was becoming increasingly elderly; if it were to remain a lively and successful team in the new age into which universities were being thrust, it should be given some opportunity to recruit new, younger staff who would at once bring in up to date scholarship and cost less to remunerate than superannuated professors. Indeed, if I were to leave C.W.A.S., and if its work in history were to be maintained, the sensible and honorable course to follow would be to give a permanent appointment to Tom McCaskie, so that the line of twenty successful doctoral students in African history that I had fostered since 1963 would not wither but continue to blossom. And this is what happened.

My last job of significance in the University, in the summer of 1984, was entirely appropriate to the times. At Senate one day, two experienced professors had ventured to suggest that conducting all the University's spending through a great central bureaucracy called the Finance Office might not be the most efficient and economical way of doing its business in times of increasing financial stringency. They wondered whether it might not be better each year to give each academic department a budget, and allow it to decide for itself how it would like to spend it – what proportions of its money it should spend, for example, on academic staff, on support staff, and on equipment – to produce the best and most economic results in its own particular job of teaching and research which it knew about better than anyone else. So I, as Vice-Principal, found myself chairing a working party to look into this idea in some detail, and to see how it might work out in practice. Our conclusion was that, given certain parameters and safeguards, and provided what we called the "budget centers" were all of a reasonable size, we thought that the scheme was well worth trying. Something on these lines was shortly established.

Soon there was really only one major decision to be taken, that of where Jean and I should live now that each day I no longer had to go into the University. Within a few years, the answer was plain enough. Living as we did in Harborne and Edgbaston on the western side of Birmingham, when we wanted to get out of the city we had soon taken to driving and exploring westwards, until we came to the marvellously scenic country of mid-Wales. When in 1973 I came into a not inconsiderable inheritance from a childless uncle, our bank manager had suggested that it would be a sound idea to invest some of the money in property. So as we explored the quite magnificent coasts and valleys, mountains and heaths, lakes and reservoirs around Aberdyfi, Dolgellau and Barmouth, we kept our eyes open and eventually found a nice house in a very pleasant village which seemed to have everything – a church and chapels, school and pub, of course, but also the luxury of two shops and a local policeman. We were able to buy this house, and so long as we continued to live and work in Birmingham we had the joy of being able to slip away at weekends, and for longer periods in the university vacations, and enjoy a life of rural contentment. We built on to the original fabric, and eventually came to have rather a splendid domicile in an attractive garden. When there was no longer any need to spend much time in Birmingham, we could see that our house there, with its costly rates and groundrent, had really become our second home, and we took the plunge to sell it and move to live full-time in Wales. In due time I think the people of the village, both Welsh and English, have come to accept us as a somewhat exotic part of the community.

---

1 It is, I think, of some interest that the University of Birmingham's other Hayter creation, the Centre for Russian and East European Studies, also achieved a 23/24 score for its teaching and a 5* rating for its research. If there is any moral in this, I think it can only be that the scheme of "centres of studies" favoured by Hayter was one that could produce first class academic results.